M000289512

MONTPELIER TRANSFORMED

A Monument to
JAMES MADISON
— *and its* —
ENSLAVED COMMUNITY

WILLIAM H. LEWIS

THE History PRESS

Published by The History Press
Charleston, SC
www.historypress.com

Copyright © 2022 by William H. Lewis
All rights reserved

Front cover: A striking view of Montpelier central area, showing the House and South Yard buildings of the Enslaved Community in late afternoon. *Photo by Kenneth Garrett, courtesy of The Montpelier Foundation (TMF).*
Back cover, bottom: The iconic Temple, the only Madisonian structure that remains, other than the House. *Photo by Rick Seaman, TMF*; *inset*: The Gilmore Cabin, after completion of renovation of its exterior. *TMF.*

First published 2022

Manufactured in the United States

ISBN 9781467151658

Library of Congress Control Number: 2022930160

Notice: The information in this book is true and complete to the best of our knowledge. It is offered without guarantee on the part of the author or The History Press. The author and The History Press disclaim all liability in connection with the use of this book.

All rights reserved. No part of this book may be reproduced or transmitted in any form whatsoever without prior written permission from the publisher except in the case of brief quotations embodied in critical articles and reviews.

For Peyton

[James Madison is] *the greatest man in the world.*

—*Thomas Jefferson, as told to Benjamin Rush*
The Autobiography of Benjamin Rush: His "Travels Through Life" Together with His Commonplace Book for 1789–1813

[Madison's administration] *acquired more glory and established more union than all his three predecessors, Washington, Adams and Jefferson, put together.*

—*John Adams to Thomas Jefferson*
Letter dated February 2, 1817

Over 200 years after the founding of the federal republic, James Madison remains the most important political thinker in American history. The prime framer of the Constitution and the Bill of Rights, Madison was also a brilliant and lucid expositor of the new republican government and its underlying principles. His eloquent and insightful writing on freedom of religion, freedom of speech and the press, and the rights of minorities are central to American political thought and continue to speak to the controversies and challenges of the day.

—*Jack Rakove,* James Madison: Writings

Despite recognizing the tragedy of slavery, Madison never freed Montpelier's enslaved people.

The magnitude of this evil [slavery] *among us is so deeply felt, and so universally acknowledged, that no merit could be greater than that of devising a satisfactory remedy for it.*

—*James Madison to Frances Wright*
*Letter dated September 1, 1825**

*At the time of Madison's death in 1836, his view of slavery was not "universally acknowledged" and was, in fact, very much out of date in Virginia and throughout the South.

CONTENTS

PREFACE

In 1984, when the National Trust for Historic Preservation acquired Montpelier, James Madison's lifelong home, the estate's future was anything but certain. The one certainty was the Trust's commitment to open the site to the public. The property had been in private hands throughout the post-Madison period. The challenges faced in presenting it as a significant historic site were many. Prior owners had expanded and reconfigured the house to such an extent that it no longer was recognizable as the home of James and Dolley Madison. Dotting the 2,650-acre landscape were 135 structures, almost all in various states of disrepair or collapse. Only one, a small, round temple, was an intact Madison structure.

After more than a decade of limited Trust progress, The Montpelier Foundation was created in 1998 for the express purpose of managing and preserving Montpelier. From the outset, the Foundation Board's vision was for it to become a "monument" to the life and legacy of James Madison. But to most advisors, this seemed an impossible dream. Architectural historians said the house could not be authentically restored. They advised leaving it as configured by William duPont Sr., the last private owner. Also, limited archaeology had been done to locate the sites where the plantation's enslaved people had lived and worked. With funding for no more than a small staff and modest maintenance of the site, developing initiatives to advance the Board's vision would be highly problematic.

Chapters 1 through 12 tell the unlikely story of the Foundation's journey in transforming Montpelier into a national monument to the life and legacy of Madison in just its first 10 years of operation. Substantial additional progress on recognition of the enslaved community would be critical in the future. I've written the book from my vantage point as Board chair of the Foundation, the position I held for the first eight of its years. The narrative proceeds step by step through the following milestones:

- a tour of the site as the journey began
- the founding directors' dreams of elements that should constitute the monument
- assembling a dedicated board of directors, gifted chief executive and talented staff
- my negotiation with the Trust to give us management autonomy
- surmounting the challenges faced in accomplishing numerous critical initiatives
- raising the huge amount of funding required
- establishing policies and developing plans to ensure the highest quality and authenticity in all aspects of the Foundation's work

Chapters 13 and 14 highlight the most significant initiatives during the Foundation's second decade. Of greatest importance were the initiatives to address more fully the tragedy of slavery and the essential role of the individuals and families enslaved at Montpelier. Together with initiatives accomplished during the first decade and a half, the establishment of a permanent exhibition on slavery that opened in 2017 and reconstruction of housing of the enslaved support the reality that Montpelier is now a monument not only to James Madison, but also to its enslaved community. The epilogue briefly summarizes the continued expansion of initiatives to present the indispensable contributions of the enslaved community.

Writing this memoir seemed important for a number of reasons. The other founding directors and I recognized that we had participated in a remarkable achievement unlike any other in our lifetime. From our efforts, momentous benefits would accrue for generations to come. A number of directors and staff strongly encouraged me to undertake this project. Some stressed the importance of there being a record for future generations of the actions involved in establishing what has already become an institution of national significance. I have been told that other historic sites of our nation's founders—for example, George Washington's Mount Vernon and Thomas Jefferson's Monticello—do not have such a useful historical record of their respective foundation's organization and early years.

It is my hope that a wide range of readers, from the merely curious to the serious student, will find the extraordinary story in this book interesting (and for professionals in a variety of careers, a helpful resource). Reliving in depth the Foundation's first 20 years has allowed me to gain an even greater appreciation of the honor and unique opportunity I had in playing a leadership role.

William H. Lewis
Charlottesville, Virginia
December 2021

PROLOGUE

Why create a monument to James Madison? True, by any criteria, his seminal contributions to founding the American system of government—Father of the U.S. Constitution, Architect of the Bill of Rights and fourth president—justify permanent national recognition. Also true, no monument to him exists on the Mall in Washington, D.C., or elsewhere.[1] But what purposes would be served by The Montpelier Foundation making the enormous financial and human commitment to transforming Montpelier into a national monument?

Underlying the founding directors' dream was the guiding mission that Montpelier become a national resource of historic significance for education about the life and legacy of James Madison and his essential role in creating the nation's founding documents. We shared the belief that education about the values and principles embodied in these documents is critical to sustaining a strong American democracy and civil society. The substantial acreage and much-altered house of the original Madison plantation held exciting promise for providing an inspirational, unique setting for this scope of education and a broad range of complementary experiential learning.

Key Initiatives. Montpelier's transformation resulted not just from our leadership, vision and actions but also from no small amount of luck. When the Foundation was organized, achieving our dream of Montpelier becoming a Madison monument seemed virtually unimaginable. In fact, undertaking the most important of the necessary actions—restoration of the main house to again become the Madisons' home—was at that time impossible. As you will learn, it was unclear whether an authentic restoration could ever be done. And raising the extraordinary funding required, while difficult to imagine being doable then, was not the hurdle that made restoration an impossibility.

Nonetheless, the Foundation did overcome the seemingly insuperable hurdles. We were able to undertake a combination of initiatives in just the first 10 years that together will ensure perpetual recognition of Madison's life, intellect and contributions and support our vision of educating a global audience about Madison and the U.S. Constitution. Among them were:

- A $25 million authentic restoration of the Madisons' home
- Establishment of Montpelier's Center for the Constitution with on-site housing in a Constitutional Village
- Construction of a new multipurpose Visitor Center and William duPont Gallery
- Extensive archaeology
- Restoration of a small home built by George Gilmore, a former Montpelier slave
- Initiation of efforts to present the life of the Montpelier enslaved community

As this list shows, much of the attention and resources during the first decade (1998–2008) was devoted to creating physical infrastructure. Throughout, however, the heart of our activities was Montpelier's education and related programs.

In the second decade, there was significant growth in the Foundation's educational capabilities, especially in telling the story of African Americans who lived at Montpelier. From the time we began to pursue our Madison dream, we recognized it was important, indeed essential, to tell the story of Montpelier's enslaved community. During the first decade and a half, the Foundation built a relationship with descendants of the enslaved workers and undertook an array of actions to begin the journey toward properly recognizing Montpelier's enslaved.

But it was not until philanthropist David M. Rubenstein made a $10 million gift commitment in 2014 that the Foundation was able to dramatically expand the scope of Montpelier's recognition of its enslaved. His gift funded both the creation of a permanent exhibition on the tragedy of slavery and the reconstruction of the housing complex of the enslaved who worked in the Madisons' home. The Foundation's extensive archaeology and prior activities with descendants provided a major part of the research needed for these projects. As a result, Montpelier has truly become a monument to the life and legacy of James Madison and its enslaved community. Reinforcing the importance of recognizing the central role of Montpelier's enslaved, the Foundation's Board took the unprecedented step in June 2021 of amending its bylaws to establish a goal of having one-half the Board be directors recommended by the Montpelier Descendants Committee.

To set the stage for the Foundation's journey, it's important to briefly review Montpelier's ownership history, the litigation that complicated the National Trust for Historic Preservation's acquisition and the Trust's management of the property.

Private Ownership. Dolley Madison sold Montpelier in 1844, eight years after James Madison's death. The property changed owners five more times before William duPont Sr. acquired Montpelier in 1901.[2] Mr. duPont created an expansive estate with a dairy, garden, pony barn, greenhouses, a general store, a train depot, a power plant, prize-winning cattle, horses and houses for staff. He expanded the main house into a mansion of 55 rooms. In so doing, he reconfigured and increased it in size to such an extent that the 22-room Madison home was discernible only in very limited respects.[3] The one other Madison-era structure that remained was the iconic Temple. After inheriting Montpelier upon her father's death, Marion duPont Scott established extensive equestrian operations. These included barns for world-class racehorses, a steeplechase course and a flat racetrack.[4]

Marion duPont Scott's Will. Mrs. Scott expressed in her Will the strong desire that, upon her death, the National Trust acquire Montpelier and open it to the public. She also stated her desire that the house be restored "to conform as nearly as possible with the architectural pattern" of James Madison's home. Under the terms of her father's Will, however, the property vested in five nieces and nephews because she had no children. Having no right to transfer the property directly to the Trust, Mrs. Scott bequeathed $10 million to the Trust to purchase Montpelier from the heirs.[5] To induce the heirs to relinquish their interests, she made their deriving benefits under a trust valued at $100 million contingent upon donation or sale to the Trust. Mrs. Scott died on September 4, 1983.[6]

Will Challenge and Settlement. Two of the heirs challenged the sale inducement provisions of Mrs. Scott's Will.[7] (See chapter 6.) In October 1984, after a year of litigation, the Trust reached a settlement with all members of the duPont family enabling it to acquire Montpelier for $7.5 million.[8] Among the Will Settlement terms was a requirement that two of the rooms Mr. duPont had added to the mansion—the drawing room and morning room—be furnished and presented as a memorial to him.[9] This provision, unless later amended, would make impossible Mrs. Scott's wish for a Madison-era restoration.[10]

Opening Montpelier to the Public. The Trust opened the mansion to the public in 1987. Its obvious objective was to create an experience that would attract significant numbers of visitors. Greatly complicating this was the need to devote substantial resources to build infrastructure for public visitation (such as reliable water wells and septic fields) and to address serious maintenance problems of the mansion and a few of the property's other 135 structures likely to be used.[11] To obtain advice on how it should proceed, the Trust convened two ad hoc groups—one in 1989, a second in 1996. A third advisory body, the Montpelier Property Council, a Trust-organized support group, prepared a five-year plan in 1995.[12]

Advisory Group Recommendations. Building on the suggestions of the 1989 ad hoc group and the Property Council, the 1996 Working Group undertook a nine-month investigation and developed recommendations addressing a broad range of programmatic, infrastructure, management and funding issues.[13] It proposed expenditures of about $15 million and an additional $10 million for endowment, with a target date of 2001 for completing the recommended actions.[14] The Working Group acknowledged, though, that significant additional expenditures would be required for infrastructure, visitor services and programs to educate about the Madisons' life. A key recommendation was its call for an entity independent of the Trust, with a national board to assume responsibility for the site by the end of 1998.[15] Not addressed was the Trust's earlier decision, based on the 1989 group's advice, that it should preserve the duPont family's twentieth-century additions.[16] The Trust's board of trustees approved the Working Group Report in October 1996.

Trust Management. In its operation of the site, the Trust hired a succession of capable executive directors and a small staff and, with substantial support from volunteers, made modest progress in attracting visitors. Also, it expended more than $3.5 million for property improvements,[17] about $1 million of which was used just to replace the mansion's leaky roof.[18] From the portion of Mrs. Scott's bequest not used to acquire Montpelier, the Trust created a $2 million endowment.

Monument Not Yet Envisioned. The blueprint the Trust's advisors provided engendered hope that in the next five years Montpelier would make advances toward becoming a successful historic site. But Montpelier's evolving in the foreseeable future into a national monument to the life and legacy of James Madison was, in 1997, beyond the vision and expectation of the Trust and its advisors.

Opposite: Map of Montpelier in 1997. *Courtesy of The Montpelier Foundation (TMF).*

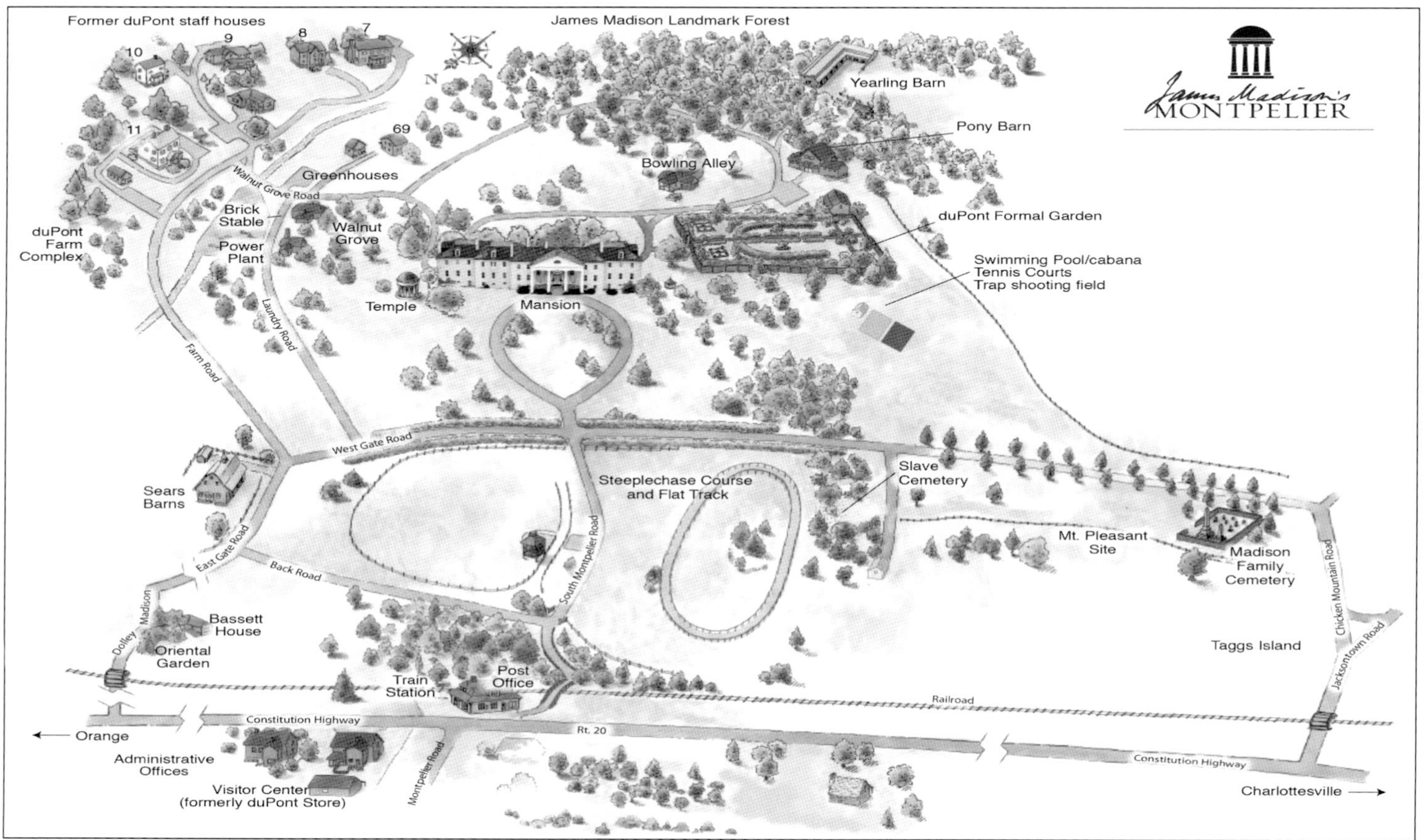

James Madison's
MONTPELIER
Former duPont staff houses
James Madison Landmark Forest
10
9
8
7
11
69
N
Yearling Barn
Pony Barn
Bowling Alley
Greenhouses
Walnut Grove Road
Brick Stable
Walnut Grove
duPont Farm Complex
Power Plant
duPont Formal Garden
Swimming Pool/cabana
Tennis Courts
Trap shooting field
Temple
Mansion
Laundry Road
Farm Road
West Gate Road
Sears Barns
East Gate Road
Back Road
Steeplechase Course and Flat Track
South Montpelier Road
Slave Cemetery
Mt. Pleasant Site
Madison Family Cemetery
Chicken Mountain Road
Jacksontown Road
Taggs Island
Dolley Madison
Bassett House
Oriental Garden
Train Station
Post Office
Railroad
Constitution Highway
Rt. 20
Orange
Administrative Offices
Visitor Center (formerly duPont Store)
Montpelier Road
Constitution Highway
Charlottesville

Mansion circa 1997. *Photo by Philip Beaurline, TMF.*

1

MONTPELIER IN 1997

A JOURNEY THROUGH THIS HISTORIC SITE

On a slight knoll, with a breathtaking, unobstructed view of the Blue Ridge Mountains, sits the main house at Montpelier. In its second-floor library, James Madison did his research and writing in preparation for the Constitutional Convention in 1787. After four months of intense debate and negotiation, the Convention produced the U.S. Constitution. In 1997, however, visitors did not see the Madison home; they saw a mansion very different in appearance.

Arriving for a Visit

Location. The Montpelier property is located on a rural section of Virginia Route 20, "Constitution Highway." It is between the small town of Orange and the village of Barboursville, about 30 miles northeast of Charlottesville and 90 miles southwest of Washington, D.C. As the highway approaches Montpelier from either direction, several modest houses with slate shingles and green siding are the first buildings a traveler sees on Montpelier property. The highway and a railroad track running parallel to it are about a quarter mile from the house.

Visitor Center. In 1997, the Montpelier visitor center was in a complex of small buildings on Route 20. The primary building had previously served

Montpelier's original Visitor Center. *TMF.*

as an Esso gasoline station and duPont farm store known as Montpelier Supply Company. (The Esso sign had not been removed.) Much of the first floor served as the gift shop, with the former store's cashier's counter still in use for customers' purchases. Among the items for sale were James and Dolley Madison biographies and books on Revolutionary War and Civil War history. Visitors paid their admission fee at a window in a building—formerly a garage—behind the gift shop. A rudimentary orientation film was shown there. Restrooms were entered from the outside and required a key. The Montpelier executive director's office was in an adjoining duPont-era house.

Entry to Montpelier. A shuttle bus took visitors to the Mansion. It had to cross over the railroad track on a charming, but rickety, decades-old bridge that was structurally unsafe for large emergency vehicles. Close by the bridge was the Montpelier Train Station, attractive but no longer in use for transportation. William duPont Sr. had it built in 1910 for travel to and from his office in Wilmington, Delaware. It was used in 1997 as a small U.S. Post Office for the community of Montpelier Station. After passing through a clump of trees, the visitor saw the duPont steeplechase course and flat track (both still in use today). In the farther distance was the

Montpelier Train Station, showing bridge in background. *TMF.*

Mansion. The 55-room house, much different in appearance than when James and Dolley Madison lived there, had a pinkish stucco-like coating on the original brick.

The House

> **House or Mansion?** For convenience in making a structural distinction about the Montpelier main house, I use the term *House* to mean the Madisons' home—that is, when referring to the house as the Madisons configured it. (It's unclear whether the structure in Madison's time was predominantly called "house" or "mansion," but it would have been considered a grand home.) I use the term *Mansion* (or mansion) when the reference is clearly to the structure as the duPonts configured it. When the context does not call for making a distinction between the two configurations, I use the term *house*.

Interior Tour. Upon arriving at the Mansion, visitors typically were allowed to tour most of it on a self-guided basis, with staff or volunteers available to respond to questions. Throughout, the Mansion's walls and floors needed significant renovation. Many walls had peeling plaster and water stains. Three first-floor rooms on the south side (to the right as you face the house) were the only ones fully furnished. The items there had been retained from the duPont ownership. Two of those rooms, the drawing room and morning room, were filled with attractive antiques. The third, the art deco "Red Room" designed for Mrs. Marion duPont Scott, Mr. duPont's daughter, was a highlight for many visitors. It was decorated with numerous equestrian photos and memorabilia and was furnished exactly as it was when she died. On the north side, two other first-floor rooms—a large warming/serving kitchen and dining room—retained a degree of the ambience of life there in the twentieth century. Montpelier Property Council members refurbished the dining room and the adjoining breakfast room in 1991. This was done in anticipation of President George H.W. Bush's visit to commemorate the bicentennial of ratification of the Bill of Rights. He flew on the Marine One helicopter, accompanied by a host of dignitaries and press traveling by special train for the ceremony. Subsequently, the rooms were used for receptions, dinners and other special events. In the cellar, one large room had a recessed floor that had been an exercise area for Mrs. Scott's former husband, Hollywood actor Randolph Scott.

Mrs. Scott in her Red Room, circa 1970s. *TMF.*

Interpreting the Mansion. In attempting to provide some sense of its Madison past, the Montpelier staff and volunteers pointed out to visitors a few details about the design and use of the house when James and Dolley lived there. However, except for copies of a few paintings in which artists depicted the nineteenth-century exterior, little was known with any confidence in 1997 about the details of the Madison House's design. This absence of knowledge was, in part, responsible for the advice the National Trust for Historic Preservation received in 1989 that the Mansion's structure be left as it existed when the Trust acquired Montpelier.

James Madison's Library. One important interior design feature that was generally accepted as authentic was the second-floor location of Madison's library in 1787. Facing west, it gave him a spectacular view of the Blue Ridge Mountains. But its exact configuration was not known. Near the room was a line of four twentieth-century bathrooms, a peculiar design that later investigation would show to have minimized the duPonts' compromising of the Madison home's fabric.

The Property

> In describing the property, I use the present tense except when specifically referring to a difference in 1997 conditions.

West of the Mansion. Looking west, the view of the Blue Ridge Mountains from the house's portico is virtually the same as the one the Madisons enjoyed. The Madisons' Temple, which covered their underground icehouse, remains within the close-in northwest view. With the exception of the house and the Temple, the 135 structures on the property when the Trust acquired it were built after the Madisons' ownership. The only built features other than the Temple in the stunning wide-angle view from the house to the mountains are the steeplechase course and flat track. Successive owners developed much of the 2,650 acres, but considerable acreage had returned to forest.

North of the Mansion. In 1997, spread out over the estate north of the Mansion were buildings and infrastructure in various states of poor condition or extreme disrepair, screened somewhat by a Madison-era walnut

Bassett House. *TMF.*

grove. They included a power plant, a stable for the duPonts' carriages, a large farm barn, a large greenhouse, seven small houses in the general area of the power plant and stable, a small pond, barns purchased from Sears Roebuck & Co. and a small home Mrs. Scott purchased from E.F. Hodgson Co. for her Thoroughbred horse trainer (Carroll Bassett).[1] The Bassett House lawn featured an impressive but poorly maintained "Oriental Garden" designed by Charles Gillette, a renowned landscape architect.[2] Also to the north were several run-in sheds, a large "schooling barn," a blacksmith shop, other barns of various sizes, extensive fencing and a system of mostly unpaved roads. Except for the farm barn, the houses and barns are still in use.

South of the Mansion. To the south, the structures were fewer, but the curious visitor in 1997 had opportunities to walk or drive to areas with features associated with the Madisons and with the duPonts. Closest to the house is an area that Montpelier staff later determined through extensive archaeology had been the site of a circa 1750 house (James Madison's parents' initial home on the site) where Madison lived as a boy[3] and quarters for slaves who worked in the Montpelier home. (See chapters 10 and 13.) Through a small grove of trees were the remains of a duPont swimming pool and cabana, with an adjoining tennis court and trap-shooting field. About 100 yards away, archaeologists were seeking to discover and learn about the home known as Mount Pleasant, built by Madison's grandfather. Madison may have lived there in his early childhood before moving to the Montpelier location. Farther south are open fields and a gravel state road with two additional duPont-built houses. Also to the southwest, in an isolated enclave close to the railroad tracks, is a group of houses (known as Tagg's Island) that verged on being uninhabitable.

Top: Madison Obelisk in Family Cemetery. *Photo by Cpl. Timothy A. Turner, TMF.*

Bottom: Snow-filled depressions marking location of graves in Enslaved Cemetery. *TMF.*

Madison Family and Enslaved Cemeteries. The Madison Family Cemetery, which could be seen from the duPonts' pool and tennis court, is surrounded by a brick wall that, like every grave within it, was poorly maintained. Obelisks mark the graves of both James and Dolley Madison. Unlike his friend Thomas Jefferson, James Madison did not specify a list of accomplishments to be carved into his gravestone—and none is listed. Madison did not even leave instructions for creation of a gravestone—much less the 20-foot-tall obelisk that was erected. Nearby is the Montpelier Enslaved Cemetery, with graves marked by pieces of quartz rock in the traditional manner for the enslaved.[4] Initially, most of the graves in the Family Cemetery also were marked in the same manner.

East of the Mansion. To the east (rear), close to the house, is one of the features of greatest interest in 1997: a tiered, brick-walled garden divided into sections with a variety of perennial flowers, boxwoods and sculptures. Annie Rogers duPont, the wife of William duPont Sr., was the primary designer of the garden, which is located in the area where the Madisons' garden had been.[5] Just beyond this formal garden are trees and plants landscaped to create a border for the house's back lawn. A path through the border leads to a narrow 1850s-era building constructed as a bowling alley, then in use for storage. A bit farther away is a large barn also used for storage. Next to it is a charming barn that Mr. duPont had built for the ponies of his children, Marion and Willie. The Pony Barn is the one duPont building the Trust extensively renovated. A $450,000 gift made this possible so that it could be used in educating children about the Madisons. East of the Pony Barn is a 200-acre old-growth forest, recognized to be the finest of its kind in the eastern United States and designated as a National Natural Landmark. Adjacent to the forest and behind the Pony Barn is a handsomely designed barn used for Mrs. Scott's yearlings, which looks over a valley of open fields.

Management

Sources of Revenue. In 1997, Montpelier's revenue from all sources was approximately $1.5 million. The Trust contributed $400,000 of that amount for operations.[6] Sources of the balance included a Virginia legislature appropriation, an endowment withdrawal, admissions revenue from about 30,000 visitors, gift shop sales, Trust memberships, rents and leases, and contributions and grants from foundations and individual donors.[7] The annual steeplechase, which Marion duPont initiated in 1929, was also a modest source of funding.[8] Property Council members and other volunteers made donations and provided assistance for events to encourage interest in Montpelier. Without a role in management, however, they had been unsuccessful in getting local supporters to make major donations. In a disconcerting development, the Trust's leadership announced that its operational funding would end in 2001. This decision was made notwithstanding its board's approval the prior year of a $25 million plan to support Montpelier. Having recently ended its dependence on federal government funding, the Trust faced its own uncertain short-term financial picture and was making plans for a $105 million fundraising campaign.[9]

Uninspiring Visitor Experience. In light of the limited funding available, Montpelier's 22 full-time and 40 part-time seasonal staff[10] and varying numbers of volunteers did not, and could not, present the inspiring experience that visitors expected when they came to the historic home of the Father of the Constitution. As the duPont Mansion, the house itself did not encourage interest in the Madisons. Visitors were able to tour the entire estate in whatever depth they desired. Typically, though, the most enjoyable part of their visit was experiencing the property, garden and mountain views, not a tour of the Mansion. A visit provided little education about the Madisons and James Madison's role as Father of the Constitution and Architect of the Bill of Rights. Visitors also received little information about the lives of Montpelier's enslaved people.

2

A PERPLEXING BEGINNING—1998

FINANCIAL SUPPORT FOR THE NEW NONPROFIT COLLAPSES

By 1998, it was clear that two building blocks would be essential for Montpelier to become a historic site worthy of James and Dolley Madison: (1) a new independent management structure and (2) a massive investment in programs and property improvement. The potential to make significant advances on both counts waxed and waned for much of 1998. A new nonprofit–The Montpelier Foundation–was organized, and an ambitious program to educate visitors about the Madisons was established. In fact, for many months, transfer of management authority to the nonprofit and multimillion-dollar funding commitments to it seemed within reach. By year end, however, these major steps forward failed to materialize, and it appeared that progress would take a much more deliberate path.

Preparation for Discussions with the National Trust

In December 1997, the Montpelier Property Council[1] asked its chair, Glen R. Moreno, formerly chief executive of Fidelity International and of other major international investment and banking corporations, to initiate discussions with the Trust for the purpose of establishing an independent foundation to assume operational responsibility.[2] Under the envisioned "co-stewardship" arrangement, the Trust would lease Montpelier to the new nonprofit, which would take over its operations.[3]

Having watched little progress being made under the Trust's management, Property Council members and local citizens in the nearby town of Orange were overwhelmingly supportive of moving forward with co-stewardship. Ongoing tension existed between the Trust's staff and Montpelier's staff and volunteers due to delay and disagreements that often occurred when decisions, of which there were many, had to be approved at Trust headquarters in Washington, D.C. This led to pessimism about Montpelier's future as long as the Trust managed the property. Given the extent of the site's programmatic and infrastructure needs, the Trust likewise fully supported using the co-stewardship vehicle to transfer management.[4]

To prepare for contacting the Trust's leadership, Glen reviewed the advice of the Trust's 1989 and 1996 ad hoc advisory groups and of the Property Council on what actions Montpelier would need to take to become a successful museum. In particular, he focused on the 1996 Working Group's recommendations and background papers. His general conclusion was that the advisors' analyses, while generally helpful, would merely provide a guide for the long term.

But a daunting short-term question had emerged: Was there a realistic possibility that Montpelier could become viable as a nonprofit? The site had always been substantially underfunded and unable to address many operational deficiencies. Experience also showed establishing a successful historic museum to be extraordinarily challenging, even one centered on the life of a founding father. Major potential donors told Glen that, absent "adequate endowment," they wouldn't become significant supporters and attracting substantial financial contributions wouldn't be possible. Therefore, it had become clear that success in fundraising would be a prerequisite to proceeding with co-stewardship.[5]

A Fundraising Challenge

To build a financial base, Glen decided to propose a joint fundraising initiative between the National Trust and the new independent nonprofit. On January 22, 1998, Glen wrote to the Trust's president, Richard "Dick" Moe, urging that the Trust issue a substantial fundraising challenge. Under it the Trust would commit to raise $8 million over the five-year period from 1999 to 2003, and the nonprofit would be required to match it.[6]

Dick sent a supportive response on March 11, outlining suggested terms for the challenge. The Trust's $8 million commitment would be met with $5.75 million in endowment, $1.5 million in capital improvements and a total of $750,000 for operating support in fiscal years 1999–2002. The Trust hoped that the source of $4 million for endowment would be proceeds from sales of a Congressionally authorized Dolley Madison Commemorative Coin. Dick's advocacy had been, in no small part, responsible for issuance of the Tiffany-designed coin. To satisfy the improvements component, the Trust intended to seek a $1.5 million special federal appropriation. The $750,000 for operations would come from its unrestricted budget and additional fundraising.[7]

Rather than an $8 million nonprofit match, however, Dick proposed that the match be $12 million. He also summarized his views on the keys to Montpelier's becoming self-sufficient. These left no question about the difficulty of the task the new nonprofit would face. He placed particular emphasis on (1) continued success in securing significant state funding; (2) increased revenue from visitation due to the soon-to-be-opened *Discovering Madison* exhibits; (3) building Montpelier's endowment; and (4) placing tight controls on expenses.[8]

Glen told Dick on May 4 that the Trust's proposed elements for its meeting the challenge were generally acceptable but that the nonprofit's match should be the originally proposed $8 million, not $12 million.[9] Dick agreed to the lower amount on May 13.[10]

Discovering Madison Exhibits

Concurrent with negotiations over the challenge terms, the Trust's Montpelier staff completed the first major action to significantly enhance the visitor experience. In the mid-1990s, Kathy Dwyer Southern, the site's executive director, had initiated discussions with Ralph Applebaum Associates of New York to design a strategy focused on presenting the Madisons' life at Montpelier. The result was *Discovering Madison*, a project that cost about $1 million.[11] Its features included a new orientation video, an audio tour with a mobile audio guide, exhibits in a number of first-floor rooms and additional supporting educational materials. The themes of the new exhibits, which consisted of narrative text framed in plexiglass on metal stands, were "A Remarkable Family," "Plantation Life: The African American Community," "Civic Culture" and "Hospitality: A Montpelier Tradition."[12]

Discovering Madison opened on July 9, 1998. A festive event accompanied the opening to show that Montpelier was turning the corner on becoming a major presidential museum. On a 90-degree sunny day on Montpelier's back lawn—with a Secret Service team scanning the crowd—First Lady Hillary Clinton made an inspiring speech to 3,000 guests. She emphasized the importance of James and Dolley Madison and education about James Madison and his contributions. After her remarks, Dick Moe announced the Trust's $8 million challenge. Not surprisingly, he received rousing applause. Then, after expressing great appreciation to the Trust, Glen Moreno informed the crowd that a local and national fundraising campaign was already underway to meet the challenge.[13]

Planning for the New Foundation

Throughout the period leading up to the July 9 event, a small task force had been developing plans to organize the nonprofit and prepare preliminary budgets and goals for it under the co-stewardship arrangement. The group consisted of three people: Glen Moreno, Kathleen "Kathy" Stiso Mullins (Kathy Southern's successor as executive director) and me. I took responsibility for having the requisite legal steps performed by Morgan, Lewis & Bockius LLP, the international law firm in which I was a partner. On July 31, 1998, The Montpelier Foundation was officially incorporated under Virginia law. The three of us were the incorporators.[14]

At the same time, while the Trust was preparing drafts of the agreements required for co-stewardship, dark clouds began to appear on the horizon. As Glen and Dick discussed details of the challenge and co-stewardship in greater depth, the Foundation team began to be concerned that elements of the proposed arrangement would make assumption of legal responsibility too risky. One significant concern was that the Trust would require the Foundation to agree to assume $600,000 in debt, primarily attributable to *Discovering Madison* setup costs and expenditures for visitor center inventory. We also were concerned that infrastructure work the Trust had promised to undertake before the management transfer had not been done.[15]

But the most critical issue from the Foundation's standpoint was whether the Trust would agree that its commitment to meet the $8 million challenge was binding. We had reasons to be apprehensive. Instead of receiving $4 million from sales of the Dolley Madison Commemorative Coin, the Trust had learned the proceeds it would receive to add to Montpelier's endowment might be much less. The Trust also had not made significant progress on Congressional enactment of a federal appropriation for infrastructure. Citing these changes in the Trust's expectations, Dick began to make clear that its commitment would be on a best-efforts basis.[16]

The Board's Organizational Meeting

The Foundation held its first Board of Directors meeting on August 14. As provided in its Articles of Incorporation, the initial Board consisted of Glen Moreno, Louise "Lou" B. Potter, Elizabeth "Bitsy" B. Waters, J. Roderick "Rod" Heller III, Kathy Mullins and me. Lou, an architect and philanthropist, had long been a major supporter of Montpelier through her work on advisory groups and in her role as a Trust board member. Both Bitsy and Rod had served on the Trust's 1996 Working Group; Rod was its chair. Bitsy was a former mayor of Charlottesville and had a long career as a consultant specializing in historic preservation, economic development and growth management. The Trust had retained her in the past as a facilitator-participant for program sessions. Rod was a lawyer, business executive and historian. He had been a partner in the renowned Washington, D.C. firm of Wilmer, Cutler & Pickering and served as chair and chief executive of National Housing Partnerships. He also sat on a number of nonprofit boards—including the Trust, for which he had been vice chair.

I was the only director who had no past formal relationship with Montpelier-related activities. Initially a corporate and securities lawyer, I next served in state and federal government for seven years, first as executive officer of the California Air Resources Board and then as director of the National Commission on Air Quality. For the 25 years prior to my Montpelier Foundation Board membership, I had specialized in environmental law, primarily air quality issues. My longtime interest in the history of the nation's founding period and extensive reading on James Madison and other founding fathers had led to my becoming involved with Montpelier. Indeed, this interest had been the impetus for my wife and me to buy a mid-nineteenth-century home as a second residence about a 15-minute drive from Montpelier.

At our inaugural meeting, the Board briefly reviewed the budget for the upcoming year and discussed the proposed governance structure. Our principal focus, though, was on negotiation of co-stewardship and concerns that the $8 million challenge would not be an unequivocal Trust obligation.[17] This led to a decision to advise Dick that the Trust's commitment must be binding. To stress our position, Glen, Rod and I met with Dick on September 9. Much to our consternation, Dick made it clear to us that he had concluded that the Trust was not in a position to guarantee its challenge obligations.

Collapse of the Fundraising Challenge

On September 18, Dick met with Kathy to address two issues related to the Board's concerns. First, he advised her that the Trust now expected to receive $1 million to $1.5 million from sales of the Dolley Madison Coin, rather than the $4 million projected when the Trust made the $8 million challenge. (The total was ultimately in excess of $3 million.) Second, the Trust would require that the amount not yet raised to cover *Discovering Madison* costs (about $350,000) be taken from the Montpelier endowment created from Mrs. Scott's bequest.[18]

Dick followed up with a September 23 letter to Glen saying that while the Trust was committed to the $8 million challenge, it would have to revisit how it would raise endowment funds.[19] At the Board meeting two days later, we asked Glen to advise Dick that we would have to reconsider co-stewardship if the Trust did not confirm that the challenge was a binding obligation.[20] After Glen sent a note to that effect, Dick responded again that he could not ask the Trust board to act as Glen requested. He added that he hoped they could continue to work together on the challenge.[21] In reality, this exchange brought their pursuit of the fundraising effort and co-stewardship to an end.

Glen and Dick held different views as to whether Dick had indicated earlier that the challenge would be a firm Trust commitment. The written record is murky on this. Supporting Glen's interpretation were Dick's initial memo agreeing to the challenge and the normal understanding of commitment regarding fundraising challenges. But there had always been an element of uncertainty. For the $1.5 million for infrastructure, for instance, Dick had said a not-yet-obtained Congressional appropriation was the intended funding source. Also, the actual revenue from Dolley Madison Coin sales was initially an unknown, with the Trust expecting enough money to cover almost two-thirds of its $5.75 million for endowment. Regretting the breakdown in their relationship, Dick said in a November 2 letter to Glen that he "probably did not articulate sufficiently the reasons why [the Trust] could not proceed with" its $8 million commitment. He further stated that he had a "high regard" for Glen, whose efforts had "helped move Montpelier significantly in the right direction."[22]

The Foundation Becomes Manager of Montpelier

After reflecting on how to proceed, I sent Dick a memo on November 5 that outlined a proposed alternative agreement under which the Foundation would manage Montpelier's operations until conditions for co-stewardship were ripe. It confirmed commitments Dick had made in conversations with Kathy and me about a Trust/Foundation management arrangement. We proposed that the Trust would (1) give a high degree of autonomy to the Montpelier staff and Foundation Board, (2) continue its operating support at the then-current level of $400,000 annually and (3) carry out $200,000 in specified infrastructure projects. Legal responsibility would continue to reside with the Trust.[23] Before sending the memorandum, I sent Dick a draft and he agreed to its terms.[24]

A Change of Founding Board Leadership

At the directors' meeting on November 6, Glen reported what most of us already knew: the Trust's position was that the $8 million challenge was not a firm commitment. He said that in light of its decision, he was resigning from the Board as a matter of honor and accordingly would not assume the role of chair. Glen believed that his failure to obtain a binding challenge required this action. He said his involvement had been premised on being able to lead an effort to rapidly build a successful Madison museum. Absent an unequivocal Trust commitment, he did not think this would be possible. (None of us at that time could foresee or had even dreamed of the circumstances that would result in the extraordinary transformation of Montpelier within just a few years.) The directors expressed great appreciation to Glen for his dedicated service in connection with organizing the Foundation and developing and pursuing the proposed challenge.[25]

Glen then recommended that I become chair, and the Board unanimously endorsed his recommendation. Rod asked if there were conditions to my accepting the chair position. I said that Dick's agreement to the terms in my November 5 memorandum were sufficient for me to accept. Particularly important were the Trust's continued funding for operations and its assurances of autonomy for the Board and staff in managing Montpelier.[26]

Glen's resignation was a major loss. His background and experience equipped him well to spearhead the fundraising necessary to make significant progress in tackling the issues the Trust's advisory groups had identified. Clearly, the Board's highest priority would now have to become the expansion and strengthening of its membership to acquire the talent Glen had brought, particularly in fundraising.

The abandonment of the $8 million challenge and Glen's resignation meant that co-stewardship would have to be postponed. I recognized, however, that there could be an upside to the delay. It would give us additional time to build a stronger organization before entering into future negotiations with the Trust and, as a consequence, more leverage to obtain acceptable terms. With greater certainty of operational success, we could insist, as a nonnegotiable condition, that the Trust agree to the Foundation's being granted a high degree of autonomy. Having this autonomy would be necessary to attract the highest caliber directors and staff and secure the massive financial support the Foundation would need. Unfortunately, based on Kathy's and my discussions with some key Trust staff, we were not at all certain they shared Dick's commitment to giving the Foundation broad autonomy.

Glen's final achievement as a director was to obtain a $100,000 grant from the Fidelity Foundation. Its purpose was for Montpelier to retain professional assistance in developing a strategic plan.[27] In supporting planning at other nonprofits, Fidelity had developed respect for Herbert "Herb" Sprouse as a facilitator for the process. It encouraged us to consider him for that role. After interviewing Herb, we selected him and scheduled the initial planning meeting for early 1999.[28]

Board Governance Structure

At the founding directors' four 1998 meetings, we devoted significant time to setting up the Foundation's governance structure. In most respects, the bylaws established a typical nonprofit organizational scheme.[29] The number of directors initially was set at a range of 6 to 15. Later, recognizing there would be advantages to having a larger board, we increased the maximum number to 25.[30] Consideration of the length of terms and whether to limit the number of them resulted in a decision to provide for staggered three-year terms and a limit of three terms. Initial partial terms would not count against the limit.

In one important respect, however, the governance structure was unusual. As initially adopted, the bylaws provided for both a board of directors and a board of governors. The governors' role was principally to elect directors at an annual meeting. We quickly concluded that this structure was too cumbersome and revised it in 1999 to authorize only one board: a board of directors.[31]

The principal intended benefit of having a board of governors had been to give a sense of ownership to an expanded group of supporters. Our hoped-for result was that they would then make substantial financial contributions. But we determined that this anticipated outcome did not justify having a second management board and the major commitment of keeping both boards functioning properly. Upon reflection, I think the "two boards" structure was the only governance decision we made in initially setting up the Foundation that was not well thought out.

The Board amended the bylaws in 2003 to provide that all Board members who serve three full terms would automatically become emeritus directors, with privileges the Board would establish.[32] (When directors began to transition into emeritus status in 2007, they continued to be invited for the next decade to all Board and Executive Committee meetings and received all Board and many committee materials.)

A fourth three-year term was authorized under a 2007 bylaw amendment, should the Board determine that special circumstances justified this exception to the term limitation. Adoption of this amendment resulted from several directors' requests that I, as well as several other founding directors, serve a fourth term.[33] They believed that the continuity our involvement provided would be important.

The First Addition to the Board

Directors devoted time at each Foundation Board meeting in the first few years to recommending and considering potential Board candidates (a task that later became a function of the Nominating and Governance Committee). The first candidate considered was Joe Grills. After learning that Joe had recently moved to Rapidan, in nearby Culpeper County, Kathy quickly identified him as a potential director. Before his retirement, Joe had worked at IBM for more than 30 years. His last role was as chief investment officer of the IBM Retirement Funds. A recognized expert in finance and investments, Joe also served as a member of boards and investment committees of numerous investment funds, retirement funds and nonprofits. After meeting with Joe in the fall of 1998, Kathy and I strongly recommended him to our Board. Following a brief discussion, he was elected.[34]

Year-End 1998

As 1998 came to a close, Montpelier's status as a historic site was on a modestly upward trajectory. The disintegration of the $8 million challenge had slowed programmatic expansion and infrastructure improvement and postponed the time when the Foundation would assume full operational responsibility. We had, however, negotiated a management agreement that would be the precursor for later favorable co-stewardship terms. Additionally, there was solid programmatic growth. The *Discovering Madison* initiative had resulted in visitation increasing by 7,000 to about 39,000. The approved budget for 1999—although it seemed overly optimistic—reflected an increase of close to $500,000, to about $2 million. A new Trust-approved system for financial management would aid Montpelier staff in operating more efficiently.[35] Lastly, the Foundation ended the year with a dedicated, albeit small, Board and prospects for attracting additional talented directors.

3

YEAR OF FOUNDATION ORGANIZATION—1999

BUILDING A STRUCTURE FOR AMBITIOUS PLANS AND DREAMS

Having ended 1998 with The Montpelier Foundation very much in its embryonic phase, the founding directors principally devoted 1999 and 2000 to organization building. Our decisions in that period established the structure and leadership that proved to be critical in transforming Montpelier into a national Madison monument. The Board and staff began 1999 focused on four complementary objectives: (1) developing a strategic plan for the next 10 years, (2) making further strides in improving the visitor experience and the property's infrastructure, (3) attracting additional talented Board members and (4) creating capability to raise significantly increased revenues. As progress was made on these goals, we continued to consider when to initiate co-stewardship discussions with the National Trust. In the middle of the year, chief executive Kathy Mullins unexpectedly resigned. After completing the strategic plan and hiring an exceptional new chief executive, we decided that in 2000 we would give serious consideration to beginning negotiations to assume legal responsibility for Montpelier (addressed in chapter 4). But the most consequential actions were two philanthropists' gifts that were the first step in a long-term commitment to Montpelier's future.

Board and Staff Collegiality

In the Foundation's 1999–2000 organizing period, one characteristic of discussions about the direction and focus for Montpelier's future may have been most important for achieving the success that followed: the collegiality that emerged from the manner in which the initial directors and staff worked together. Difficult issues had to be tackled, and disagreements were inevitable—and did occasionally occur. But by selecting directors and staff who would respect others' opinions and recognize collegiality as a priority, the Foundation throughout its history has made decisions on policies and actions through consensus without significant dissent.

Development of a Strategic Plan

An early action that benefitted from collegiality was the development of a detailed strategic plan. The planning team consisted of directors Joe Grills, Lou Potter, Bitsy Waters and me and staff members Kathy Mullins, Carol Christensen (director of administration) and Randy Huwa (director of development and marketing). The team, with Herb Sprouse's guidance, met for eight daylong meetings. Before each, we received extensive background materials.[1]

During our discussions, several considerations significantly affected our decision-making on what projects to include. Perhaps of greatest importance was the Trust's limited success in making progress over the prior 12-year period. A factor likely contributing greatly to the Trust's record was Montpelier's being in a rural setting, with no nearby urban area. Madison's being so underappreciated clearly was another major factor. And overhanging our future was the daunting reality that we were only beginning to build the Foundation's fundraising capability. Put simply, to be a blueprint that would be useful, the plan's initiatives had to be tempered by highly uncertain prospects.

Early in our discussions, Herb asked us to consider whether the mansion, because of its many changes and expansion over the years, should be interpreted to show the evolution of a great American home, from the Madisons to the duPonts. Up to this time, although the *Discovering Madison* exhibits had begun to shift the focus, visitors often seemed more interested in the duPonts than the Madisons. Unanimously rejecting Herb's suggestion, we stressed that the Foundation's mission was to be centered on educating the public about the Madisons and the U.S. Constitution. Indeed, this was a primary, or in some cases the sole, reason for directors being involved. We nevertheless wanted to give the duPonts appropriate recognition. To accommodate both James Madison's centrality and the duPonts' history, we titled our plan "Madison, an Extraordinary Man; Montpelier, a Memorable Place."[2]

Final Strategic Plan

When finalized, the plan had 44 initiatives, to be carried out in three phases over a 10-year period.[3] Of its 100-plus pages, 34 consisted of narrative description. The rest of the pages were tables detailing the content and timing of specific initiatives, a budget with best-estimate scenarios and explanatory financial notes.[4] These were the most important initiatives:[5]

- Establishment of an Institute for Madison Studies—in a new facility separate from the house—to educate the public on Madison's role as Father of the U.S. Constitution and Architect of the Bill of Rights
- Restoration and interpretation of the first-floor wing of the house's north side known as "Dolley's Wing," and development of programs to use other parts of the house more effectively
- Planning and design of a new major visitor center and gift shop (The plan did not provide for construction of the visitor center.)
- Significant expansion of the archaeological program
- Celebration in 2001 of the 250th anniversary of James Madison's birth through a year of programs on his life and contributions
- Expansion of education programs on Dolley Madison
- Undertaking major infrastructure improvements
- Securing broad autonomy for operation of the site
- Recognition of the duPonts and their preservation of the home and estate
- Expansion of the collection of Madison artifacts and period furniture and art
- Interpreting James Madison's innovative farming and reforestation methods in *Madison on the Land* programs

- Development of a site master plan
- Creation of a comprehensive long-term interpretive program
- Recognition of Montpelier as a national resource for education about James Madison

Once developed, our strategic plan, like many plans, was not routinely consulted in determining Board and staff action. But the initiatives did continue to embody consensus judgments on some of the future actions to be implemented.

The Founders' Dreams for Montpelier's Transformation

In retrospect, the plan seems somewhat unambitious in light of the extraordinary transformation of Montpelier that occurred—and its happening in a very short period. The directors' *dreams* at the time, however, were ambitious. After the team's last meeting, each of us prepared a list of accomplishments that we hoped could be celebrated in the annual report 10 years hence, in 2009. The list was not to be constrained by the strategic plan's content. Many of the accomplishments mirrored actions in the plan, but a number had either been deemed too ambitious or not been considered. These significant initiatives were not included in the plan:[6]

- Full restoration of the House so that its configuration would reflect the Madisons' home in every respect (no serious consideration had been given to including this in our plan, for several reasons: the Trust advisors' assessment that discovering the details of the original design would likely be impossible, the almost certain astronomical cost of restoration even if the design could be determined and the Will settlement's requirement to retain two duPont rooms; chapter 6 discusses resolution of these issues)
- Construction of a major visitor center by 2006, with both a Madison museum and a separate duPont facility (incorporating the design of duPont rooms and re-creating Mrs. Scott's Red Room)
- Development of a campus for the proposed Madison study center
- Research and telling of the Montpelier enslaved community story

- Achievement, within 10 years, of projections of increased annual visitation ranging from 200,000 to 400,000, a budget of $10 million and an endowment of $50 million
- Recognition of Montpelier as *the* national memorial or monument to Madison

Astoundingly, almost all of the actions *not* included in our plan would be achieved in our first decade. Not met were the projections for visitation, budget and endowment (and still not achieved are the visitation and endowment goals). In the case of the enslaved community initiative, we took significant steps in the first decade to recognize the enslaved people's contributions. Appropriate recognition of the essential role of the enslaved was always an integral part of the founding Board's dream in transforming Montpelier. But it was not until the Foundation's second decade that it became possible for actions to be taken that would result in Montpelier being known as a monument to the enslaved community, as well as to the life and legacy of James Madison. (See chapters 13 and 14 for more on the second-decade progress.)

Program and Fundraising Advances in Early 1999

During the period the team prepared the plan, the staff achieved a number of significant successes and pursued initiatives that would provide the groundwork for future progress. In an exciting beginning to 1999, First Lady Hillary Clinton hosted the Dolley Madison Coin Commemoration ceremony at the White House. Revenues added to the endowment from Dolley Madison Coin sales reached about $3 million in the next two years.[7] A yearlong "Celebrating the Women of Montpelier" program was begun in February with a speech by Dolley Madison scholar Dr. Holly Shulman.[8] Visitation continued to increase based on the favorable response to the *Discovering Madison* exhibits and the press coverage they received.[9]

Fundraising progress in 1999 also was encouraging. The Board inaugurated a new category of supporters called the Madison Cabinet, which we expected (and which happened) to generate an ongoing major base of support. Members would contribute $5,000 or more annually; their benefits would include special programs, events and an annual dinner.[10] (See chapter 11 for more on the Cabinet.) The Foundation also received substantial contributions or pledges for these specific projects: (1) archaeology at the site of one of Madison's boyhood homes (Mount Pleasant), which was built by his grandfather; (2) significantly expanded education programs; (3) a substantial portion of the $950,000 cost of rehabilitating the Montpelier Train Station (built by William duPont); and (4) restoration of the Madison Family Cemetery. Among the donors were the Virginia Daughters of the American Revolution and the Mary Morton Parsons Foundation. Both organizations continued to be important financial supporters in future years. In addition, the Trust pursued a federal appropriation for the Dolley's Wing restoration project that was included in the strategic plan.[11]

An Unexpected Resignation Occurs

Throughout 1999, as in past years, Kathy Mullins and other Montpelier staff continued to be required to devote considerable time to seeking approvals and obtaining financial information from the Trust. While its leadership had generally seemed to be willing to transfer authority in accord with the 1998 alternative management agreement, frustrations remained an annoying part of working with Trust staff. For Kathy, challenges associated with meeting the fiscal year 1999 revenue targets also were an ongoing concern. More troubling, Kathy realized, was that even if budgeted revenue levels were achieved, the funding still would not be adequate to build enhanced programming to significantly increase visitation. For these reasons and personal considerations, Kathy informed Dick Moe and me on May 18 that she was resigning to head up a living history museum in New England.[12]

The cumulative impact of Kathy's resignation, Glen Moreno's withdrawing from the Board and the collapse of the $8 million challenge, together with the backdrop of the past lack of progress, caused at least one director to question whether our vision of creating a national Madison monument might be unachievable. Lou Potter had worked unceasingly for more than a decade in an advisory role and attracted the few significant contributions individual donors had made. Reflecting her concern about Montpelier's future, she said, "Bill, if you will give this [effort to build a successful historic site] another year, I will too." Unlike Lou, I had been involved for only a couple of years and was not as disheartened as she understandably was. In general, other directors also saw Kathy's departure as just another hurdle we would have to surmount. Lou continued in her longtime role as a leader and, as will become clear, was essential to the future success that followed.

Hiring a New Chief Executive

Upon receiving Kathy's resignation, the Trust began a search for a new executive director. After it narrowed the applicants to three well-qualified candidates, Joe Grills and I joined Dick Moe and two other Trust executives, David Brown and Greg Coble, to interview candidates. Michael "Mike" C. Quinn was the most impressive candidate—despite visibly suffering from a broken collarbone he'd incurred in a bicycle accident the previous weekend—and our unanimous choice. Mike was then the deputy director for programs (the number-two staff person) at George Washington's Mount Vernon and previously had been director of education there. Prior to that, he had held positions at several historic-preservation nonprofits. He had also been highly recommended by, among others, Daniel Jordan, president of the Thomas Jefferson Memorial Foundation. Shortly after that single interview, Dick extended an offer to Mike.[13]

In addition to being the Trust's executive director, Mike would become president and CEO of the Foundation. In preparation for accepting the positions, and after collaborating with me, Mike sent Dick a memo outlining conditions of his acceptance. Dick immediately approved them. Mike's highest priority conditions were that the Trust (1) fulfill commitments that Dick had made to give the Foundation autonomy in operating Montpelier and (2) support making the Madisons the focus of Montpelier, including restoring the house as much as possible to its appearance when they lived there.[14] After Mike joined Montpelier, and at a time when full house restoration seemed inconceivable, one staff member privately questioned Mike's interest in restoration, saying it seemed to be his only priority. But Mike proved to have the vision we needed.

New Relationships Key to Montpelier's Future

The importance of relationships with two philanthropists that developed in 1999 cannot be overstated. We learned that renowned philanthropist Paul Mellon, who died in February 1999, had bequeathed $1 million to the Trust for Montpelier.[15] To take advantage of this much-needed bequest, we reached an agreement with the Trust for it to do the following: (1) transfer about $350,000 to Montpelier's endowment to cover the amount the Trust had withdrawn to pay *Discovering Madison* expenditures; (2) reimburse the Trust for Dolley Madison Commemorative Coin marketing expenditures and a portion of the operating budget it had provided; and most importantly, (3) build fundraising capability with about $500,000. Later, the estate's executors, Frederick "Ted" A. Terry Jr. and Beverly Carter, advised Dick and Mike that Montpelier could be considered for possible additional support from Mr. Mellon's estate. This development had the effect of dramatically changing Montpelier's future (as discussed in chapter 5).

Philanthropist Robert H. Smith also was responsible for a $1 million commitment in 1999. Lou Potter and her husband, Alan, had previously introduced him to Montpelier. Working with The Nature Conservancy, Mr. Smith offered to contribute $800,000 to purchase an easement that would protect Montpelier's 200-acre old-growth forest. He additionally committed $200,000 to renovate two small houses for use in connection with Madison-related educational activities for teachers, scholars and interns. As with the Mellon bequest, Mr. Smith's gifts would begin a multiyear relationship resulting in momentous physical and program changes.[16]

In a precedent-setting development, Montpelier also entered into a partnership with James Madison University in 1999. Initially, the principal focus was on JMU's joining in Montpelier's archaeological investigations and planning for celebration of James Madison's 250th birthday.[17] JMU staff also designed a logo for the new name Mike and I, with Board support, selected for the site: "James Madison's Montpelier."[18]

Other Notable Developments in 1999

Wishing to express appreciation to the founding members of the Madison Cabinet, Mike and I hosted a "Hunt Breakfast" in the duPont dining room prior to the annual steeplechase races.[19] Attendance was small, but Cabinet members were quite enthusiastic about Montpelier's prospects. As she did for many events while Mike, her husband, was president, Carolyn Quinn planned and oversaw all the details for the breakfast. This became an annual opportunity to entertain donors. The steeplechase races have been run since the 1920s on the first Saturday in November. A separate nonprofit that the Trust organized, the Montpelier Steeplechase and Equestrian Foundation, remains responsible for managing the races—a highlight of the fall social calendar in Piedmont Virginia. Under an agreement with the Trust, it is a de facto Foundation subsidiary.[20] To assure that the steeplechase will continue, a duPont descendant set up an endowment to support the event.[21] The steeplechase foundation covers Montpelier's costs for the course's maintenance and makes a financial contribution to the Foundation each year.

Toward the end of 1999, at Mike's urging, the Board reviewed whether it should change the manner in which visitors came onto the property. Instead of visitors being transported in shuttle buses, Mike proposed that they drive onto the property and park, after paying for admission and getting a mobile audio guide at the Visitor Center on Route 20. For parking, lots could be created where the duPonts' swimming pool and tennis courts had been. Agreeing that the proposal offered an improvement from both cost and visitor-convenience standpoints, the Board approved it.[22]

Mike envisioned this change as part of a larger "Open Gate" initiative. In addition to creating a parking lot and access road to it, the initiative included a figure-eight trail network. One loop began at the parking area and led to the mansion, with return through the back gate of the garden. The other loop went to the Madison Family Cemetery and site of Mount Pleasant, with return to the parking lot by way of the Enslaved Cemetery. The local landscape architect for the project, John James, helped us recognize the viability of the pool/tennis court site for parking and as a possible location for a future visitor center (see chapter 9). We implemented "Open Gate" in 2000. This meant that the property would be open in 2001 when Montpelier celebrated Madison's 250th birthday.[23] Dick Moe agreed to the National Trust's lending the Foundation the necessary funding, estimated to be $258,000. This one-time expense would result in eliminating the $120,000 annual cost of shuttle buses.[24]

Taking another organizational step, directors developed a list of proposed Board committees to work with staff. Initially, with our small Board, only a few were created. Committees set up over the next few years were for finance, development, education and visitor experience, marketing and buildings and grounds. Either an ad hoc subgroup or the entire Board would handle human resources and director nominations. The bylaws authorized formation of an executive committee of six to nine directors and gave it authority to act for the Board. At the outset, however, there were too few directors to establish one.

New Board Directors in 1999

The Board was strengthened in 1999 by the addition of three new directors:[25]

- Hunter R. Rawlings III, PhD, a classics scholar and professor, was president of Cornell University and previously president of the University of Iowa. A scholar of the nation's founding period, Hunter has read extensively and is highly knowledgeable about Madison. His expertise had been widely remarked on after he made a commencement speech focused on Madison at nearby Woodberry Forest School.[26]
- Walter W. Craigie was an investment banker who previously had been the first elected treasurer of Virginia and secretary of finance for the Commonwealth. He also served as chair of the board of Woodberry Forest School and on boards and investment committees of numerous other organizations.
- Margaret "Peggy" B. Boeker (now Rhoads) is a collateral descendant of James Madison[27] and was a director of the Madison Family Association. She had extensive public relations experience, serving in roles in overseas U.S. embassies and other federal offices.

Both Walter and Peggy had been members of the Montpelier Property Council.

The major strides in 1999 laid the groundwork for our considering whether to pursue co-stewardship with the Trust. The strategic plan had established the vision and initiatives for Montpelier to become a fitting presidential historic site. The visitor experience and operation of the site had been improved. Perhaps most important was that we had hired a talented chief executive with decades of relevant experience. We were optimistic that these strengths would put us on the path to future success.

4

MANAGEMENT TRANSFERRED TO THE MONTPELIER FOUNDATION—2000

BROAD AUTONOMY AND RESPONSIBILITY GRANTED

For much of 2000, negotiating co-stewardship with the Trust was the principal focus of the Foundation's attention. Negotiations with Dick Moe and his staff throughout the process were amicable. But they became increasingly intense in the latter stages as we dealt with terms governing decision-making over building and landscape changes. In the end, though, the Trust agreed to give the Foundation the promised high degree of autonomy. This was unprecedented for a Trust-owned site. Other Trust sites have expressed envy about the Foundation's autonomy, while regretting that their agreements don't provide it. We also made advances in 2000 on a number of other fronts: (1) preparation for celebration in 2001 of the 250th anniversary of James Madison's birth, (2) hiring key staff, (3) expanding the Board, (4) gaining funding support for restoration of Dolley's Wing, (5) improving physical access to the property and (6) building donor support.

Preparations for Negotiating Co-Stewardship

Before deciding to pursue co-stewardship, the Board devoted considerable time to discussing whether the time was propitious to assume full responsibility for Montpelier's management. Having been in existence for little more than a year, the Foundation had little experience and success in raising significant financial contributions. On the other hand, we were confident we would continue to attract talented directors and were optimistic about the leadership Mike Quinn would provide. After weighing the pros and cons, the Board ultimately concluded that the prospects for building Montpelier into a nationally significant historic site and a monument to James Madison were sufficiently strong to justify proceeding with negotiations. Furthermore, we felt strongly that the future was brighter with the Foundation becoming the site's steward than if the Trust continued in that role.

Agreements Required for Co-Stewardship. The Trust's legal framework for co-stewardship involved three separate agreements: a Cooperative Agreement, a Lease and a Loan Agreement.[1] The Cooperative Agreement would provide a comprehensive statement of the terms governing the nonprofit's management of the site. The Lease would establish the length of each term, provide for renewals and prescribe the maximum Lease period. The Loan Agreement would set forth the terms for the use and handling of collections of furnishings and artifacts the Trust owns that the nonprofit would retain for its use. Once the maximum length of the Lease is agreed on, reaching an understanding on the terms of the Lease and Loan Agreement should generally be quite straightforward, as would be the case in our negotiations.

Categories of Management Responsibilities. Management of a historic site with buildings in various physical conditions and real property of varying importance involves two basic categories of actions. One is the day-to-day operation of the site. This includes development of programs, fundraising to support its operations, employing staff and allocation of responsibilities, maintenance of facilities and financial accounting and oversight. The other involves stewardship of buildings and the landscape, including restoring, modifying or demolishing existing buildings; siting and construction of new buildings; and protection of sensitive viewshed and resources on the land.

Research for Developing Co-Stewardship Terms. In late 1999, Mike and I began to pull together our preliminary thoughts on terms that should be included in the co-stewardship agreements. For background, we reviewed a number of agreements that the Trust had entered into with other nonprofits. Unlike Dick Moe's autonomy commitment to us, those agreements required that other sites obtain approval from the Trust for all major actions—particularly ones that involved building or property changes. The nature and extent of the Trust's oversight role would obviously determine whether the Foundation would have the autonomy we were seeking. Up to this time, I had intentionally not discussed this in detail with Dick. I thought it best to use the autonomy concept as a touchstone for working out specifics of the Foundation's powers and responsibilities in our negotiations.

General Negotiation Objectives. Not surprisingly, our objective was to start with a framework that set the outer bounds of Foundation authority we believed to be reasonable. We were confident that negotiating terms to give the Foundation responsibility for day-to-day management would not present a significant challenge. But negotiating terms to govern actions involving existing and new buildings and the landscape would likely be much more difficult. Complicating reaching an agreement would be our intent that co-stewardship continue for decades. Understandably, the Trust would want to ensure that current—and future—Foundation Boards would manage Montpelier consistent with stewardship appropriate for this historic site. Nonetheless, by carefully circumscribing the Trust's role, we were confident that the Foundation could obtain sufficient authority to carry out any reasonable future plans.

General Limitation on Trust Oversight. Developing terms to give the Foundation sufficient authority over an estimated 135 buildings and approximately 2,650 acres would require creating a much different oversight regime than in any existing Trust co-stewardship agreements. In preliminary discussions, Trust staff had said that while the Trust would continue to be interested in all of the site's buildings and landscape, it would require a major role in connection with only four buildings. They were the Mansion, Temple, Train Station and Montpelier Farm Store, which was then in use as the Visitor Center.[2] Appropriately, the Trust's greatest level of involvement would be with respect to proposed changes to the Mansion and the Temple, the only two buildings with known Madison provenance. It would be essential that any changes to them meet the most rigorous preservation standards. Mike and I believed that the Trust's oversight role should be minimal in connection with other buildings. Some would need to be modified or restored, if they were to be used. Others would not be able to be used productively or were collapsing and would need to be demolished. For these buildings, the Foundation needed to have final authority over what actions would be taken.

Development of Draft Co-Stewardship Provisions

Trust Oversight of Important Buildings. In February 2000, Mike prepared a proposed set of instructions for outside counsel to use in drafting the co-stewardship agreements.[3] The principal focus was on Cooperative Agreement terms related to stewardship of existing buildings. The outline did not address new construction. The instructions envisioned that the Trust would have the opportunity to review and approve changes to only the four buildings the Trust staff had said would be of principal interest. We believed that terms to govern actions affecting the Temple, Train Station and Farm Store would be easy to develop. In contrast, we knew that crafting provisions related to the Mansion would be challenging. We intended to provide the Trust with an approval role in connection with major changes. At the same time, we wanted to specify the conditions under which the Trust must approve a future Foundation request to restore the house to be the Madisons' home. Unfortunately, one of these conditions would have to be amendment of the Will Settlement to eliminate the requirement to retain two duPont rooms. I feared that this might not be achievable.

Agreement on Key Financial Terms. Among the other terms to be included were a number relating to the Foundation's current and future financial condition. Obviously, raising revenues to support Montpelier's operations would become a basic Foundation responsibility. But there were several important financial terms involving the Trust to be addressed. A key consideration in the Board's decision to pursue co-stewardship in 2000 was the Trust's commitment to continue funding operations at the same level through fiscal year (FY) 2003. These were the specific amounts:

FY00 $430,000
FY01 $445,000
FY02 $460,000
FY03 $475,000

Terms for the Trust's management of its Montpelier endowment also were needed. Most important was the withdrawal amount that the Trust would pay annually to the Foundation. We recommended that it be at least 5 percent of the endowment principal. More controversial would be our proposal of terms under which the Trust would transfer its Montpelier endowment to the Foundation. We proposed that the transfer could be triggered, at the Board's option, when the Foundation raised $5 million in endowment contributions. We also included the terms for applying the $1 million Mellon bequest, consistent with our prior discussions.[4]

Lease Terms and Control of Property. Another critical term to be negotiated was the Lease's duration. We wanted to propose that the Foundation would have the right to continue as steward for as long a time as the Trust might agree. We recommended that the Lease's maximum length be 100 years, not 25 as Trust staff had suggested. We expected that other provisions would be noncontroversial. Each Lease term would be five years, with automatic renewal for successive terms unless the Foundation gives notice of intent to terminate. The Foundation would have authority to grant subleases without Trust approval. The consent of both parties would be required for the sale of a portion of the Montpelier land or for creating an easement on it.[5] The Will Settlement prohibited sale of the historic core of about 800 acres where the house is located.

Board Consideration of Terms. The most important agenda item for the Executive Committee's February 18 meeting was consideration of the proposed instructions for drafting co-stewardship terms. After reviewing the instructions, directors made several minor suggestions and then authorized development of draft documents for submission to the Trust.[6] Thereafter, throughout the period in which Mike and I prepared for, and engaged in, negotiations with the Trust, I held numerous conference calls with directors. The principal purpose was to discuss the substance of terms under consideration and obtain support for, or modify, positions we proposed. Joe Grills, Mike and I also had regular conversations to supplement Board discussions.

Preliminary Discussions with Trust Staff. Later in February, Mike met with Trust assistant general counsel Thompson "Tom" M. Mayes to begin discussions on the scope of the Trust's role in reviewing proposed actions affecting existing buildings. Shortly thereafter, Mike had further conversations on this issue with Tom and other Trust staff. The discussions had these results:

- In Mike's initial conversation with Tom, Mike was told that it would be necessary to *notify* the Trust of proposed major changes to all buildings, structures or features and to thoughtfully consider any Trust objections.

- Trust staff indicated that they intended to identify a small group of buildings for an explicit Trust role that would be less significant than for the Mansion and the Temple. For these other buildings, if the Foundation proposed to remove all or a portion of a structure, any Trust objection to the proposed *removal* would have to be resolved to its satisfaction. The implications of this would be that the Trust could veto the removal of any portion of those buildings. Not wanting the Trust to have this authority, we decided not to incorporate this provision in our instructions to counsel for preparing the first draft of the agreements.
- The Trust staff proposed a requirement that the Foundation maintain all buildings. We agreed to accept this obligation, but only if it would be subject to a proviso that the Foundation would not be required to carry out maintenance, preservation or restoration for a building at a level greater than what the Trust had provided.[7]

We had made significant progress in crafting a narrow role for the Trust with regard to the Foundation's making changes to buildings. The only buildings for which Trust approval would be required for all major changes would be the Mansion and the Temple. Our principal objective of limiting Trust oversight seemed within reach. Even if we agreed to the Trust staff position that the Trust would have the right to object to *removal* for a small number of other buildings, making building decisions would not be too greatly constrained.

Importance of the Foundation Being Final Decision-Maker. The Trust staff's acceptance of the Trust not being the final decision-maker on proposed changes to almost all existing buildings had important long-term implications for the Foundation. The Trust had performed little or no maintenance to address the massive needs of a high percentage of the buildings. The Foundation would not have the requisite substantial resources to impede the buildings' further decline. Not having to perform greater maintenance than the Trust had, we would be protected from a claim that we were carrying out insufficient maintenance. Making decisions about adaptive reuse or demolition would be solely within the Foundation's discretion. In the unlikely event the Trust concluded that preserving a building proposed for demolition would be important, it could exercise an option to provide necessary funding for renovation and maintenance.

Trust's Request Regarding Changes to Landscape. As we had anticipated, the Trust staff said that it would also be necessary for the Trust to have a role in reviewing proposed new construction and other material changes affecting the landscape. In response, we included a provision that called for the Foundation to notify the Trust of proposed major landscape changes and take into account any Trust objection, but with the Foundation having final decision authority.[8]

Preparation and Negotiation of Co-Stewardship Agreement Drafts

I asked Celia Roady, the partner responsible for the Morgan Lewis law firm's nonprofit practice, to take the lead in preparing drafts of the co-stewardship agreements. (Although then a partner, I was not the Lewis in the name of the firm, which was formed in 1873.) She secured the assistance of her colleague Carolyn "Morey" Ward. Celia, Morey and other Morgan Lewis lawyers provided many hours of invaluable legal assistance to the Foundation on a pro bono basis throughout the co-stewardship negotiations and on a number of future matters. Morey prepared drafts of the agreements using the instructions we had developed. Mike and I then reviewed and revised five rounds of drafts over the next two months.

Trust Concerns with First Draft. On April 25, I forwarded drafts of the three co-stewardship agreements to Dick.[9] After reviewing the draft Cooperative Agreement, the Trust informed us that, in a number of respects, the draft did not provide it an adequate role. For day-to-day management, the Trust agreed with the Foundation's having authority to operate without Trust approvals being required. Only if material changes in the Foundation's plans were proposed would it be required to consult with the Trust. But the Trust raised objections to its having only the limited role provided in connection with proposed changes to buildings and new construction.[10]

Dispute Resolution Added for Building Changes. Mike and I went back to the drawing board to develop terms that might be acceptable to the Trust. But we wanted to do this while still making certain that the Trust would not be in a position to block reasonable Foundation actions. As Mike explored concepts with Trust staff, we realized that the Trust might insist on a role somewhat similar to what it had for the Mansion and Temple in reviewing material changes to a small group of additional buildings. Also, a more significant role would be necessary for it in reviewing new construction. In one major respect, though, we were able to negotiate a major improvement: the inclusion of a dispute resolution process. This would be available for addressing unresolved Trust objections in circumstances in which the Foundation alone would not be the final decision-maker. We thereby eliminated the possibility of a Trust veto of proposed changes to any building, including the Mansion and the Temple, without an opportunity for further review.

Allocation of Roles for Building Changes in Second Draft. On May 31, I sent Dick a revised draft. We proposed an oversight scheme for building changes and new construction that we believed would resolve almost all, if not all, the areas of disagreement:

- The Foundation would have final decision-making authority over actions involving all buildings, except for material changes to the Mansion and the Temple and significant changes to the *exterior* of a small number of other identified buildings. If any Trust objection to those actions could not be resolved, the dispute resolution process would be the vehicle for reaching a decision. Before making significant changes to any buildings, we would have the obligation to consult with the Trust and seriously consider any objections.
- For new construction *within the house's viewshed*, the Trust would be consulted and participate in reviewing the Foundation's plans. Here also, the dispute resolution process would be available for any unresolved Trust objection. For new construction *outside* the viewshed, however, the Foundation would have final decision-making authority.
- The dispute resolution process would be set up in the typical three-person format. The Trust and the Foundation would each appoint one member, and those two appointees would select a third.[11]

Specific Authorization for House Restoration. A new provision, which Mike stressed as being essential, would specifically authorize full restoration of the house, as long as the Foundation complied with applicable Will Settlement terms and with the U.S. Secretary of the Interior's restoration standards. Because it was our understanding that some Trust staff opposed approving the potential for restoration, Mike and I felt that the Trust's agreement to the authorization may have been due to the belief that the Foundation would never be able to surmount the high hurdles for restoration. Happily, any who had that belief proved to be wrong.

Finalization of Agreements and Signing Ceremony

Frustration of Negotiators. As discussions with Trust staff ensued, it appeared that the Trust would still not find acceptable a few key terms that we had proposed. For a time, this led Dick and me to engage in conversations that raised the specter of our not reaching an agreement. Both of us thought we had been especially reasonable in working out compromises and were frustrated that any disagreement remained. The principal unresolved issue at the end was the Trust's position that it should be able to invoke the dispute resolution process for any unresolved objection to new construction anywhere on the property—not just new construction within the house's viewshed. We had good reason to limit the Trust's role outside the viewshed as much as possible. Our paramount concern was that resolving Trust objections might take so much time that the Foundation could lose support of major donors and doom new construction projects.

Final Issue Resolved. After a number of conversations with Dick, I realized that the Trust's unstated, reasonable concern might be that the Foundation could potentially undertake expansive construction inconsistent with the integrity of the property. This might include residential development, hotels or motels or large-scale retail development. We had no interest in making any of this possible, certainly not solely at the Foundation's option. To alleviate the possibility of any Trust concerns, I proposed that unresolved Trust objections to such "non-mission-related" activities anywhere on the property be addressed through the dispute resolution process. For "mission-related" activities outside the house's viewshed, however, the Foundation would have the final decision-making authority. The Trust ultimately accepted this compromise, after I agreed to include an appeal condition that Dick requested. The Trust would have the opportunity to present its concerns to the Foundation Board if an objection was not resolved satisfactorily.[12]

Agreement on Remaining Details. With few exceptions, the Trust accepted terms we proposed on other topics. The principal change of consequence we agreed to was a 75-year maximum Lease period, not 100 years as we had proposed. Also, the endowment annual payment was not fixed at 5 percent. Instead, it would be the same percentage applicable to all other Trust-owned properties. In the past, it had been as low as 4.5 percent. The Trust would not agree to setting an endowment threshold, which, if met, would give the Foundation the right to have the Trust-controlled endowment transferred to it to manage. We obtained the option, however, to have the Trust manage the endowment that the Foundation raises. Later, we exercised that option. The Trust had a history of hiring capable investment advisors and achieving favorable results. To involve the Foundation in endowment oversight, the agreement provided that we could appoint a member of the Trust's investment subcommittee, which oversees investment of the Trust's entire endowment. We appointed Joe Grills, and he became, in effect, our permanent representative. (See chapter 11.)[13]

Foundation Achieves High Degree of Autonomy. As we wound up negotiations, the co-stewardship terms, in our view, provided the high degree of autonomy that we insisted on to control Montpelier's future.[14] The Foundation would have final decision-making authority on all actions, except where the Trust had unresolved objections to major changes to the Mansion, Temple and the exterior of thirteen other buildings (all of which were important to protect),[15] and to new construction within the house's viewshed or any outside it that is not mission-related. For those exceptions, the dispute resolution mechanism would be available for any unresolved Trust objection. Obviously, the Foundation and the Trust would have a strong incentive to be reasonable and constructive in working out disagreements. Both would surely recognize the value of maintaining a spirit of cooperation and avoiding a breakdown in their important relationship.[16]

Parties Herald Agreement at a Signing Ceremony. The ceremony to execute the co-stewardship agreements was held at Montpelier in September. Representing the Trust were Dick Moe, president, and William "Bill" B. Hart Jr., Board chair; representing the Foundation were Mike Quinn, president, and me, Board chair. It was an opportunity to highlight the significance of the agreement for Montpelier's future and acknowledge those who had made it all happen. Dick said, "Under the strong leadership of Bill Lewis, Montpelier has turned an important corner." He then recognized the Foundation's "skillful and capable Board whose breadth of experience will greatly benefit Montpelier." Mike added that the "new arrangement brightens the prospects" for making Montpelier "a fitting memorial to the life and legacy of James Madison." Pointing out that the "new arrangement yields many benefits," I noted the importance of the "Trust's national visibility and stature." Of particular value, the Foundation's "dedicated Board of Directors" will provide "on-site, entrepreneurial decision-making."[17] Bill Hart said that the Trust/Foundation agreements reflected a "new paradigm" for the Trust's relationship with its historic sites. Montpelier board members Lou Potter, Bitsy Waters and Walter Craigie also witnessed the signing ceremony.

Program Activity and Fundraising

During the period that negotiation of the co-stewardship agreements was underway, the Board and staff took a number of actions to advance Montpelier's becoming a nationally recognized historic site. Mike's ambitious leadership was evident in many spheres.

Madison Birthday Celebrations. Realizing an important opportunity for Montpelier, Mike intensified planning for the 2001 celebration of the 250th anniversary of James Madison's birth. At Mike's request, Foundation director Hunter Rawlings contacted James H. Billington, the librarian of Congress, to propose a joint gala in the Library's Madison Building, in the nation's capital.[18] After agreement was reached, Mike began to retain speakers and set up a planning committee. In 2000, on Madison's birthday (March 16), we held the first Madison Cabinet dinner in the duPont dining room for the increasingly sizable number of donors making annual gifts of $5,000 or more. Stanford University professor Jack Rakove, a distinguished Madison scholar and later a Board member, delivered a thought-provoking speech focused on Madison's legacy.[19]

Government Funding. We also received the following significant federal and state funding commitments:

- Largely due to the Trust's advocacy, Congress appropriated $1 million through the Save America Treasures initiative for restoration of the first-floor Dolley Madison bedroom (Dolley's

Wing). Montpelier had to raise a matching amount.[20] In 2002, in connection with the feasibility study for the house's restoration, we learned that, although Dolley had used the room as a bedroom, Madison-era construction plans for expanding the House in 1809–12 called for the room to be a first-floor library for James.

- Congress appropriated TEA-21 (Transportation Equity Act for the 21st Century) federal transportation funding of $300,000 for restoration of the Montpelier Train Station and improvements for the access to the site. Virginia legislator John J. "Butch" Davies III, federal transportation advisor, provided critical support.[21]
- Following presentations to Virginia legislators by Board member Walter Craigie and Mike Quinn, the legislature increased its appropriation to $500,000 for the next year.[22] State funding abruptly ceased after that due to state budget shortfalls.

Projects for Visitors. The Board and staff also focused on projects to improve the visitor experience, including the following:

- One involved implementing the "Open Gate Project," approved in 1999, to discontinue use of shuttle buses and create new parking areas and visitor walking paths.[23]
- Hiking trails were created in the old-growth forest subject to the easement that Robert H. Smith had purchased.[24] The easement transaction had resulted in $800,000 being added to endowment.
- Renovation of the poorly maintained Madison Family Cemetery moved forward thanks to a $170,000 fundraising effort led by Susan Gonchar, regent (head) of the Virginia Daughters of the American Revolution.[25]
- New director Bud Ince, in his first year on the Board, successfully led the effort to have high-quality highway signage established throughout the surrounding area to direct travelers to Montpelier.

Board Finance Oversight. Having assumed full control of Montpelier's operations, the Board established a Finance and Investment Committee to play a major financial oversight role. The committee's initial members were

Joe Grills (chair), Walter Craigie and David Gibson.[26] Under Joe's leadership, the Foundation compiled an impressive record of fiscal soundness.

Staff Changes. Mike prioritized changes during 2000 to augment the staff's capability. One outstanding addition was Dr. Matthew Reeves, who became director of archaeology and quickly expanded the number and scope of investigations. His talent and enthusiasm allowed him to support archaeology at Montpelier primarily through grants he secured. Over time, he came to be recognized as a leading national expert in his field.

New Directors

The Board elected four new directors in 2000 with diverse talents.

- David E. Gibson, a retired Citicorp senior executive, had worked in areas of corporate and private banking, directing the company's growth in Europe, the Middle East and Africa. He also served as a trustee on several University of Virginia boards.
- Eugene "Bud" St. Clair Ince Jr. had a distinguished career in the U.S. Navy. He was a naval aviator in Korea and later a cryptologist for the Seventh Fleet. He rose through the ranks of naval intelligence and became deputy director of the National Security Agency. He retired as rear admiral, director of Naval Security Group Command.
- Ralph Ketcham, PhD, was emeritus professor of history and political science at Syracuse University. Recognized as the nation's leading scholar on James Madison, Ralph had written extensively on him. His biography had long been the most highly regarded study of Madison.[27] The University of Virginia Press advised me that more than 50,000 copies of the biography had been sold, the most for any book it had published. Ralph also was a member of the Montpelier Property Council.
- David B. Smith, formerly an executive with Charles E. Smith Realty Companies and son of Montpelier philanthropist Robert H. Smith, was an author, editor, publisher and business executive.

The Quinns Settle In

When Mike became the Foundation's president and CEO in 1999, his knowledge of James Madison was not extensive. Within a year of his arrival, he had devoted so much energy to the study of both James and Dolley that he had become a veritable expert on their life and legacy. Widely recognized to be an exceptionally talented speaker, he made numerous presentations on the Madisons at Montpelier events and in other venues. Shortly after Mike arrived, I urged him to be the emcee for all events and thereby become known during his time as CEO as the face of Montpelier. It was a wise decision; his remarks were always thoughtful, well-organized and inspiring.

Throughout 2000, Mike and Carolyn were settling into Bassett House, their new Montpelier residence. Despite improvements made while prior executive directors lived there, the home and surrounding property needed substantial updating and maintenance. Among the improvements the Quinns had to have made immediately were installation of a new roof (it leaked when it rained), measures to obtain potable water (they were advised not to drink it because the water had bacterial contamination) and insulating and replacement of some water lines (three water breaks occurred the first winter, with one causing significant flooding).[28] A garden walk, designed in the 1950s by renowned landscape architect Charles Gillette, adjoined the house, but it was so overrun with vines and weeds that it was almost unrecognizable.[29] A Gillette-designed Oriental Garden on the grounds had received more staff attention, but was badly deteriorated as well. The Quinns, with assistance from Montpelier facilities staff, continued to pursue efforts to improve the Bassett House and property during the time Mike was CEO. They created a tradition of inviting Board members, donors and other Montpelier friends for relaxing lunches and dinners.

5

MADISON MONUMENT ADVANCES TOWARD REALITY—2000–2002

THE FOUNDATION HAS UNEXPECTED, TRANSFORMATIVE OPPORTUNITIES

With management now fully in our hands, we wanted to jumpstart Montpelier's becoming a fitting monument to Madison. Yet the Foundation's limited staff and financial resources in 2001 were barely adequate for existing operations. Undertaking major new initiatives would be possible only with a significant infusion of funding. One already-planned program, however, held much promise: the yearlong celebration of James Madison's birth. This was expected to give Montpelier greater national visibility and increase awareness of Madison's essential role in founding the nation. And indeed, the festivities did result in substantial media coverage and a huge increase in annual visitation. Visitor totals increased by 44 percent, even though visitation all but ended after the September 11 attacks.[1]

What was not expected, and in fact not even imaginable by the most optimistic among us, was the extent to which our dreams and long-term plans to transform Montpelier would be realized over the next 20 months. By late 2002, though, Montpelier's emergence as a national monument to Madison would be on a seemingly secure, well-defined path. By then, we had tangible expectations and prospects to accomplish these goals: (1) restoration of the house so it would truly be the Madisons' home, (2) construction of a new visitor center,

(3) creation of a Constitutional studies center and on-site housing, (4) construction of a new bridge and entryway from Route 20, (5) expanded archaeology and (6) restoration of a cabin of a freedman who had formerly been a Madison slave. To fund these initiatives, financial resources already committed or projected to be obtainable with a high degree of confidence totaled about $40 million. To satisfy conditions established to secure this funding and to implement all the projects, however, would require sustained efforts over a five-year period.

Celebration of Madison's 250th Birthday

House Interpretation Improvements. Since 1998, we had placed heavy reliance on *Discovering Madison* exhibits to tell the story of the Madisons' life. In early 2001, Montpelier's curatorial staff, led by Lee Langston-Harrison, completely redesigned and made more authentic the presentation in the mansion.[2] The most dramatic change was in the room where the Madison dining room had been located. The staff decorated it to present an imagined re-creation of the dinner on November 17, 1824, when Marquis de Lafayette came to visit. Key features included the walls painted bright yellow (believed to be Dolley's choice, but later determined not to be so); more than two dozen original Madison pieces; a Venetian carpet; damask curtains; use of translucent screens to mark the size of the original dining room; a table set for the first course; and life-size cutouts of the Madisons, Lafayette and House servants. Madison family descendants, museums and private collectors donated or loaned many of the items. Several other rooms featured furnishings recently acquired to add to Montpelier's limited Madison collection.[3] We opened the reinterpreted dining room and other house improvements on Madison's 250th birthday.

Front Lawn Celebration. On the birthday morning of March 16, after months of staff planning and making necessary school contacts, about 2,500 elementary-grade children from nearby schools created a "Living Flag" on Montpelier's front lawn. On cue, the children raised red, white or blue placards to form the 15-star, 15-stripe flag that flew when Madison was president. They had to hold them while a helicopter carrying a photographer circled to get the right vantage for a photo. Then they had to face west (looking toward a television cameraman in a bucket truck) and, when all were in position, shout "Good morning, America."[4] Prior to the celebration, Foundation staff had sent information about the Madisons, other relevant historic individuals and Montpelier to participating children and their teachers. To select which students would hold the flag's 15 stars, an essay contest was held. Francis Scott Key immortalized the flag when he wrote the poem that became "The Star-Spangled Banner" after seeing it flying the morning after Fort McHenry's bombardment in the War of 1812. Images of the Living Flag, which measured 228 feet by 135 feet, were seen across the country in hundreds of newspapers and on ABC's *Good Morning America* and PBS's *NewsHour with Jim Lehrer*.[5]

Gala Dinner. The day's celebration concluded with a formal dinner in the Madison Building of the Library of Congress. Before dinner, guests had an opportunity to view original Madison documents displayed specially for the occasion. James Billington, librarian of Congress, and I hosted the event, which was attended by an impressive array of distinguished guests and members of the Foundation's Madison Cabinet and the Library's Madison Council. Chief Justice William H. Rehnquist and Dr. Hunter R. Rawlings III, Cornell University president and Foundation director, presented remarks focused on Madison's significance. Another feature of the evening was a performance on the "Crystal Flute," which is maintained in the Library of Congress's collection. Made of lead crystal, the flute had been presented to Madison when he was president.[6] Among those present were Justices Sandra Day O'Connor, Stephen Breyer and Antonin Scalia of the U.S. Supreme Court. The evening concluded with the appearance of actor–impersonators portraying George Washington, Thomas Jefferson and James Madison, all of whom gave brief remarks.[7]

"Finest" Washington Event. In a letter expressing appreciation for the evening, Justice O'Connor said that she and her husband thought the dinner celebration "was the finest such event we have attended in our 20 years in Washington, D.C."[8] The evening's lead organizer was Mike Quinn, who secured the high-profile speakers. Jean Ince, wife of board member Bud Ince, chaired a committee that was responsible for all the necessary details; members included Carolyn Quinn, Marge Grills, Peyton Lewis, Beese Craigie and Kay Heller.

Recognition of the Enslaved Community

First Descendants Reunion. In April, the Foundation held Montpelier's inaugural event to recognize the enslaved community's all-important role in building and operating the Madison home and plantation. Rebecca Gilmore Coleman, president and founder of the Orange County African American Historical Society and descendant of Madison slave George Gilmore, organized the three-day Slave Commemoration Gathering. Many dozens of descendants of the enslaved people who lived at Montpelier came from across the country. Participant activities included genealogical seminars, reenactments of people who lived during Madison's life, special house tours, an archaeology discussion of Montpelier enslaved housing sites and a tribute to ancestors. Former Virginia governor L. Douglas Wilder, a grandson of Virginia slaves, presented remarks on the legacy of African Americans and their contributions to the nation. Like the celebration on Madison's birthday, the gathering received extensive media coverage.[9] Over the next six years, Montpelier staff worked with Mrs. Coleman and the historical society in developing an extensive registry of descendants. This laid the groundwork for the second Slave Descendants Reunion in 2007. (See chapter 10.) Montpelier's ongoing commitment to recognize the tragedy of slavery and the essential contributions of the enslaved culminated in 2017 in the nationally acclaimed, multimillion-dollar *The Mere Distinction of Colour* permanent exhibition and reconstruction of the housing and ancillary buildings of the enslaved who worked in the House. (See chapters 13 and 14.)

Restoration of Freedman Cabin. After his emancipation, George Gilmore and his wife, Polly, built a cabin in 1870 as a home for their family on Montpelier property. They later acquired the property from a Madison family member. At the time of the first reunion, our staff had almost completed restoration of the exterior of the cabin, which made it of particular interest. The cabin is a small two-story log structure chinked with clay and has a fieldstone chimney.[10] Before its restoration, it faced almost certain collapse. Initial restoration work continued for more than a year. The cabin has been the focus of much attention, due in part to the fact that few homes of former slaves remain. Also, it became important in research focused on George Gilmore and African American life in Virginia. The more in-depth discussion of the Gilmore Cabin in chapter

Freedman cabin of George Gilmore while being renovated by Montpelier team. *TMF.*

10 points out that the Gilmore descendants donated the four-acre parcel associated with the cabin to Montpelier.

New Education Programs

***Sponsor of* We the People *in Virginia*.** Placing increased emphasis in the birthday year on expanding Foundation education programs, we sponsored the national *We the People: The Citizen and the Constitution* program in Virginia. Created by the federally funded Center for Civic Education, *We the People* is aimed at challenging students in high school government classes to become experts on the Constitution. Using the Center's well-designed materials, Montpelier provided teachers free textbooks on the Constitution and the Bill of Rights. To demonstrate their expertise, teams of students participated in simulated Congressional hearings. After presenting testimony, they responded to questions from a panel of experts who challenged their knowledge and understanding of Constitutional issues.[11] Recognizing the value of the *We the People* program, the Foundation sponsored it throughout the next decade and a half. Subsequent to that, a Foundation director established a nonprofit to continue operation of the program in Virginia.[12] (See chapter 8.)

Madison Prize for Students. To broaden students' knowledge of James Madison's contributions, the Foundation and the Center together developed a lesson on Madison that was sent to 8,000 teachers across the country and to every Virginia high school. As part of *We the People* state and national competitions, the Foundation sponsored a Madison Prize. Participating students made presentations on Madison's legacy; to recognize their knowledge, winners received awards in the 51 state (plus D.C.) competitions.[13]

Additional Programs. In 2001, the Foundation also initiated its seminar programs on the Constitution. It held a number of one-day professional development seminars for teachers at Virginia schools and a weeklong summer institute cosponsored by James Madison University and the Center for Civic Education.[14] Altogether, 55 Virginia teachers received instruction on the Constitution from historians and other scholars to enhance their ability to provide students a deeper understanding of founding principles.[15] Complementing Montpelier's emphasis on education, playwright Peyton Cockrill Lewis wrote a musical play, *Mr. Madison Remembers*, which was sent on CD-ROM to all fourth-grade classrooms in Virginia.[16] The setting of the play is Montpelier's front portico. Madison reminisces in his retirement years about his life and lessons learned. The Madison Family Association awarded Peyton the Madison Family Cup in 2002 in recognition of her contributions to advancing knowledge and appreciation of Madison.[17]

Mellon Estate Supports Restoration Study

Potential Mellon Support. In spring 2001, we received the tantalizing news that there was a possibility of obtaining additional funding from the estate of Paul Mellon. The executors of the estate, Ted Terry and Beverly Carter, had contacted the National Trust in April to discuss the possibility of providing support for initiatives at Trust properties. They specifically inquired about Montpelier. The site was a candidate for funding by virtue of its being a designated beneficiary in Mr. Mellon's will. A few weeks later, the executors came to Montpelier and took a tour of the property with Mike Quinn. In the course of their visit, the executors discussed a number of potential projects with Mike. Among them were education programs, restoration of the house, infrastructure improvements and equestrian activities.[18] They asked Mike whether he had an estimate of how much restoration would cost. Mike said he did not but speculated it "would not be a penny less than $10 million."[19] We were quite encouraged when we soon realized that Mike's speculation had not ended the executors' interest.

Request for Education and Restoration Proposals. In early June, Mike and I, together with Dick Moe and David Brown (Trust executive vice president), met with Mr. Terry and Ms. Carter at the Trust offices. At the outset, the Mellon executors informed us that they were interested in potentially providing funding support for education and restoration of the house. Believing these areas had been of great interest to Mr. Mellon, they invited us to submit proposals on initiatives for them. The education initiative was to be of sufficient scope to give Montpelier's programs a national impact. They were most interested in Montpelier's summer institute for teachers and its other teacher training seminars on the Constitution.[20] They also indicated support for improving the Montpelier website and for developing and distributing educational materials. The restoration proposal was to provide for determining the feasibility and costs of restoring the house to its configuration in Madison's time (that is, removing additions and reversing interior changes). The Mellon executors expressed a willingness to fully underwrite the study's cost. If restoration proved feasible, the estate would provide help in funding it. They believed others also would be willing to contribute. We got the impression that the estate might not be willing to fund more than half the costs. Recognizing that we had limited fundraising capability, the executors said the estate would underwrite at least some portion of the costs for us to build a development team.[21]

Management of Expectations. In a June 26 memo, Mike and I advised the Board of the exciting, transformative possibilities arising from the Mellon executors' interest. We stressed the need to proceed with care in pursuing this opportunity, especially in how we would share the news and answer inquiries. We thought that the most sensitive issue might arise with the duPont family. It was critical that the family understand we intended to honor the agreement to retain and interpret two duPont rooms, unless we could reach an alternative agreement with them. We also did not want those in the local community to gain the impression that the bulk of Montpelier's financial needs would be met by funding from the Mellon Estate. The executors specifically limited their interest to the educational and restoration areas and emphasized the importance of our increasing Montpelier's base of support.[22]

Education Endowment Proposal. To encourage support for funding a transformational education program, Mike prepared a detailed proposal calling for the establishment of the Paul Mellon Endowment for Education. He proposed an endowment donation of $5 million. Revenue from it would be dedicated to education on the Constitution: in particular, to providing training opportunities for teachers, focusing on those in Virginia and neighboring states; developing and distributing resources to teachers across the nation; and enhancing the educational experience for visiting students from nearby schools and Montpelier interns. The Mellon Endowment would also create the framework for a Foundation-organized national institute for teachers. Our proposal included a request for $50,000 to support planning for a Constitutional Studies Center. The Center was conceived as a program that would contribute to Americans' understanding of Constitutional principles and to upholding them in their professional and private lives.[23]

Restoration Feasibility Proposal. To satisfy the broad intent of the executors' expressed interest—and contribute to achieving our dream of a Madison monument—our restoration proposal was aimed at funding an investigation comprehensive enough to produce at its conclusion full architectural and construction plans to restore the house. To emphasize the importance of restoration, it stressed Madison's roles as Father of the Constitution and Architect of the Bill of Rights and the role of his restored home in making Montpelier a national leader in Constitutional education. Also, it indicated our optimism that restoration would be possible. A team of experts with stellar national credentials would carry out the study for a projected cost of $760,000. Architectural design would be led by John Mesick of the Albany, New York firm of Mesick Cohen Wilson Baker. He was regarded as the most knowledgeable restoration architect of historic homes of the late eighteenth and early nineteenth centuries in Virginia. The team also would include recognized leaders in other required disciplines. To provide peer review, a Restoration Advisory Committee would be created, with members having relevant expertise and experience.[24]

Mellon Funding Support. Mike submitted the two proposals to the Mellon executors in August 2001, just a little more than two months after their visit to Montpelier.[25] Shortly after receiving the proposals, the executors advised us that the estate would fund the restoration feasibility study (its ultimate cost was $897,000) and would contribute $250,000 toward education programs relating to Madison and the Constitution.[26] They expressed appreciation for the detailed presentations in both proposals. Mike quickly retained the team to carry out the feasibility study and assembled the Restoration Advisory Committee. (Chapter 6 discusses performance of the study, amendment of the Will Settlement and securing funding for the restoration.)

Smith Support for the Center for Constitutional Studies

Houses Renovated for Education Programs. During the time the Mellon executors were considering whether to support the education endowment initiative, we took actions that would advance plans for creating the Center for Constitutional Studies. With $200,000 Robert H. Smith had committed in 1999, we renovated two duPont-era houses for interns, teachers and others visiting for education programs. As a byproduct of phone conversations and meetings about the renovations, Mr. Smith and Mike began to have increasingly serious discussions about the Foundation's vision for Montpelier. This led to Mr. Smith in late 2001 inviting Mike to make a presentation on our highest priority projects.

Proposals Submitted to Robert H. Smith. In a February 2002 letter to Mr. Smith, Mike followed up on this extraordinary opportunity. He described the four initiatives that he and the Board agreed were of the greatest importance: (1) restoration of the house, (2) establishment of a Center for Constitutional Studies, (3) a new visitor center and (4) a new entryway.[27] Mike included a lengthy description of the proposed Center for Constitutional Studies and a draft of the design for the new entry project. In his description of the Center, he incorporated elements of the education initiative that the Mellon executors had declined to support. Since the entryway project was already in the final design phase, Mike provided an in-depth description of it. The project would accomplish a complete redesign of the entrance onto Montpelier from Route 20.

Smith Commitment for Constitutional Studies Center. Mike's letter led to a meeting with Mr. Smith at his historic estate (Heronwood) in Upperville, Virginia. Joining Mike was Montpelier advisor Dennis A. Kernahan (subsequently a Foundation director and Board chair). Following the meeting, Mr. Smith informed Mike in a June 2002 letter that he would make a major commitment to support the creation of a Center for

Constitutional Studies (later renamed the Center for the Constitution).[28] He emphasized how impressed he was with Montpelier's vision and leadership by pointing out that he rarely supported nonprofit "start-ups."

Funding Allocation for the Center. Mr. Smith committed a total of $6 million to fund the Center. Included would be $1 million to create a Constitutional Village. This would fund planning, infrastructure improvements and building renovations. Five duPont-era houses located in close proximity would provide the initial nucleus of the Village. All of them needed significant renovation. Four would provide housing for teachers and others attending educational sessions. The fifth would be for a library. Funding was already available for renovating two of the houses from Mr. Smith's earlier support. The new commitment would fund renovation of the other three. A total of $1 million over a five-year period would support operations. To create a permanent source of funding, Mr. Smith would donate $4 million over a similar period for an endowment.[29] Each year's increment of support would be dependent on meeting the progress goals Mike had outlined. (Establishment of the Center and its programs and their success are discussed in chapter 8.)

Gateway Project

Inadequate Existing Entryway. As discussed in chapter 1, the inadequacies of the entrance to Montpelier were numerous. After stopping at the Visitor Center (formerly a farm store), visitors had to cross Route 20, a rural highway, to a poorly marked main entrance next to the Montpelier Train Station. A ramp led to a single-lane wooden bridge that brought visitors across a railroad track onto the property. The severely weight-restricted bridge would not accommodate tour buses and large emergency vehicles. In short, the Visitor Center and entrance to the property created an uninviting, unsatisfactory introduction to the site.

> Montpelier has three entrances. In addition to the main entrance, there is a west entrance on Jacksontown Road and an east entrance on Dolley Madison Road, both of which are reached from Route 20. The east and west entrances were not used for general access to the site. The access to the east entrance is across a wooden bridge that was in better condition than the original main entrance bridge, primarily because it has a much shorter span and was, and is, maintained by the state. The west access is reached by traveling over a dirt road.

Planning an Improved Entryway. The Foundation had begun developing plans and seeking funding for an improved entryway in 2000. The proposed project's elements included relocating the entrance, improving the bridge or constructing a new one and making improvements to the train station. By April 2001, the Foundation had secured $675,000 in federal TEA-21 funding.[30] Recognizing the need for ongoing oversight of the entryway and other construction projects, the Board had created a Building Committee chaired by director Bitsy Waters earlier that year.[31] At the committee's first meeting on April 9, considerable time was devoted to outlining a process for developing the design of the entryway (called the "Gateway"). The committee's first major decision was to retain outside expert assistance. After obtaining guidance from Mike, the committee hired the highly regarded Kapps and Robbins consulting team. As its first task, the team was asked to develop three design scenarios for the project.[32]

Review of Consultant Scenarios. Shortly thereafter, the Montpelier team received the consulting team's scenarios and reviewed them at a Gateway workshop in May. The scenarios called for improving conditions at the existing main entrance, moving visitor admission operations to a site just across the railroad tracks from that entrance and creating a new entryway at the existing west gate.[33] After discussions in that meeting and several follow-up sessions, the design team reached a consensus that the entrance should continue to be in the same general location. However, we concluded that the design should be different and that significant landscaping and other aesthetic improvements should be incorporated.[34] The committee considered, but ultimately rejected, making sufficient improvements for the west gate to be the property's exit.

New Bridge Required. The design team gave extensive attention to redesigning the main entrance so that it could both serve as the primary entrance and have a positive effect on visitors.[35] It quickly became clear that the old wooden bridge that brought vehicles onto the estate would have to be replaced. The National Trust had improved it with some repairs, but no amount of remedial work could bring it up to current standards or make it consistent with creating an inviting entrance. As the design team began to consider replacing the bridge, it quickly discovered a thicket of constraints. The current restrictions imposed by Norfolk Southern would require two major changes. First, the new bridge must provide for an additional nine feet of vertical clearance for trains. This appeared to necessitate a steeper road approach. Second, the horizontal span would have to be increased to accommodate three tracks (only one track existed). The Virginia Department of Highways' policies would require that any upgraded public entrance provide a right-angle turn off Route 20, as well as turn lanes for traffic in both directions. At first, because Route 20 and the railroad track were so close to each other, it seemed impossible to satisfy all of these requirements.[36]

Realignment of the Entrance. After spending much time considering the various restrictions, the design team finally realized that, by moving the Route 20 entrance a quarter mile south, it would be possible to meet every one of the conditions. Satisfying regulatory slope requirements would cause the ramp to be somewhat elongated, and this would unfortunately necessitate removal of a considerable number of large trees. However, with thoughtful landscaping, the redesigned entry would be much more aesthetically interesting. As a consequence, the realignment would contribute to visitors feeling that they have arrived at an important destination. Adding the turning lanes would contribute to creating this impression as well. The contemplated booth for payment of admission fees could be located along the entry lane as visitors travel onto the property.

New Bridge Options. Perhaps the most challenging issue the team had to address was designing the bridge.[37] The cost implications of each component option would be significant. Three structural options were considered: two that would be constructed of laminated timber and one of steel plate girder (with a concrete deck).[38] Other considerations were whether to have one or two vehicle lanes and a pedestrian/bicycle lane. The consulting team recommended construction of a two-lane concrete bridge with a pedestrian lane. It also proposed that the bridge be built with the optimum size and features in a single project.[39] Adopting a phased-in approach would, of course, result in less cost in the short run. But the overall cost would be greater when the total project was completed. And a phase-in would cause substantial inconvenience to Montpelier's operations. The estimated cost for the single-project option was approximately $2 million.[40]

Agreement on Gateway Design. The design team decided to delay its final decisions until the Foundation had secured all the required funding. But it reached a consensus in 2002 on the fundamentals of the design. These were the key elements:[41]

- Realigning the entry to the south and adding new turning lanes from each direction
- Building a ticket booth to be positioned on the entry lane[42]
- Constructing a two-lane steel girder and concrete bridge with a pedestrian lane that would be reached by a ramp with a relatively minimal slope from the booth
- Incorporating substantial landscaping that would involve removing many trees

Project Funding. Dramatically slowing progress on the Gateway project, in 2002 the Federal Highway Administration ruled that its prior approval of funding did not authorize its use for the new roadway and bridge. Under the changed ruling, TEA-21 funding of approximately $1 million was not available for the project. Our appeals, joined by Virginia's U.S. senators and representatives in Congress, took two years to achieve an acceptable resolution. Ultimately, the Highway Administration authorized reallocating $1,080,000 of Scenic Highway funding to the Gateway project from another Virginia project.[43] The TEA-21 funding originally allocated to Montpelier would be transferred to the other project. For the necessary additional funding, the principal sources would be a Mary Morton Parsons Foundation grant of $300,000 and Foundation directors' personal contributions totaling $300,000 to match the grant. At Director David Gibson's suggestion, the bridge would be named Directors' Bridge.[44] The train station improvements, initially a part of the project, were postponed until funding could be obtained.

Finalizing Design Details and Opening of New Gateway. After federal funding issues were resolved, the Building Committee, together with other design team members, met in August 2004 to address details relating to a host of issues. It finalized decisions on the bridge's height and width, turning lanes, signage, landscape and the bid process.[45] The committee retained the team of Bartzen & Ball to design landscaping and architectural elements, including the ticket booth, guardrails, gate and wall. (See chapters 8 through 10 for descriptions of the Bartzen & Ball team's important role on other projects.) After Kapps and Robbins withdrew from the project, the premier engineering firm of Wiley Wilson was hired to design the bridge and entry road. The Lynchburg, Virginia firm of English Construction was awarded the construction contract.[46] Using a number of local subcontractors, English began work in 2005 and completed the project with exemplary workmanship.

Montpelier Gateway, showing new road, kiosk and bridge. *TMF.*

The final project cost was about $2.8 million, $800,000 higher than the estimate two years earlier. The new Gateway opened on Presidents' Day weekend in February 2007, five years after the design had essentially been agreed on and federal funding was thought to have been approved.[47]

New Visitor Center Plans

Preliminary Considerations. The fourth major project critical for the envisioned Madison monument was construction of the new Visitor Center (the other three being house restoration, a Constitution Studies Center and the Gateway). The location that seemed best suited for the Visitor Center was adjacent to the recently created parking area—a particularly desirable site because the house was within easy walking distance. Archaeology did not seem to present an issue because the duPont tennis courts and swimming pool had previously been constructed in the area. (See chapter 9 for discussion of an unexpected hurdle that had to be overcome.)

The Potters' Essential Role. Recognizing the importance of a new Visitor Center, Board member Lou Potter and her husband, Alan, pledged $100,000 in 2001 for development of the design. Subsequently, construction of a new Visitor Center was one of the funding options Mike submitted to Mr. Smith. After reviewing Mike's description, the Potters let him know they would support its construction and committed $3 million in March 2002. This was the amount then projected to be sufficient for a single facility or a complex that would accommodate visitor orientation, a small exhibit area, a gift shop, bathrooms and possibly food service.[48] (The necessity for a more expansive complex is discussed in chapter 6. Obtaining the required additional funding and construction of the complex are covered in chapter 9).

New Staff Management Position. In light of the number and complexity of construction projects to be carried out in the next few years, Bitsy Waters and Mike realized that greater management capability would be needed than in the past. As a result, they reviewed options for ensuring that the work would meet standards for high quality and efficiency. After considering whether to retain outside consultants or hire staff, they recommended, and the Board approved, creating a high-level staff position.[49] The person in this role also could provide support for the Building Committee and supervise facilities, grounds and gardens. Up to this point, Russell Childs, a retired architect, had been handling many of these responsibilities, but he decided to return to retirement.

New Directors in 2001–2002

The Board elected four new directors in 2001 and 2002 who further broadened the Foundation leadership's expertise:

- Benny Sedwick was president of a local building supply company and had extensive experience in the building industry. The Board indicated a desire for either Benny or his wife, Carolyn, to become a director. Carolyn had been a key member of the Montpelier Property Council for many years. She encouraged Benny to accept the invitation to join the Board, and he was elected.
- Adding distinguished Constitutional law expertise was the renowned A.E. "Dick" Howard, the White Burkett Miller Professor of Law and Public Policy and holder of the Earle K.

Shawe chair (later the Warner-Booker Distinguished Professor of International Law) at the University of Virginia Law School.

- Peter C. Rice was an entrepreneur and a founder of a number of businesses, including Plow & Hearth Inc.
- Arthur J. Collias was an entrepreneur who had founded and taken public a number of corporate ventures.

Both Dick and Peter also were longtime members of the Montpelier Property Council.

At this point, the Foundation had 16 directors with diverse experience and expertise: a lawyer with extensive leadership and negotiation experience, two investment experts with long finance and investment management careers, an architect, a consultant specializing in historic preservation and economic development, a retired senior corporate executive in the banking and finance industry, a building management executive, three entrepreneurs, a university president, the leading Madison biographer, a nationally recognized Constitutional law professor, a retired rear admiral, a Madison family descendant and the National Trust's president. The majority of directors had a history of substantial service on nonprofit boards and fundraising experience.

6

SURMOUNTING RESTORATION HURDLES—2001–2003

ACHIEVING THE SEEMINGLY UNACHIEVABLE

Authentically restoring the house would be both the most necessary and most challenging undertaking for Montpelier to become the national monument to Madison. The property would not truly be James Madison's Montpelier and have national stature as long as the house remained the duPont Mansion. Not restoring the house would compromise Montpelier being, and being recognized as, a leader in Madison and Constitution education. Thus, findings of the feasibility study the Mellon executors funded would play a defining role in shaping not only Montpelier's future appearance but its importance as well.

It was by no means certain that the study would find "restoration" to be possible. Earlier, a respected architectural historian had asserted that restoration could never be more than an "elegant fake."[1] To not keep the house configured as expanded and changed by the duPonts would, he said, be a "monumental blunder."[2] His opinion had been a major factor in the 1989 Trust working group's recommendation that the mansion should be preserved as is.[3] Many local residents, in less dramatic terms, expressed a strong preference that "Mrs. Scott's home," where they had attended her annual steeplechase and other events for decades, remain unchanged. Mrs. Scott had been the most generous philanthropist in Orange County for decades. Indeed, the duPonts–as a consequence of their economic, social, philanthropic and cultural contributions–had been the most important residents since their arrival in 1901.

Even if the study found that a true restoration would be possible, two potentially insurmountable impediments would still have to be overcome. Most daunting would likely be amendment of the provision in the settlement of Mrs. Scott's Will calling for retention of two duPont rooms. It would require that possibly as many as 41 duPont family members sign the amendment. A local court would then have to hold a hearing and issue an order approving it. Securing the necessary funding was also expected to be challenging. The amount required might well be more than the total revenues raised in the entire decade and a half of Trust management.

The Feasibility Study

Structuring the Study

Investigation Team. Under the leadership of the Mesick firm of architects, the Foundation assembled a team with the diverse talents required to carry out a feasibility study of the highest quality.[4] Over the prior few years, experts from the Colonial Williamsburg Foundation (CWF) had been retained to investigate the building fabric[5] of the north wing, Dolley's Wing,[6] to identify the Madison House evidence that remained.[7] The CWF experts' role

Team of staff and advisors studying plans for determining feasibility of restoration of house. *TMF.*

was expanded in the feasibility study to give it the structural investigation responsibility for the entire house. A separate team organized and recorded investigation results. Carpenters and structural engineers were retained as specific assistance was needed. The Mesick firm—which had played a leading role in restoring Thomas Jefferson's Monticello and Poplar Forest, historic University of Virginia buildings and other eighteenth- and nineteenth-century structures—was responsible for undertaking architectural aspects of the study and coordinating with the other project team members.[8]

Restoration Advisory Committee. Mike Quinn assembled a committee with a broad range of relevant expertise to meet periodically and review all facets of the restoration study. The purpose of its involvement was to provide a high level of comfort to the Foundation's leadership that the team's findings and conclusions would receive the preservation community's respect and acceptance. Initially, the Advisory Committee members were skeptical that the investigation would satisfy them that restoration was supportable. The committee's members were:[9]

- William L. Beiswanger, Director of Restoration, Monticello
- John C. Larson, Vice President of Restoration, Old Salem Museums and Gardens
- Calder Loth, Senior Architectural Historian, Virginia Department of Historic Resources
- Travis McDonald, Director of Restoration, Jefferson's Poplar Forest
- Dennis J. Pogue, Director of Archaeological Research and Preservation, George Washington's Mount Vernon
- Orlando Ridout V, Architectural Historian, Maryland Historical Trust
- James M. Vaughan, Vice President, Stewardship of Historic Sites, National Trust for Historic Preservation

Overview of Study Elements. The investigation would consist of two basic parts: (1) exploration of the house's structure to identify evidence that remained, as well as of other buildings for any original House components and (2) research to track down and study archival evidence, which ultimately encompassed visitors' letters and diaries, builders' records and invoices, insurance maps, newspaper accounts, old photographs and other pictorial representations.[10] The Madisons built the House in three phases. Investigators would need to review the building fabric in such depth as to determine the House's design in each phase, even though the restored House's architecture would be as it was ultimately envisioned and configured by James and Dolley Madison.

History of Madison House Construction. Built in the 1763–65 period by Madison's father, James Madison Sr., the House initially had two stories, with four rooms on each floor and a raised basement. At the time, it was the most notable home in that part of Virginia. The House was first enlarged circa 1797–1800 following James Jr.'s marriage to Dolley Payne Todd and his 1797 retirement from Congress.[11] An addition was constructed to create a duplex to accommodate both the James Sr. and James Jr. households. The second and last expansion, in 1809–12, significantly altered the House design. Among the changes were the addition of a centrally located front door, reconfiguration of the first floor to eliminate the duplex design and provide an entry vestibule and a large central drawing room, construction of a rear colonnade, addition of one-story wings on both the north and south ends of the house and reconstruction of several chimneys.[12]

Archival Evidence

James Dinsmore Building Accounts. Fresh from working at Monticello for Thomas Jefferson, master carpenters James Dinsmore and John Neilson and brick mason Hugh Chisholm took the lead in constructing the expanded House.[13] Probably the most important archival evidence was a copy of Dinsmore's building accounts documenting in extraordinary detail the work he and Neilson carried out at Montpelier. The account was some 40 pages long and listed in great detail the elements made and installed in each room and their prices (e.g., baseboard, chair rail, trim, flooring). Mike says it was "like the Rosetta Stone of the investigation." It may have been a copy that Dinsmore created to demonstrate the reasonableness of his pricing to John Hartwell Cocke. This gesture must have been successful, because Cocke hired Dinsmore to build the main house on his plantation, Bremo, with its classical Jeffersonian-influenced architecture. When the study team visited Bremo, its members were able to review work of Montpelier's original craftsmen who would have used the same tools (molding planes, joinery tools, etc.) at Bremo as at Montpelier. Particularly helpful was their gaining insight into original chimneypieces, as well as hardware used on the doors.[14]

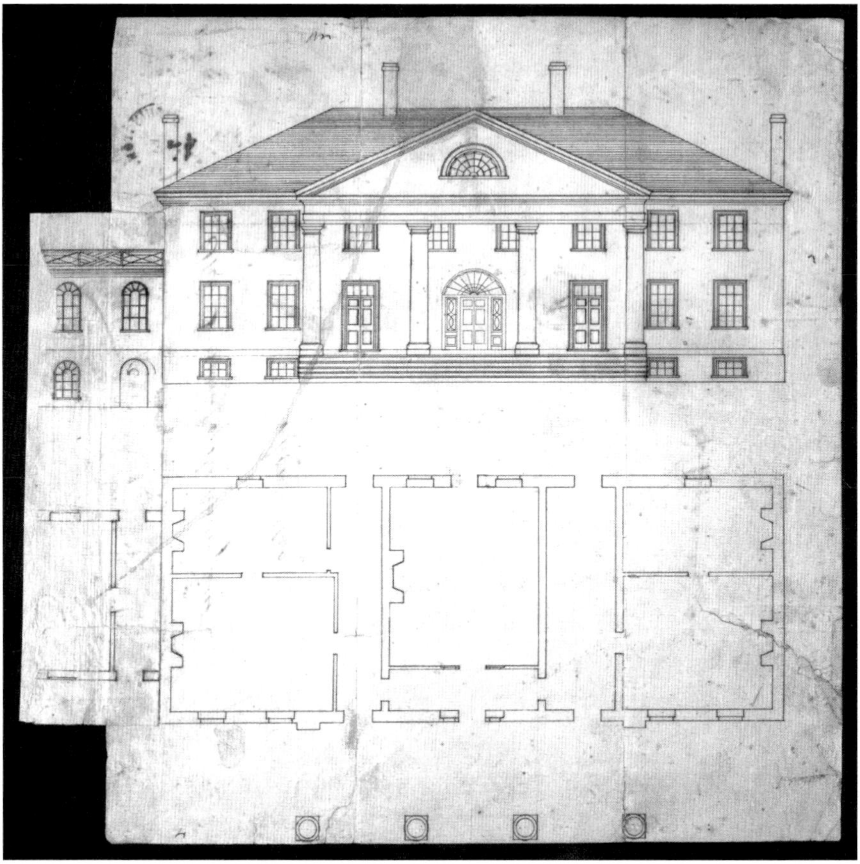

Above: Drawing in 1808 of Montpelier floor plan and elevation attributed to James Dinsmore. *Virginia Museum of History & Culture (Mss5:10 B5628:1).*

Left: Back of Dinsmore 1808 Montpelier Drawing, believed to show handwriting of Thomas Jefferson. *Virginia Museum of History & Culture.*

Original Builders' Drawing. The archival investigation also produced a number of surprises that played a key role in conducting the study. The most important was discovery of a previously unknown drawing. Rarely found in the surviving record of historical homes of that period, the drawing consisted of both an elevation (exterior design) and interior first-floor plan. The investigators believed that James Dinsmore drafted it in 1808, the year prior to the last expansion. Found in the archives of the Virginia Historical Society, the drawing was donated just two years prior to the study's initiation. It had been among the architectural drawings collection of Thomas R. Blackburn. A teenager at the time the drawing was made, Blackburn later began an architectural career working for Jefferson at the University of Virginia. The drawing was instrumental as a guide to providing confirmation of the House's final exterior design. Notes on the drawing in Jefferson's handwriting were consistent with letters between Jefferson and Madison.[15] They contributed to understanding Jefferson's role in expanding the House.

Other Nineteenth-Century Evidence. Researchers also found other significant archival material. For example, they located in a private collection an 1802 watercolor of Montpelier painted by Anna Maria Thornton, wife of Dr. William Thornton, a friend of the Madisons (and to whom the painting until recently was attributed). It represents the only painting known to exist of the House prior to the 1809–12 changes.[16] Rough drawings of

Watercolor, Anna Maria Thornton, circa 1802. Purchase made possible through the generosity of several Montpelier patrons. *TMF.*

the House in the pre- and post-construction configuration were found in Montpelier insurance policies. Mutual Assurance Society issued the policies in 1799, 1808 and 1813.[17] Photographs from the late 1800s showed original walls, doorways and windows in several rooms. Numerous builders' letters and records of their work and material purchases also contributed greatly to understanding design details.[18]

Evidence from the Building Fabric

House Investigation Techniques. Under the capable hands-on direction of CWF investigators Mark Wenger and Myron Stachiw, researchers explored the structural fabric using the latest techniques to find the evidence obtainable from the building itself. With great care to preserve architectural details and disturb them as little as possible, investigators peered into every surface. Over 300 subsurface study units were opened to determine where walls, stairs, doors and windows had been located. They also looked for and examined as many nails and nail holes as possible. Every layer of the fabric—plaster, paint, wallpapers, floors, lath and roof—and associated details were scrutinized so that a comprehensive analysis could be conducted. To document the basis for their conclusions and guide restoration, the team assembled extensive records of their findings in detailed notes, photographs, drawings and measurements.[19]

Structural Discoveries. Throughout the study, important evidence of the House's original fabric was identified in myriad ways. The following are examples of findings:

- Because the Madison stairs no longer existed and had been in different locations than those of the duPonts, determining their design was difficult. However, while investigating a small office that William duPont added to a post-Madison period bowling alley (circa 1850s), researchers found boards from a Madison stairs plank-enclosure with original painting that showed the outline of steps.[20] It was particularly useful because it belonged to one of the stairways to the cellar for which little other evidence survived.[21] Also found in the office addition, used as floor beams, were the original north and south wing roofing members that provided physical evidence of the exact configuration of the Jefferson-designed serrated roofs.

- The design and materials of the roofing shingles were determined from a few shingles that had fallen into the attic when the original roof was replaced in the nineteenth century. The 1765 central core's shingles were mostly white oak and chestnut. On the 1797 addition, they were heart pine.[22] Not only did the overlooked shingles give the original wood species, but also their shape revealed an important design feature: the shingles "fanned" out to the "hipped" exterior corners of the roof, butting to smaller narrow shingles that ascended along each hip. At interior corners, the valleys of the roof were installed with a "swept" design (i.e., shingles sweeping continuously from one roof slope to the adjacent slope).[23]
- In assessing narrow window sashes on either side of the front door and corresponding sashes in the drawing room doorway, investigators found that the windows, which had been painted shut, were movable to provide cross-ventilation. The ones on either side of the front door were designed to drop down into cavities in the wall—and they retained the original six-strand hemp rope attached to the sashes. The windows in the interior wall moved sideways on small brass rollers.[24]
- Stucco on the House's exterior brick walls was initially believed to be from the Madison period. But through photographs and testing, it was determined to have been added in the mid-nineteenth century after the Madisons' ownership. This was most clearly discernible where stucco at each end of the central section of the House had stopped next to the 1840s hipped roofs of the adjoining wings—*after* the Madison-era serrated roofs had been replaced.[25]
- Through various techniques, the House was found to have had 65 doorways. About 38 of the doors were located despite the House's substantial later renovations and expansions. More than half, however, were found in new locations. Paint ghosts on the doors provided details on how doors were hung and on the hinges and locks used.[26]

Study Conclusion

Authentic Restoration Is Achievable. After reviewing the abundant evidence amassed in the eight-month investigation, researchers concluded that, even though less than 1 percent of the house had been opened up, perhaps as much as 90 percent of what needed to be known had been discovered.[27] Based on their experience with restoration of other buildings, they were confident that work required in restoration would lead to further knowledge that would allow the house to be fully returned to the Madisons' configuration.[28] Given the extensive changes over a 200-year period, reaching this conclusion was no mean feat. Researchers emphasized that one critical key to restoration being possible was Mr. duPont's obvious care to maintain the Madison home's fabric as he expanded the House, originally with 22 rooms, into a 55-room Mansion.[29]

The History in Digital Images. Using evidence from the investigation, the recordation team produced digital images of the House as it existed after each of the three construction phases. This allowed the Foundation to educate a wide audience about the study and the House's evolution and final design.[30]

Digital image of Montpelier's first phase, built in 1763. *PartSense Inc., TMF.*

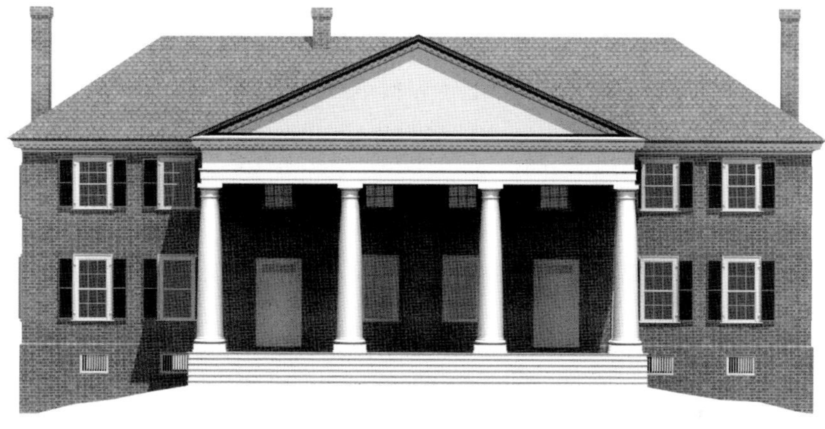

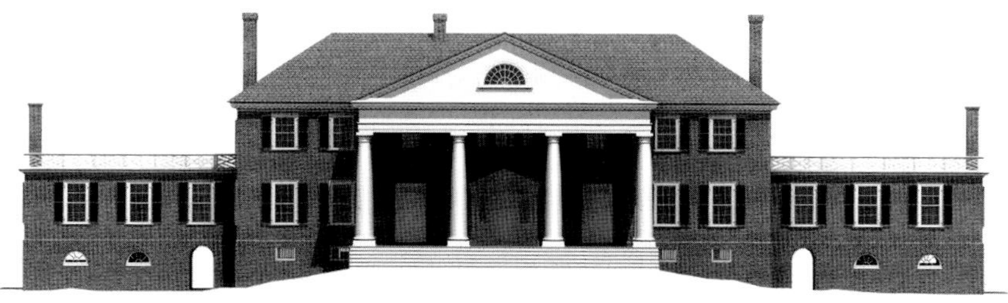

Top: Montpelier representation after second phase, built in 1797. *PartSense Inc., TMF.*

Bottom: Digital image of Madisons' House after final construction phase, in 1809. *PartSense Inc., TMF.*

Plan for Restoration

Details of Work to Be Required. After determining that restoration was feasible, the Mesick team developed a detailed plan for undertaking it and prepared a cost estimate for all aspects of the work.[31] The construction sequence and restoration methodology called for the work's performance over a 56-month period.[32] Phasing of work—from the demolition of post-Madison elements and removal of salvageable building fabric, to the reconstruction of lost features and addition of necessary building support systems—would allow there to be continuous, complementary activities throughout the almost five-year period. To illustrate the plan, the team developed detailed drawings and a meticulously prepared timeline.[33]

Precise Cost Estimate. Using the drawings, it was possible to describe, with great specificity, the work that would be required. More than a dozen expert craftsmen prepared detailed cost projections of specific tasks. The entire team that expected to participate in the restoration worked with architects to develop the final project estimates. They proudly advised that, due to the study's scope and intensity, the construction cost estimate could be prepared with "considerable confidence," and was far more detailed than would normally be possible.[34] The estimated cost was $21,767,500. It was summarized in a comprehensive five-page breakdown and included amounts for contingencies to reflect the inherent uncertainties due to the nature and duration of its work.[35]

Advisory Committee Study Findings. After meeting with the investigation team throughout the study and completing its review, the Restoration Advisory Committee gave its seal of approval, saying, in part:

> *This committee affirms its belief that the case has been made to restore the house to the Madison period. It is clear to us that the extremely high quality of the research has set a new standard for architectural investigation and documentation. It is important that this same high standard be maintained throughout the restoration, and we recommend that the project be guided by an ongoing process of peer review.*

The committee completed oversight activities in July 2002 and issued its formal statement on January 29, 2003.[36]

Mellon Estate Financial Support

Transmittal of the Final Study Report. On July 15, 2002, Mike transmitted the final study report to the Mellon Estate's executors.[37] Accompanying the report was a strategy for operating Montpelier through the period of restoration and undertaking other major initiatives to build it into a nationally recognized historic site. The strategy contained three discrete parts:

- Most important, of course, was conducting the actual restoration itself, which was estimated to cost $21,423,300, an amount slightly less than the Mesick report indicated due to final review and refinements.

- The second category was "initiatives associated with restoration," a smorgasbord of actions with a projected cost of $15,820,000. These included vacating the mansion, maintaining visitor programs, undertaking a development campaign, building a gallery to honor William duPont, raising substantial endowment and furnishing the restored House.
- The third group was made up of other major projects already planned—creating the Constitutional Studies Center, building a new Visitor Center and undertaking the Gateway Project—with a total cost then projected to be $15,350,000.

Altogether, the three-pronged strategy called for an aggregate investment of $52,593,300, a staggering amount for a nonprofit only four years old.[38] It showed, though, that the restoration's cost would be less than half of the total for the initiatives that taken together would elevate Montpelier to be recognized as a national Madison monument.

Strategy for the Funding Meeting. A meeting with the Mellon Estate executors to discuss restoration was held on July 17 in the Trust's Washington, D.C. offices.[39] In a pre-meeting, Mike, Joe Grills and I met with the Trust's Dick Moe and David Brown to prepare a strategy for seeking funding from the estate. Recalling that the operative assumption when the study began was that the Mellon executors might not be willing to contribute more than half the cost, Dick questioned whether we should request more than that. I insisted that we should boldly ask that they contribute the total cost. The key to our request would be its obvious rationale: the project could not be started unless we had all the funding. We could not interrupt the work—with, say, the house partially demolished—for extended periods due to lack of funding. If the Mellon Estate did not provide the funding, it might be years before we would be able to obtain it and begin demolition. The team agreed to have me present our case that the estate fund all or almost all of the cost.

Request for Funding. The executors listened to our presentation and seemed to recognize the logic and merit of our funding request. They expressed great admiration for the study's quality and the detailed 56-month work plan. At one point, Mellon Estate coexecutor Beverly Carter asked whether we thought we could raise *any* portion of the cost. We responded that we were confident we could—if we had their commitment to fund almost all of it. We believed that the executors' demonstrated belief in the project would allow us to attract other donors. One point the executors emphasized was that the restoration must fully return the home to its Madison configuration. This meant we must negotiate an amendment to the Scott Will Settlement so that the duPont drawing and morning rooms could be removed. At the meeting's conclusion, the executors said they would consider our request and get back to us with their response.[40]

Funding Agreement. The executors quickly transmitted a draft agreement proposing to grant $20 million for restoration. They included a provision authorizing use of $2 million to build fundraising capability for both restoration and other initiatives. As expected, the draft provided that no funding would be distributed until the Will Settlement had been amended. The draft agreement also called for restoration completion by the end of 2007. After the intent of several provisions was clarified, the executors' counsel prepared a final agreement.[41] With great enthusiasm, the Board's Executive Committee approved it on September 13.[42] The full Board approved the agreement on October 16.[43] By the end of October 2002, all parties, including the National Trust, had signed it. Mellon Estate coexecutor Ted Terry told me later that during a visit to Charlottesville in 2000 he had come to Montpelier and concluded then that the house should be restored to the way it was in Madison's time. Needless to say, it would have been nice to know about his interest when we considered what funding amount to request.

Amendment of Will Settlement

Honoring the duPonts. With the requisite knowledge for authentic restoration and a commitment for funding in hand, the remaining essential element was amending the Will Settlement. From the time the Foundation was formed, as we stressed in our 1999 Strategic Plan, we had placed a high priority on honoring the duPont family. Montpelier would not have become a national historic site devoted to James Madison without the family's extraordinary generosity. Consistent with Mrs. Scott's stated desire that the Mansion be returned to the Madisons' configuration, her grandnephew James "Jamie" H.T. McConnell Jr. encouraged Mike Quinn, Joe Grills and me soon after the Foundation was incorporated to pursue the possibility of revising the Settlement. Doing so would entail gaining support from all (or almost all) the living descendants of William duPont Sr. For this reason, we understood, as Jamie emphasized, it would be necessary to devise an appropriate alternative way to honor Mr. duPont. See the prologue for a discussion of the legal challenge to Mrs. Scott's Will and the negotiations that ensued to resolve the litigation.

The Relationship with the duPonts. The National Trust's relationship with duPont family members, as well as with many local Orange County residents, had become strained since the Trust acquired Montpelier in 1984. Indeed, this dated back to the litigation over Mrs. Scott's estate. For the Foundation to begin building a relationship with the family, Jamie McConnell arranged a meeting with Henry E.I. duPont and Martha duPont, his wife, at their estate in Greenville, Delaware, to be held on August 29, 2001.[44] Henry and his brother John, grandsons of William duPont, had taken the lead in challenging Mrs. Scott's bequest, which resulted in the Will Settlement. Jamie joined Mike, Joe and me for the visit.

The Delaware Meeting. We talked with Mr. and Mrs. duPont for several hours at their home about Montpelier developments since the Foundation had become responsible for its management. Our focus was on plans to improve the visitation experience and expand education opportunities. Along with our commitment to the property becoming a Madison monument, we emphasized that we placed a priority on honoring the legacy of William duPont and his family at Montpelier. To give the duPont family a meaningful advisory role, we told Mr. and Mrs. duPont that we wished for two family members to become ex officio directors and hoped they would become the initial family representatives. This would ensure that they would receive all Board materials and have an opportunity to provide the Board and senior staff with advice on matters of interest to them.[45]

The duPonts' Concerns with the Trust. As we were concluding our discussion, Mr. and Mrs. duPont asked us to join them for lunch at a nearby restaurant. When we finished a relaxing lunch and were about to leave, Mr. duPont commented favorably on the Foundation's work but expressed frustration about the Trust's stewardship. He was particularly troubled that the "first thing [the Trust] wanted to do" was to remove the Mansion's wings. It was my understanding that he had been opposed in 1984 to making it possible for the Trust to restore the house. We feared that his comment might indicate that it would be difficult for the Foundation to obtain his support for restoration, which would, after all, involve removing almost 66 percent of the Mansion. More time would likely be needed to gain his confidence.

Not having obtained the final feasibility study results, we thought we had at least a little time for this. Also, not having discussed funding with the Mellon executors, we were not yet certain we would be able to fund restoration, even if it were found to be feasible.

Brainstorming Recognition Possibilities. By late 2001, it was clear that the study would find that we could carry out an authentic restoration. After returning from our visit with the duPonts, we began to brainstorm about how to honor William duPont Sr. in a more effective and significant way than could be done in the drawing and morning rooms. Because we were planning to build a new visitor center, Mike's initial thinking was to include a room or rooms in it that would tell the duPonts' story at Montpelier. Before developing a proposal, however, we wanted to have additional opportunities to talk with Mr. and Mrs. duPont and Jamie McConnell. In January 2002, Mr. duPont died. To be respectful of Mrs. duPont's loss, Mike postponed contacting her for several months.

Preliminary Views on William duPont Recognition. In April, Mike met with Mrs. duPont at her Key West, Florida home. In a wide-ranging discussion, she expressed her support for proceeding with restoration plans. As to modification of the Will Settlement, Mrs. duPont discussed possible ideas for telling the duPont story by re-creating rooms in a separate facility or establishing an exhibit in a new visitor center. But she had concerns about how to incorporate some of the duPont rooms' design features and the finest pieces of furniture. At the meeting's conclusion, they agreed that Mike would develop draft plans for her consideration.[46]

Initial Recognition Proposal Unacceptable. Having received support for restoration from the widow of the principal challenger of Mrs. Scott's bequest, we pursued discussions with Jamie McConnell with a renewed sense of urgency. In addition to his having long been a proponent of our negotiating a Will Settlement amendment, he was the one duPont descendant who was a local resident. Initially, Mike developed a proposal to establish an exhibit room to honor William duPont Sr. in the planned new visitor center. The room would incorporate key features of Mansion rooms and present information about Mr. duPont's life. In early May, following a meeting with Mike and Joe, Jamie made it clear that the visitor center room proposal was a nonstarter.[47] Since his support was essential, we intensified our negotiations with him to develop an acceptable proposal.

William duPont Gallery Proposal. Over the next two months, Mike, Joe and I met a number of times with Jamie and Charles "Charlie" H. Seilheimer Jr. (a friend of Jamie, who participated at his invitation) to discuss how to honor William duPont. After their rejection of the sufficiency of a room or rooms in the visitor center, we began to discuss construction of a separate facility (the William duPont Gallery) adjacent to the planned new visitor center. The Gallery would have three public spaces. As our conversations with Jamie proceeded, Mike and I began to focus on the fact that Montpelier, once restoration occurred, would not have any large space for dinners, lectures and similar events. So, we recognized that a significant benefit would result from one room being a great room, at least as large as the combined drawing and morning rooms. To make amending the Will Settlement even more acceptable, we suggested that the large room could feature significant elements of the drawing room and be appointed with appropriate duPont furnishings. The amendment we proposed listed some of the elements and furnishings to be included. A second public area would be an interpretive space devoted to telling the duPont story at Montpelier.

Recognition of Mrs. Scott. Re-creation of Mrs. Scott's art deco Red Room with her equestrian memorabilia would be the third public space. It had been a highlight of many visitors' tours. Since her bequest had been responsible for the Trust acquiring Montpelier, it seemed essential to us that her interests be presented in the Gallery.

Additional Honoring of the duPonts. Even though the Gallery would recognize William duPont and his family in a far more impressive fashion than could ever be done in the two mansion rooms, Jamie and Charlie insisted that we provide additional means to recognize the family. We then agreed to name the formal garden for Annie Rogers duPont. Although aspects of the garden had other progenitors, she had been responsible for most of its architectural features and plantings. The Madisons created the garden's terraces, and renowned landscape architect Charles Gillette later made minor design contributions. The Foundation also would formally agree to establish a weekend of equestrian activities of the type conducted during the residency of the duPont family (ideally, the steeplechase races in the fall) as a permanent annual event. To give further continuing assurance of duPont family recognition, I agreed in a phone conversation with Jamie at the conclusion of our discussions to provide that there would be no buildings in Montpelier's historic core devoted to presenting or interpreting individuals or families other than the Madisons and duPonts.[48]

Support for the Amendment. The Will Settlement amendment, when finalized, was an eight-page document.[49] In addition to the meetings Mike, Joe and I had with Jamie and Charlie, Mike and I had discussed details of the amendment numerous times with Jamie. Joe also had talked individually with Jamie and Charlie on a number of occasions. By mid-June, after several conversations about minutiae, Jamie said he was prepared to support the amendment. As the owner of the Montpelier property, the Trust also advised that it would formally support the amendment. Of great concern to the Board was the cost that would be entailed in building the separate William duPont Gallery, rather than including recognition in a visitor center for which we had a $3 million commitment. But obtaining the support of Jamie and family members would not have been possible without our having negotiated the much grander duPont tribute. One important benefit—recognized then and of continuing value—was that the Gallery would serve as the needed venue for major Foundation events. To assure that no delay would occur in the Gallery's construction, Jamie insisted it must be completed no later than completion of the house's restoration (i.e., 2007).[50]

The Approval Process Begins. On June 25, Mike and Jamie met with Mrs. Martha duPont to discuss the amendment. She began the meeting by saying her husband would have wanted the house restored, setting the stage for a productive discussion. Jamie gave her background on his role in discussions and why he felt it was appropriate to revise the Will Settlement. He pointed out the amendment afforded the family much more recognition than was provided under the existing agreement. Mrs. duPont reviewed the amendment terms and expressed appreciation for inclusion of the ex officio director authorization, under which a duPont family member would always hold that position. They discussed the process for getting signatures and decided she would sign first. Also, it was agreed that it would be best for Jamie's mother, Mrs. Jean Ellen Shehan, to handle contact with John duPont, who had challenged Mrs. Scott's Will.[51]

Family Approval. On August 21, Mike and Jamie traveled to Mrs. Shehan's summer home in Easton, Maryland, to review the amendment to the settlement agreement with her. After reviewing its terms, she agreed to endorse the amendment and assist in obtaining other family members' support.[52] To encourage their support, Mrs. Shehan, a niece of Mrs. Scott and granddaughter of William duPont Sr., sent family members a letter supportive of restoration that advised them of the need to amend the Will Settlement.[53] Mike followed up by sending a letter in late October to all who would be required to sign. It provided substantial background on Montpelier developments, a copy of the draft amendment and the procedure to follow in signing it.[54] Over the next five months, Mike coordinated an effort with Jamie to obtain signatures. Most of the 41 family members who needed to be served with the amendment quickly indicated support. But in the end, five family members did not sign. Happily, none of the non-signers, likely due to Jamie's influence, responded to us with any objections or concerns.

Court Approval. In preparation for seeking court approval, we had retained the Fairfax, Virginia law firm of Blankenship & Keith in mid-2002. From that point until the hearing on August 18, 2003, the firm (primarily through partner William Porter) provided advice and assistance for securing favorable court action.[55] On the day of the hearing, when we arrived at the court, we observed that three of the non-signers were in the courtroom. We had not been told whether any of the three might object to the court's issuing an order granting approval. We also didn't know what the judge might do if there was such an objection. As a result, there was quite a bit of tension among the Montpelier team when the proceeding began. Judge D.R. Bouton of the Orange County Circuit Court quickly relieved our concerns. After dealing with several preliminary matters, the judge announced his favorable views about plans for Montpelier's restoration and the anticipated local community benefits. The counsel for the Foundation and the National Trust, Hugo Blankenship, an avuncular senior barrister, and William Porter quickly handled introduction of the Montpelier team and recounted the necessary procedural history of the petition to modify the Will Settlement.[56] The judge did not ask if there were objections to the petition, and none was made. He then signed the order approving the petition.[57] And we breathed a collective sigh of relief. So, as of August 18, 2003, the Foundation had satisfied all prerequisites for restoration to begin. Funding to supplement the $20 million commitment of the Mellon Estate would be necessary, but the Board was confident it could be raised.

7

HOUSE RESTORED—2003–2008

THE MADISONS RETURN TO MONTPELIER

Restoration began immediately following the court's approval of the Will Settlement amendment. In quick order, we received the first $5 million of the Mellon Estate's $20 million commitment[1]—at the time believed to be the largest single gift to a historic property. The estate provided the balance in increments based on staff annual budget projections. The Mesick feasibility report had premised its detailed restoration roadmap and 56-month timeline on work beginning in August 2002,[2] but the time required to amend the Will Settlement delayed its start until fall 2003.[3] Although already widely known locally, restoration's commencement was publicly announced in an October press release. "Montpelier is the last home of a founding father to become a public site and to undergo restoration," CEO Mike Quinn proudly pointed out. "No restoration project of this significance to the founding of the American republic will ever be undertaken again."[4] The interest nationally was reflected in the extensive press coverage the announcement received, including a lengthy, favorable article in the *Washington Post*.[5]

One of the most important purposes in my writing this history was to create a narrative record of the major projects that were essential to transform Montpelier into the national monument to James Madison—and at the head of the list is the restoration. The scope of the work involved in restoring the house was so extensive that it is quite challenging to summarize the hundreds of tasks that were necessary to accomplish the authentic restoration. Nonetheless, this chapter provides an in-depth review of the restoration process and the performance of the multitude of required individual projects. In doing so, it will describe one remarkable discovery of the original House's details after another. Because of its importance, the restoration is described in more detail than some readers may wish to delve into. The following is a chronology of the highlights:

- Assembling a world-class team to design, manage and perform many complicated projects
- Removing and relocating all the contents of the Mansion (this required special care for those items to be included in the William duPont Gallery)
- Preparing a permanent record of the duPont rooms through photography, maintaining samples of architectural features and other techniques
- Creating an interim visitor experience to provide education on the Madisons in the Pony Barn Education Center
- Demolishing 66 percent of the Mansion that was built post-Madison, while ensuring that walls and floors of the original House did not collapse and interiors were not compromised[6]
- Installing scaffolding and enclosing it to allow work to continue throughout the year
- Performing extensive masonry work, which included removing stucco from the brick exterior, repairing damaged brick where possible and obtaining necessary replacement bricks in the many original colors
- Creating a state-of-the-art heating and cooling system that called for installation of 12 geothermal wells, as well as a bunker under the rear lawn for a vault for the associated equipment system
- Taking steps to avoid intruding on the House's interior spaces in providing heating and cooling, which included building an underground duct and installing ducts in chimneys and wall cavities

- Constructing roof systems with the original design, which included first determining the design for the House's central part from shingles discovered in the attic and installing a "serrated" roof over the wings, as designed by Thomas Jefferson
- Re-creating the exact interior design and restoring numerous features, which included building walls in their original location and relocating arches, windows and doors—and, where necessary, producing and replacing floors, doors, windows and plaster
- Identifying structural features not observable during the feasibility study, including ones as difficult as locating nail holes for the Madisons' extensive collection of mounted art objects
- Returning the front portico to its original design and re-creating the rear colonnade
- Performing archaeology investigations for all areas likely to be disturbed and ones not previously studied near the House, which led to discovering the location of the original front lawn fence and its postholes

The description of the restoration process in the balance of this chapter elaborates on the process in great detail. But in reality, to tell the full story of this historic endeavor would by itself require a book-length treatment.

Overall Management Responsibility

A threshold decision was whether we should retain an outside general contractor (GC) or serve in that critical role ourselves. We devoted considerable time to assessing the advantages and disadvantages before deciding which approach to take. The advantages of an outside GC were that it would (1) be a firm with more experience than we had, (2) give us a guaranteed price (or at least give us control of expenses) and (3) have insurance in case of a disaster (such as collapse of a portion of the house). One director strongly encouraged retaining a GC. The negatives would be that workers would not be selected by us or under our direct control. Thus, they might not have the training to be sensitive to new evidence of original fabric revealed during demolition or construction. Valuable evidence might be inadvertently destroyed. Even worse, driven by the GC's concern about price and schedule, its team might intentionally not disclose possible evidence that turned up. We felt that having full control would allow us to achieve the highest possible restoration quality, although it meant that we would be assuming much greater risk. As stressed in several earlier chapters, an uncompromising commitment to authenticity was paramount.[7] Based heavily on Mike's advice, we decided to act as GC. This proved to be an excellent decision.

The Restoration Team

Project Architect. Building on the relationship developed during the feasibility study, we negotiated a contract with the Mesick firm to be the project's architect.[8] Its principal responsibilities were to prepare construction drawings for all aspects of the work, revise the drawings as necessary throughout the restoration and make twice-monthly visits to the site.[9] Timely production and revision of drawings were essential to complete restoration by the end of 2007, the deadline the Mellon executors emphasized must be met.[10] Given that restoration was beginning one year later than the study's schedule had provided, any further delays would create significant concerns about our retaining the executors' confidence. Later, when drawings necessary for interior work were delayed, or revisions were required, tension sometimes ensued between the Mesick and Montpelier teams.[11] Importantly, though, Mesick continued to be a key advisor, and the working relationship remained strong. Helpful advice also was received in the periodic reviews of the Restoration Advisory Committee.[12]

Restoration Crew Management. The feasibility study report proposed that a crew manager be designated for the project's central management responsibility. The manager would have the challenging jobs of coordinating with the Mesick team and overseeing activities of Montpelier's crew and numerous craftsmen and contractors. Mesick encouraged integration of outside specialists with an in-house crew as a proven method for accomplishing a high-quality restoration. The Montpelier crew would have the lead day-to-day role, just as in Madison's 1809–12 House expansion. It would primarily be made up of skilled carpenters. Specialized tasks—millwork, masonry work, plastering, roofing and paint analysis—would be the responsibility of experts in each trade.[13]

John Jeanes Named Director of Restoration. In consultation with Mesick, Mike made the decision to have the crew manager be a Montpelier employee. During the feasibility study, John Jeanes, a master carpenter Mike had hired for varied Montpelier tasks, played an increasingly significant management role. Mesick recommended that John be crew manager. He said John had demonstrated the managerial and master carpenter talent required to lead the restoration team. With the concurrence of all who had worked with John, Mike named him director of restoration.[14] This would prove to be perhaps the single most important decision to having restoration carried out in the world-class manner called for by the Restoration Advisory Committee. Of great significance, John also managed the costs and schedule to meet the study's projections. His attention to detail and master-level carpentry skills—combined with his engaging, unflappable demeanor—made him the ideal leader for the project. Later, to assist John, Steve Chronister, a master carpenter throughout the project, was named deputy crew manager.

The Key Role of Mark Wenger. Shortly after we made the final decision to proceed with restoration, Mark Wenger left the Colonial Williamsburg Foundation and joined the Mesick firm so that he could play a key role. At the Montpelier team's request, Mesick agreed to have Mark be on-site full time to guide the architect's detailed work.[15] Having been the principal leader in conducting the feasibility study, he was perfect for that responsibility. He was a genius at interpreting the evidence and explaining it to others in a way that inspired their enthusiasm and dedication. With less than 1 percent of the structural fabric so far investigated, details still needed to be learned from further investigation.[16] Mark's unrelenting work ethic—oftentimes he'd revise drawings overnight—alleviated timeliness concerns with the Mesick firm. Mike referred to John Jeanes and Mark as "the heart and soul of the day-to-day work of restoration."[17]

Continued Importance of Key Feasibility Study Team Members. We also employed other members of the study team to play key roles.

- Montpelier's architectural research staff (directed by Alfredo Maul, 2003–05, and Gardiner Hallock, 2005–08) had primary responsibility for recording and digitizing the evidence discovered.[18] Digital animation of the three stages of the Madisons' home that Alfredo prepared showed how each stage was modified to create the next.[19]

Director of Restoration John Jeanes examining windows that had been painted shut. They were designed to slide into the front wall to provide ventilation. *TMF.*

Architectural historian Mark Wenger investigating subsurface study unit. *TMF.*

- The Foundation's archaeological staff under Matt Reeves's leadership was tasked with evaluating subsurface areas that were expected to be disturbed.[20] Its focus would be areas below the basement and adjacent to the House, as well as locations for temporary roads, a mechanical vault and a geothermal well field required for the heating and cooling system.[21]
- Historical research was primarily the responsibility of Ann Miller, a historian, author and researcher with expertise on the Virginia Piedmont during the time of James Madison's life.[22] Her in-depth familiarity with records of that period ensured that the team would have access to relevant historical research.

Nationally Renowned Specialists Are Retained. The restoration's historic nature facilitated our attracting numerous specialists who were highly respected in their fields and willing to make the time commitment necessary over an extended period.

- Among the most important specialties was woodworking (millwork). While most of the doors and window frames from the Madisons' home ultimately were located in the duPont Mansion, all would need repair and missing ones would need to be replicated. Numerous other specialty wood features—wainscoting, arches, stairs, doorframes, mantels, exterior shutters and others—would have to be created. For this, Montpelier retained Blaise Gaston, a native of nearby Charlottesville and a nationally recognized, architectural woodworking specialist.[23]
- For the sensitive tasks of surgically removing stucco from exterior brick walls and making extensive brick repairs and reconstructions, Ray Cannetti was the ideal choice.[24] He was a renowned brick and stone specialist with significant experience at George Washington's Mount Vernon and Colonial Williamsburg. Based in St. Mary's City, Maryland, he was originally trained as a stonemason; as an apprentice, he carved sculptural elements on the Washington Cathedral.[25]
- Similarly challenging was the analysis of samples of plaster and paint to determine their characteristics during the Madison period. Selected for this was Dr. Susan Buck, a highly regarded

Top: Archaeological investigation under the house's front portico. *TMF.*

Middle: Woodworking specialist Blaise Gaston performing one of many detailed window projects. *TMF.*

Bottom: Masonry work by Ray Cannetti. *TMF.*

Dr. Susan Buck analyzing stain on a chair for the house. *TMF.*

conservator and paint analyst whose experience includes analogous work at Mount Vernon and Winterthur Museum, Garden and Library in Delaware.[26]

Preparations for Restoration

Sequencing Work to Keep the House Open. Underlying the study report's sequencing of restoration tasks were several considerations important to ongoing Montpelier operations. First and foremost, it was essential that the house, or at least some parts of it, remain open to visitors throughout restoration, except for a limited period during demolition.[27] While interior restoration was underway, spaces open to visitors would have to be shifted from time to time based on the nature of work being done. Visitor admission fees, albeit not substantial, were necessary to keep Montpelier viable. A concern, though, was whether visitors would be willing to pay to tour the property when the house would have the appearance of a construction site. Board member David Gibson viewed the issue differently; he believed that the result might be increased visitation. Mike decided to address this issue by offering a money-back guarantee to any visitors with concerns. Happily, few requested to be reimbursed and relatively few chose to forego taking a tour. Indeed, many expressed the feeling, as David had speculated, that it was a memorable opportunity to see the house while restoration was in progress.

Removal of House Contents. To minimize inconvenience to visitors caused by removing the duPont additions—and to maximize access to the house—all major demolition work was done during the first year (2003–04), principally during the winter months.[28] This necessitated prior removal and relocation of all of the rooms' contents. Furnishings with duPont provenance required special handling. Items in three rooms, some of them valuable antiques, would later be exhibited in the William duPont Gallery. The design and decoration of the duPont drawing and morning rooms would be the inspiration for design of the Gallery's great room. Mrs. Scott's art deco Red Room, while not part of the duPont additions to be demolished, was carefully deconstructed so it could be re-created in its entirety in the William duPont Gallery.[29]

Documenting the duPont Mansion. The restoration team went to great lengths to create a permanent record of every duPont room.[30] Documentation began with detailed photography and photogrammetry (taking perspective-corrected photographs for making accurate measured drawings). The team kept and organized samples of the distinguishing architectural features of each room, including the baseboard, window trim, flooring, wall paint and wallpaper. It also preserved a mantel, stair handrail and other features. Additionally, a cross-section of all decorative ceiling treatments was cut out and preserved. The large volume of duPont building artifacts was initially housed off-site in a rented warehouse in nearby Orange. Later, after a Morton Building barn was built on-site, the items were moved into a considerable portion of this new building. The documentation was created in such detail that it would permit a later researcher to understand, as well as obtain a sample of, almost any aspect of the duPont home.[31]

Interim Visitor Experience and Education Facility. The curatorial staff reorganized the Pony Barn, which housed the Montpelier Education Center, and furnished it to create an interim visitor experience.[32] The staff modified its two large first-floor rooms and mostly displayed furnishings previously in the duPont Mansion. In one, they arranged furnishings to create two Madison rooms: Dolley Madison's bedroom and the dining room. While preparing to furnish the restored House, the staff learned, however, their interpretation did not accurately represent the Madisons' décor. In the other large room, a substantial number of period furnishings, several of which had Madison provenance, were displayed in museum style on platforms. A third first-floor room was used for showing a film on the Madisons that had been commissioned for the *Discovering Madison* exhibit. In the reception area, an exhibit, *James Madison: Architect of the Constitution and the Bill of Rights*, presented Madison's role in not only the creation of the two founding documents but the ratification and implementation of them as well.[33] The curatorial staff used the upstairs for office space. To replace education space no longer available in the Pony Barn, the restoration team acquired two trailers and located them close by. The education staff used one as a classroom and dining area; the other had a kitchen and bathrooms.

Demolition of Post-Madison Additions

Magnitude of the Demolition. The restoration's first phase was to deconstruct portions of the Mansion that post-Madison owners had added.[34] This shrank the house so that the exterior footprint was the same size as the Madisons'. The staff placed in storage all structural elements they deemed to have any value. Reuse or disposal decisions were to be made later. Items that deserved special protection were crated. As with the samples selected before demolition, the volume of the material to be stored was so great that storage was necessary in off-site warehouse space.

Ensuring the Structure Is Not Compromised. Demolition required an extraordinary level of care to ensure that the house did not collapse. The restoration team knew that certain walls adjacent to the duPont additions would require special care.[35] But the team did not expect to find that parts of walls were so unstable they would require significant repair and reinforcement to ensure their structural soundness.[36] This instability had multiple causes: water intrusion, mortar deterioration, inadequate bonding in the original masonry and walls having been overloaded by the weight of duPont floors added. There was a general feeling that, if restoration had not been undertaken, at least one exterior wall would have collapsed within a few years. John Jeanes's attention to detail and anticipation of possible problems during demolition avoided this catastrophe. Mike believes that the magnitude 5.8 earthquake that occurred in the Piedmont region of Virginia in 2011 "would have brought most of the house down!"[37]

Demolition Sequencing. Demolition started with removal in entirety of the rear of the southeast wing (on the right-hand side of the mansion, which included the duPont drawing and morning rooms and rooms above them).[38] Next was removal of the attic and second floor over the front section of the southeast wing. The first-floor space below was referred to as Nelly's Wing because it had been the living space of James Madison's mother. The portions of the northeast wing not part of the Madisons' home were then demolished. The section that remained was known as Dolley's Wing. The northernmost wings, which were outside the Madison House footprint, were not demolished at that time. They housed the duPont boiler that would be used during the project for heating and the former kitchen that became the on-site millwork shop. A donated trailer was placed nearby as an additional workshop to make repairs needed on original Madison fabric, such as window frames, sashes and doors.[39]

Restoration—2004–05

Preliminaries to Interior Work. The restoration team scheduled work on areas that were part of the Madisons' home so that it generally began after demolition of the duPont additions.[40] Some work on them, though, was required during demolition to protect newly exposed areas, as described below:

- Before beginning any demolition adjacent to a Madison space, the team disconnected power, plumbing and fire protection.
- To stop water infiltration and hold in heat from the duPont boilers, the house was surrounded with a system of scaffolding to support a plastic membrane. This allowed temperature-sensitive lime mortar to be placed throughout the winter. At this point, the house was effectively hidden from view and had the appearance of a construction site.[41]
- Shoring (temporary installation of props) of the house's entire interior—cellar to attic—stabilized failing floor systems while extensive repairs were made. Prior to restoration, the floors' weakness and instability had been a serious concern for Mansion tour safety.
- Most of the first-floor beams had suffered some rot in the ends that were pocketed into the walls and had to be repaired. Because of the extent of termite damage to one massive beam in the oldest part of the house, the team had to hollow it out in order to at least retain its exterior surface. The inside was then reinforced with a composite laminate beam.[42]
- Special steel "cradles" were fabricated and installed to restore second-floor structural beams that had been severed by openings cut for the later stairways.[43]

- Ultimately, the house structure was lifted with a complicated system of hydraulic jacks to return the entire frame to its correct position.

Initial Masonry, Structural and Archaeological Work. Concurrent with demolition, a variety of other activities also were undertaken.[44]

- The masonry team removed much of the stucco on three of the four walls of the House and on the front portico columns. In some places, removal of stucco was complicated by prior repairs done using a Portland cement product that was almost impossible to extricate.
- Brick repair was then begun on the walls and the columns. This involved repairing bricks wherever possible and, where replacement was necessary, using custom bricks from Old Carolina Brick Company. The bricks were handmade to match the dimensions of the Madison-era bricks and carefully fired to replicate the original range of colors. Blending the colors from among the approximate dozen present in the House's historic brick required great skill to make the repairs undetectable.[45]
- Restoration of the front portico required increasing the height of the plinths (or piers) under the columns to their original level. A subsequent owner had cut away the plinths to extend the portico columns to the ground. Archaeologist Matt Reeves fortunately recovered from under the portico a number of the original bricks that had been cut away.[46] They provided clues to the original construction of the plinths and the column bases. Fragments included pieces of the cut brick moldings that had formed the bases of the columns. These assisted in forming the columns correctly and they also revealed the manner of finishing the columns during James Madison's lifetime.
- Structural work was initiated on the Madisons' drawing room and adjacent vestibule in the House's central section (main block) to return them to their original design.
- Work in the basement was required to stabilize the House structurally, which included repairing and banding together overstressed brick walls and installing some steel supports.
- Since toilets were not in the Madisons' home, the feasibility study called for them to be installed under the front portico. This

Masonry team rendering portico columns. *TMF.*

proved impractical once the restoration team fully understood the portico's construction. Instead, one small bathroom was installed in a closet on the first floor of Nelly's Wing. Our intent was to build bathrooms just off the backyard. But this was not done until years later due to other budget priorities.[47]

Completion of Roof Restoration. The roof required significant additions and changes to return it to the original design.[48]

- Re-creating the flat roofs of the Madison wings involved much detective work. Happily, the original joists had been recycled as floor joists in a nearby building. These had been extensively altered to be reused, but they did show the roofs' exact serrated profile, one of several designs for flat roofs that Jefferson had invented for use at Monticello and elsewhere. The Jeffersonian design originally used at Montpelier was re-created exactly. But, to protect against leaks, it was covered with a rubber membrane and stainless-steel sheathing. The deck in the Madison-era design was then installed. It provided a cover over the modern materials.[49]

- The timber frame of the House's center section required extensive repairs to address major damage from water leaks and previous alterations.[50] In order for many Madison timbers to be restored to their original length and strength, they had to be repaired by fitting them together with timber segments reclaimed from other period buildings. Only lumber of matching species and dimensions was used. To attach and strengthen the timber segments as a single piece, a scarfing (attachment) technique was often used.[51] It created "splay-squint scarf joints with opposing wedges." After the relatively new copper roof was removed during restoration, old-growth cypress shingles were installed over the timber frame of the center section. Scalloped by hand to be the same style and shape as the originals,[52] the shingles' design was based on samples found in the recesses of the duPont attic.[53] Shingles also were installed on hips of the roof.

Activities Required for Utilities' Installation. Creating the systems to provide necessary utilities and maintain a precisely controlled internal environment required extensive work both outside and inside the House.

- The approach used at major historic homes like Monticello and Mount Vernon was to install infrastructure systems in the basement/cellar. We rejected this approach because we believed fully restoring the cellar, the domain of the enslaved workers, was equally as important as fully restoring the floors occupied by the Madison family. This important decision, and the millions in additional costs it incurred, was indicative of our strong commitment to preserving and telling the history of people enslaved at Montpelier.[54]
- The energy source selected for heating and cooling was a state-of-the-art geothermal system that depended on 12 wells drilled in the northeast lawn. The selection of this system meant that no modern HVAC features would be seen or heard in the environment around the House. Each geothermal well has a closed loop of pipe that draws from the 55-degree ambient temperature of the earth. That heat is fed through heat pumps

to efficiently heat or cool water for the air handlers serving the House. In a bunker created close to the geothermal well field, the restoration team built a vault for heating and air-conditioning equipment, as well as for electrical and security systems.[55] Before any of this work was done, archaeologists investigated the affected landscape.[56] Due to the well field's size, the area to be investigated was substantial.

- Inside the House, protecting the integrity of its design presented significant challenges. For heating and air-conditioning, ductwork had to be installed. To avoid intruding on spaces in the cellar or the upper floors, the restoration team built large underground ducts, below the grade of the cellar. These extended from the bunker to risers in the chimneys and wall cavities created by post-Madison changes. The system would distribute conditioned air throughout the House. Wiring and outlets for electricity were added with similar sensitivity to appearance. For fire protection, a Marioff HI-FOG® mist system that emits far less water than the typical sprinkler system was installed.[57]

Major Interior Work Begins. Having completed most of the exterior restoration and stabilized the structure, the focus shifted primarily to the interior. The projects in some areas primarily involved extensive carpentry. Among these were work in Dolley's Wing and the northern portion of the House. When this was completed, the library where James Madison had done his seminal research in preparation for the Constitutional Convention of 1787 was restored. The Madisons' drawing room and other rooms where they entertained also were almost fully returned in 2005 to their original design.[58]

Re-Creation of Interior Design and Restoration of Features. Design changes, however, required to re-create the Madison house's interior were extensive.

- Before beginning interior restoration, numerous architectural elements, including two upstairs Madison-era arches, had to be removed and, in the case of the arches, relocated. In the feasibility study, the arches were determined to have been at the ends of the Madison vestibule connecting the north and south sections of the House. Re-creating rooms in the house commonly required removal of partitions and installation of others.[59]

- New stairs were produced and installed to connect the first and second floors. They were east–west oriented, rather than north–south, as in the duPont home.[60] Because both stairs predated the James Dinsmore expansion of the house, there was no paper trail for the elements. Fortunately, the house itself provided detailed direction on configuration and detailing. While most of the original flooring survived, much had been covered by later floors and damaged by installation of heating and plumbing systems. In many places, flooring required patching. Broad-width heart pine was used to patch and replace missing floorboards.[61]
- Remarkably, plaster on the drawing room's walls was sometimes found to be original to the Madison House and required only repairs, rather than full replastering. In other spaces, plaster with the same characteristics as the original was applied using the same techniques as in the early construction.[62]
- The survival of the original plaster in the drawing room also enabled the restoration team to determine the location of the artwork the Madisons had hung. The nail holes in the original plaster in that room could be distinguished from later nail holes because the walls had been refinished with a skim coat of plaster immediately after the Madison residency. Dolley had made a list of art as she prepared to move to Washington after Madison's death. By matching the geometry and placement of the holes with the paintings' sizes, the location of each could be determined.[63]
- Masonry reconstruction was necessary to repair and re-create fireplaces, repair walls, create window and door openings in places where they had been eliminated, and expand window and doorway openings.[64]
- Basement restoration also required further attention. With archaeological and other investigation completed and the House stabilized, the restoration team removed post-Madison partitions in the basement and re-created the Madison-era design. This involved installation of partitions and basement doors, masonry repair, reconstruction of the kitchens and plastering walls.[65]

Completion of Masonry, Roof and Utility Work. Many of the remaining exterior projects were primarily to complete activities already begun.[66]

- Stucco was removed on the east (rear) wall, the one wall on which this had not yet been done. Brick repairs for this wall and others were completed later in the year.[67]
- Wood decks, cornices and rails with a Chippendale design for the roofs of Nelly's and Dolley's Wings and the east colonnade were built and installed.[68] The railings were based on an early nineteenth-century engraving of the House and on physical evidence shown where the railings had pocketed into the walls. Molding profiles and other details were borrowed from balustrades James Dinsmore had completed at the University of Virginia, after he left Montpelier.
- The bunker where the utility vault had been built was backfilled and restored to its former grade. Toward the end of the year, the plastic membrane enclosures over both wings were removed.[69]

Celebration of the Exterior Unveiling

We celebrated the unveiling of the Madisons' home in a ceremony on the front lawn attended by hundreds of guests on April 29, 2006. The original appearance of the House's exterior had not been seen for about 150 years. Extensive work remained to finish interior restoration, but the work was well on its way to completion. Virginia's U.S. Senator John Warner, Congressman Eric Cantor and Mike each made inspiring remarks and emphasized Madison's enduring importance to the nation. Joining Senator Warner and Congressman Cantor to pull the ropes to release the massive red curtain shielding the house were John Macon, a Madison family descendant; Rebecca Gilmore Coleman, a descendant of an enslaved person at Montpelier; Louise Potter, a member of the Boards of the Foundation and National Trust; and me, as Foundation Board chair. The ceremony concluded with the arrival of "James" and "Dolley" in a horse-drawn carriage. After walking up the steps, they talked with "James Dinsmore," one of the two master builders for the House's 1809–12 expansion.[70]

Unveiling of the exterior of the Madisons' home, not seen for a century and a half in its original appearance. *TMF*.

Restoration—2006

Nelly's Wing and Southern Main Section Work. Among the areas for focus in 2006 were Nelly's Wing and the southern part of the House's center section.[71] The Nelly's Wing projects mirrored those undertaken the previous year for Dolley's Wing. Every space required the same work: removing post-Madison architectural elements, installing partitions, producing and installing stairs, repairing and replacing floorboards, plastering walls and completing extensive masonry work. Throughout the House, the restoration team repaired and installed original windows. As was the case with the doors, they found some of these in different locations than where originally installed. The Madison triple-sash windows in the drawing room had remained in place. To return them to their original appearance, later-added modern glass was removed and replaced with restoration glass.[72] Where a replacement window was needed, a window with the exact design of one in a comparable location was produced and installed. To make windows functional, they were equipped with new six-strand hemp sash cords, the same as used in the House originally.[73] By the end of 2006, the climate-control system for the entire House was in place and in full operation.[74]

Final Demolition Project. The principal exterior construction project in 2006 would be demolition of the northernmost section of the duPont mansion. The restoration team soon would no longer need its boiler and kitchen. When climate control was established in the House, the boiler was removed. Progress toward restoration completion allowed the workshop in the kitchen space to be phased out. After demolition, the surviving rear wall of Dolley's Wing was exposed. In light of its poor condition, the wall required significant repairs.[75]

Major Archaeological Discoveries and Follow-up Restoration. The archaeology team made numerous significant discoveries in 2006.[76]

- The last phase of investigation in the basement involved jackhammering through the century-old concrete floor. Hidden under that slab was a remarkable record of the floors that existed in the three stages of the Madison home. Preserved in the clay floor of the Dolley's Wing cellar was the herringbone impression left by the original brick floor. The team found brick laid in a running bond design under the cellar floor of Nelly's Wing. The cellar floor in the first addition to the Madison home was made of wood planking; in the original House, it was clay hardened with lime. Later in the restoration, the floors were returned to their original appearance. Archaeological evidence also was critical to determining how the spaces were used—based on artifacts and the presence of subfloor pits where slaves stored personal items and food.[77]
- Remarkable, unexpected archaeological discoveries were made in front of the House. Outlines of fence postholes and tiny bits of charcoal from the ends of posts led to finding the location of the fence that enclosed the front yard and a road running alongside the fence. The posts had originally been charred to inhibit decay. The fence's front gate was located 90 feet from the steps, which corresponded with the 90-foot width of the House. This corroborated the theory that Madison followed classical geometric guidelines in laying out the gardens and grounds around his home. For welcoming arriving visitors, a carriage pull-off had been built outside the fence's gate and paved with river stones.[78] To provide a safe

approach, the surface was paved after restoration using river stones similar to the original, but held in place with a special elastic bonding agent (Klingstone Path).[79]

Restoration—2007

Final Projects. The principal work left to complete restoration involved finishing carpentry work throughout the House and ensuring proper operation of fire protection and climate-control systems. One significant discrete project remained: restoration of the east (rear) colonnade.[80] Restoring it involved a microcosm of tasks required for the entire house restoration, including these: removal of features not original to the Madison house; floor and steps re-created and installed; and rendering, or stucco, applied to the portico and colonnade columns.[81] A lift to accommodate individuals with disabilities was designed and installed at the east end of Nelly's Wing. The lift proved not to be user-friendly and has not been used. It requires more attention of guide staff than does use of the temporary ramp built and installed to connect to the colonnade.[82]

An Unfinished "Restoration Room." In the final stages of restoration, we made the decision not to restore an upstairs room overlooking the rear colonnade.[83] To show the physical clues that guided the restoration, we left it in an unrestored "raw" state with most of the post-Madison fabric stripped away. The room was perfect for this purpose. It seemed unimportant for interpretation; the research staff had found few clues about its use. Not having a fireplace, it was likely not a bedroom. It also contained almost every form of physical evidence important in ensuring the restoration's authenticity, including the following features:

- Examples of original wood lathe and plaster
- Evidence of the room's original chair rail that was identifiable by plaster in the gap that was created when it was removed, as well as the chair rail's detailed profile in the paint of a surviving door surround
- The location of a later arched door opening revealed by a large patch in the wall's plaster
- In the room's closet, a remnant of decorative "fresco" painting of original plaster, dating to 1760

Discovery of fresco in closet of the "restoration room" that was not restored to show the underside of restored rooms. *TMF.*

- The initial paint layer on wood trim that experts exposed, showing the room's color the Madisons had selected
- The location of a silver Madison candle snuffer found inside a wall, apparently hidden there by a mouse or other rodent
- A remarkable truss installed in the second floor during the 1809–12 expansion, from which the second floor was suspended, and was needed because the weight-bearing wall that supported the second floor was removed at that time to create the large drawing room on the first floor
- A "dragon beam," exposed in the ceiling, which was part of the diagonal framing needed for the hipped roof of the house's center section, illustrating the original 1763 construction of the home[84]

Restoration—2008

At the end of 2007, restoration of the House's structure was complete, although an extensive punch list of work and landscape improvements remained for attention in much of 2008 and part of 2009. Restoration had been done in slightly more than the 56 months projected, and the total cost was only several million dollars more than the estimated $21.7 million in the Mesick feasibility report.[85] For a project of this magnitude and degree of inherent uncertainty as to what difficulties would arise, this was an extraordinary result. Some walls were painted, but installation of wall coverings would not be done until further investigation had been carried out. Faux graining was carried out on the stairs and interior doors.[86] Building on years of research and analysis by Montpelier staff and consultants, the multiyear project to furnish the House began in 2008. Assembling the interior décor would require years of further research and planning in order to acquire items with Madison provenance and ones of the period that were of the Madisons' style. With great confidence, the House could now be stated to be an authentic structural restoration of James and Dolley Madison's home.[87] (Celebration of this monumental achievement is discussed in chapter 12.)

Digital Restoration Archive

Throughout restoration, the Foundation accumulated "one of the largest digital archives of data relating to restoration of a historic site ever assembled and one of the first to be entirely digital."[88] The archive includes "over 80,000 digital photos; scans of historic maps and photographs; over 1,000 digital measured drawings; tens of thousands of pages of text documents; over 100 GB [gigabytes] of cloud point data; and over 500 GB of digital video." To make this collection more accessible to the public, the National Endowment for the Humanities funded the Digital Montpelier Project to present the most important elements of the archive. Using three-dimensional models of the Digital Montpelier Project, visitors are able to explore all three Madison construction phases, the last being the 1812 phase reflecting the House's current form. "Embedded in the models are links to slideshows that present the documentation that reveals how individual architectural elements were investigated and restored." The Project was a collaboration between the Institute for Advanced Technology in the Humanities at the University of Virginia and architectural historian Gardiner Hallock.[89] Its web address is www.digitalmontpelier.org. In late 2019, Montpelier received an Institute for Museum Library Services (IMLS) grant to digitize the main house collection of architectural and archaeological records from the restoration. The IMLS Project places the models in Geographic Information System Mapping technology, which allows individual elements to be clicked on to explore the restoration process. The models will ultimately give access to all of the records. The web address of the start of the models is http://arch.is/1njHCW.[90]

8

CENTER FOR THE CONSTITUTION—2002–2008

THE EVOLUTION OF MADISON AND CONSTITUTION EDUCATION

After receiving Robert H. Smith's generous funding commitment in 2002, we established Montpelier's ambitious Constitutional Center "to promote excellence in teaching, understanding, and appreciation of American constitutional principles and to honor the legacy of James Madison."[1] A survey in the early 1990s had found only about half of graduating college seniors were familiar with basic Constitutional principles. Only 23 percent correctly selected Madison as Father of the Constitution—on a multiple-choice question![2] In a talk at Montpelier in 2001, David McCullough, the renowned historian and biographer of the founding period, addressed the deficit in understanding of the nation's history and founders. He attributed it to the failure to train teachers to present history in a manner reflecting its interesting and passionate drama.[3] We believed that Montpelier would be an obvious venue for educating teachers to impart such drama.

This chapter reviews the evolution of the Center for the Constitution chronologically, from its precursor seminar programs through its dramatic growth by the end of the Foundation's first decade. To assist in clarifying the Center's appropriate role, we commissioned a study of other nonprofits with missions related to the Constitution. Based in part on that study, we concluded that Montpelier was indeed uniquely situated—as the home of the Father of the Constitution—to build a national program of Constitutional education.[4] Also, no other nonprofit had the same mission. To guide the Center's creation, an ambitious five-year operations plan was developed. It would initially build on programs Montpelier had offered in the two previous years.[5] Significantly expanding its programmatic content and reach, the Center made its mark in the ensuing years as a highly respected institution. It thereby achieved our goal for Madison and Constitutional education to be a pillar of the Madison monument.

Pre-Constitutional Center Programs for Teachers. The Foundation's first teacher seminars on the Constitution, held in 2001–2002, received very favorable evaluations (also see chapter 5). Fifty-five Virginia teachers attended its weeklong summer institutes. Fourteen one-day and half-day seminars were held on-site in schools in the state.[6] Both approaches for organizing seminars would become models for the Center to introduce teachers to advanced education methods and programs.

We the People: The Citizen and the Constitution *Program*. After assuming the leadership for *We the People* in 2001 (see chapter 5), the Foundation continued to run the national program in Virginia for a decade and a half. To encourage and expand student participation, its manager met on an ongoing basis with teachers throughout the state. Each year, the Center (1) provided teachers and students educational materials on the Constitution and the Bill of Rights, (2) held training seminars for teachers and (3) organized a statewide competition for high school seniors. Although the competition in 2001 attracted only four classes in Virginia schools, by 2003, 16 classes participated and one won the national competition.[7] Since that time, the number of classes participating has continued to be substantial, with the Virginia champion in some years winning or at least being a finalist in the national competition.[8]

Contents of Our Operations Plan. Building on the 2001–2002 seminar programs, the Foundation developed an operations plan for the Center with a primary focus on educating teachers.[9] Education was to be principally offered through a retreat experience with weeklong and multiday weekend seminars. The weekend program format, in particular, had a number of

Landscape and some of the housing of Constitutional Village to provide retreat setting for the Center for the Constitution. *Photo by Peggy Harrison, TMF.*

advantages. By offering programs throughout the year, rather than just in the summer, the Center greatly increased the number of teachers who could attend. It accommodated teachers' schedules while, at the same time, increasing usage of the Center's facilities.[10] The Center's retreat setting initially comprised five houses renovated with a portion of Robert H. Smith's funding (the Constitutional Village). Within the Village were a classroom, a library and housing for 20 participants (see chapter 5).[11] Planned as well were on-site programs for policymakers, government officials and journalists.[12] The objective would be to inform their actions as they address public policy issues.

The Center's Five-Year Goals. Mike Quinn convinced Dennis Kernahan, who had wide experience as a senior financial and technology executive, to serve as the Center's volunteer interim director. As discussed in chapter 5, Dennis had assisted Mike in developing the funding and program proposals they presented to Mr. Smith.[13] In their meeting with him, they set the teacher training objective for the Center's initial five years. The goal was to reach 1,000 high school teachers in Virginia, Maryland and the District of Columbia. Mike projected that by training this number of teachers, the program would influence Madison and Constitution education of an estimated 150,000 students in the region's nearly 500 high schools.[14] A key to meeting this goal was continued operation of the summer institute for teachers, with the joint sponsorship of James Madison University. Through these activities, the Center would aim to create a "national model for teacher training."[15] Also proposed was building the Center's capability to provide web-based support and classroom resources that could reach 10,000 teachers and 1 million students nationwide. To supplement Mr. Smith's $1 million commitment for operating programs, a goal was set to raise $1.35 million of additional support over five years.[16] Other sources of funding would include earnings derived from Mr. Smith's $4 million endowment contribution and from future endowment gifts.

Advisory Committee of Scholars. For guidance on setting up the Center, the Foundation's Board created a Constitutional Studies Committee. Its members initially were three directors with scholarly credentials: Dr. Ralph Ketcham, Dr. Hunter Rawlings and Professor A.E. Dick Howard.[17] During their years on the Montpelier Property Council, Dr. Ketcham and Professor Howard had made considerable efforts to interest Madison and Constitutional scholars in Montpelier. Later, Dr. Garry Wills, a Northwestern University professor of history, became a scholar-advisor. He had written numerous books on the founding period, including a biography of James Madison during his presidency. Princeton professor Dr. Stanley Katz, a leading expert on legal and Constitutional history, also accepted an advisory role.[18] Among the initial matters for their advice were (1) qualifications in choosing the Center's director, (2) possible selection of partner organizations, (3) establishing the curriculum for training and retreat programs, (4) selection of faculty and (5) criteria for classroom resources.[19]

Hiring an Executive Director. The most urgent need for advancing the Center's development was employing a permanent director. After soliciting applications and holding preliminary interviews, Mike scheduled an interview with the leading candidate, Dr. Will Harris, a Constitutional scholar and teacher. As a professor of political science at the University of Pennsylvania, Dr. Harris had established and directed a doctoral program on Constitutional theory. He also had extensive experience in teaching seminars for educators on the Constitution and related subjects. The interviewers were Dr. Wills, Dr. Rawlings, Mike, Dennis and me. At the conclusion of the interview, we recommended—subject to results of reference checks—that Mike extend an offer to Dr. Harris.[20] He accepted the offer and became the Center's executive director, effective August 1, 2003.[21]

A Constitutional Program for Teachers. Will hit the ground running and quickly created a program for teachers, which he titled the "Montpelier Weekend Seminar." He held the first one in October.[22] Subsequently, the format for that weekend evolved into Will's standardized approach for weekend programs. The heart of each program was several seminars over a three-day period, which he personally led, on a single Constitution-related theme. In advance, a bound volume of extensive background material was sent to participants. Other Montpelier staff provided instruction on the site's archaeological program, curatorial research and acquisitions and Madison's legacy. Staff also gave participants an in-depth tour of the house and surrounding 2,650-acre property. Opportunities for group discussion at meals and other scheduled times were an ancillary benefit of the retreat experience. Continuing his important role, Andy Washburn managed the Center's administrative activities. Prior to the Center's creation, he had coordinated Montpelier's Constitution-related programs.[23]

Initial Weekend Seminars. The theme of the initial Montpelier Weekend Seminar was "'A Constitution'—What Is It?"[24] Materials sent to participants in advance consisted of copies of the Declaration of Independence, the Articles of Confederation, the U.S. Constitution and Bill of Rights, thirteen Federalist Papers, selected anti-Federalist writings, three opinions of the U.S. Supreme Court and a current document on "Constitutionalism, Human Rights and Citizenship." Will also developed weekend programs on two other themes—the "Bill of Rights" and "Citizenship."[25] For each, he prepared a similar volume of background documents.

History and Success of Weekend Seminars. Beginning in 2004, the Center generally held between 6 and 10 Weekend Seminars each year,[26] with 15 to 20 participants at each.[27] In most years, more than 150 teachers participated.[28] Teachers initially were primarily from Virginia. But over time, consistent with the focus of Mr. Smith, a significant number from Maryland and the District of Columbia participated. The geographic reach extended to North Carolina teachers after the Center received funding from the William R. Kenan Jr. Charitable Trust, a North Carolina–based foundation.[29] The response to the programs was overwhelmingly positive. In their evaluations, so many teachers referred to the program in glowing terms that I wondered if Will might have suggested in the opening session that he expected favorable reviews. But it became clear that the responses reflected genuine appreciation. Among the reviews were references to the program being "truly inspiring," "eye-opening" and "transformational." One teacher said the experience would "result in my taking an entirely new approach in teaching my students."[30]

Seminars for State Supreme Court Justices. In 2004, with support from the national Center for Civic Education, Montpelier's Center had the prestigious honor of holding a weekend seminar for 13 state supreme court justices.[31] The program, titled "James Madison: The Man and his Political Philosophy," incorporated Madison's political theory with a focus on his role in writing the Constitution and Bill of Rights.[32] At the conclusion of the weekend, the chief justice of one state, reportedly with tears in his eyes, said that all state justices should have the benefit of participating in the program. In the two following years, a weekend program for state supreme court justices was also held. Since then, funding has not been available.[33]

The Initial Weeklong Seminar Program. The Center organized and held its first weeklong program in 2004. The content for it was a combination of the substance for the weekend seminars on the Constitution, the Bill of Rights and Citizenship. This initial program was for twenty Washington State teachers.[34] Foundation vice chair Joe Grills had introduced George F. Russell Jr., founder of the Russell Indexes and a Washington State resident, to Montpelier and the Center's programs. This led to Mr. Russell's funding the summer institute for the Washington teachers. The State's Department of Education assisted in the Center's teacher recruitment. Its observer of the program was so impressed that he helped secure state funding for the summer institute for a couple of additional years.[35] Faculty for the program included Constitutional scholars from a number of universities. This broad representation assisted the Center later in developing a network of faculty experts.

The Second Summer Institute. Montpelier's Center also held a weeklong summer institute in 2005 for 21 educators from Catholic schools in various states.[36]

NEH-Funded Teacher Workshops. Indicative of the Center's growing national reputation, the National Endowment for the Humanities (NEH) granted funding for the Center to hold two "Landmarks of American History Teacher Workshops" in the summer of 2005. A total of 82 teachers from across the nation participated in weeklong programs titled "James

Madison and Constitutional Citizenship."[37] Nearby Woodberry Forest School was a cosponsor. The programs' focus was on "six phases of James Madison's life as a Constitutional citizen."[38] NEH again funded 82 teachers' participation in weeklong Teacher Workshops in 2006.[39] Later, to help the Center institutionalize its Constitution-related education, NEH created a 3-to-1 $4 million challenge grant under which we would be required to raise $3 million to receive $1 million from NEH.[40] To assist us in meeting the challenge, Mr. Smith made a $1.5 million challenge match. As a result, we secured the total needed.[41]

One-Day and Half-Day Programs. Beginning in 2005, the Center added both one-day and half-day Constitutional educational training sessions at individual schools for teachers from the same school system. Between 10 and 15 of these programs were held each year.[42] Another format begun during that period was one-day, one-night seminars at Montpelier. In 2006, 87 teachers from Virginia and North Carolina participated in these "In-Service Retreats."[43]

Informal Board Oversight. Until 2005, the Foundation Board's involvement with the Constitution Center was loosely structured.[44] As described earlier in this chapter, the Constitutional Studies Committee had served as an advisory committee of scholars, chaired by Dr. Ketcham. In addition, an ad hoc group was organized and led by Board member Lou Potter and her husband, Alan, to work with Will Harris and other Center staff on nonscholarly needs, such as operations and new construction.

Creation of the Constitution Center Committee. In October 2005, the Board strengthened its oversight of the Center. It divided the advisory and oversight roles between two new committees. An Advisory Committee made up of directors and outside experts led by Dr. Ketcham would provide advice on programs' substantive content. The ad hoc group's work would be continued under the Constitution Center Committee made up exclusively of directors. After the Potters requested that someone else chair the committee, William "Bill" C. Remington agreed to become chair.[45] Bill joined the Board in 2003 and had an intense interest in the Center. During the balance of his time on the Board, he played a major role for the Center by working with Dr. Harris and leading the committee. Over the next year or so, because of the extent of overlap of the two committees' memberships and interests, the Board merged the role and Board membership of the Advisory Committee into the Center Committee. Non-director Advisory Committee members continued to provide advice on an ad hoc basis.

Outreach and Networking. Also in 2005, the Center developed an extensive outreach and marketing program. It began to coordinate with organizations and conferences that were involved with teachers and other educators having responsibility for civic education. To inform teachers about its professional development activities, the Center set up exhibits at conferences and educational fairs. To make the public aware of major programs such as the Montpelier Weekend Seminars, it issued press releases to local and regional media. For teachers who participated in Weekend Seminars and other Center programs, a network was created to encourage communication among themselves and with Center staff.[46] The Center also provided more extensive program information on the Montpelier website.

Program Additions in 2006. Two new Center programs on the Constitution were added in 2006. One was for faculty of schools of education, teachers who teach teachers. That program had 20 participants. The other was a series of "Teaching American History" seminars funded by grants that school systems could obtain from the U.S. Department of Education. The Center presented two of the seminars for Washington State teachers and one for teachers from Hampton, Virginia.[47]

A New Academic Facility. From its inception, the Center's teaching facility was limited to a small house that had been converted into a library. Because this space was inadequate, it increasingly cramped any expansion of the Center's education program. Moreover, there was no kitchen or dining area. In 2007, the Foundation significantly increased the Center's teaching and administrative capacity. It achieved this by renovating an expansive brick stable to become its new academic building.[48] The stable, which was built about 1905, had numerous uses in the duPont era. On the first floor were horse stalls, a carriage storage area and a workspace for hitching and cleaning horses. At one time, the stable had a cockfighting pit. The second floor had a small apartment and bathroom in one half and a loft to store hay and grain in the other.[49] To design a facility that would meet the Center's needs, the Board's Building Committee retained Maynard Ball of the architectural firm of Bartzen & Ball. Consistent with the Foundation's preservation commitment, the design retained many of the stable's original features, including massive sliding doors, and provided for only a small addition. By meeting the Secretary of the U.S. Department of the Interior's Standards for Rehabilitation, its renovation received a historic-rehabilitation certification that would permit sale of tax credits (later sold for $271,000).[50]

Celebration of James Madison's 250th birthday in 2001, with "Living Flag" created by 2,500 schoolchildren at the Mansion (before restoration). *Photo by Richard MacDonald, courtesy of The Montpelier Foundation (TMF).*

Re-creation in 2001 of the Madisons' dinner for Marquis de Lafayette when he came to visit in 1824. *TMF.*

The Pony Barn after renovation to serve as the Montpelier Education Center. *TMF.*

Annie Rogers duPont Garden. *TMF.*

Visitors entering for a tour of the house while it's being restored. *TMF.*

Scaffolding covered by plastic membrane to stop water infiltration and retain heat from boilers during restoration. *TMF.*

Looking through basement window to observe masonry and other restoration work. *TMF.*

Aerial view of underground vault being created to install equipment for heating and air conditioning. *TMF.*

Key participants at the inaugural Dolley Madison Legacy Luncheon (*right to left*): renowned journalist, author and luncheon speaker Cokie Roberts; Montpelier CEO Mike Quinn; and luncheon co-chair Peyton Lewis, who introduced Ms. Roberts. *Photo by Kevin Lamb, TMF.*

The Gilmore Cabin, after completion of renovation of its exterior. *TMF.*

Visitor Center and William duPont Gallery as planned and constructed. *Photo by Maxwell MacKenzie, TMF.*

Entry of William duPont Gallery to provide interpretive space for telling the story of Mr. duPont's family at Montpelier. *TMF.*

Great room/salon of the William duPont Gallery, which is used for lectures and other major events. *TMF.*

Mrs. Marion duPont Scott's Red Room, re-created with all the furnishings and memorabilia reinstalled. *TMF.*

Robert H. Smith, Center for the Constitution's founder and philanthropist, cutting the ribbon in 2007 at Lewis Hall, the Center's initial academic building to provide classroom, dining and office spaces. *TMF.*

Celebration on Constitution Day in 2008 of the restored House's opening and Montpelier's transformation into a Monument to James Madison—in just 10 years—featuring thousands of local children creating a "Living Flag." *Photo by James Roney, TMF.*

Above: The Madisons' Drawing Room after it was furnished in the restored House (looking from its south side). *TMF*.

Left: Painting owned by the Madisons, *Pan, Youths and Nymphs*, that once again hangs on the wall in their Drawing Room. *Photo by Jen Fariello, TMF*.

James Madison's refurnished Library on the second floor, facing the Blue Ridge Mountains, where he prepared for the Constitutional Convention in 1787 (shown here with "Mr. Madison" interpreter John Douglas Hall). *Photo by Eduardo Montes-Bradley, TMF.*

Madison Family Cemetery after it underwent significant renovations. *Photo by Ken Porter, TMF.*

Left: The renovated Enslaved Cemetery showing its peaceful setting at sunrise. *Photo by Bryan Parsons, TMF.*

Below: Statue of James and Dolley Madison commissioned by philanthropist Robert H. Smith. *TMF.*

Aerial view of administrative buildings, with the newly constructed home of the Robert H. Smith Center for the Constitution, Claude Moore Hall (*right*) and Lewis Hall (*left*). *TMF.*

The iconic Temple, the only Madisonian structure that remains, other than the House. *Photo by Rick Seaman, TMF.*

Reconstruction of double quarter housing for enslaved domestic workers and their families in the South Yard, next to the Madisons' House. *TMF.*

Aerial view of reconstructed South Yard dwellings and other buildings for enslaved workers. *Photo by Will Kerner, TMF.*

Telling the story of slavery at Montpelier in the House's cellar in *The Mere Distinction of Colour* permanent exhibition. *Photo by Proun Design LLC, TMF.*

Names of Montpelier enslaved written on a wall in *The Mere Distinction of Colour* exhibition. *Photo by Proun Design LLC, TMF.*

Director of Archaeology Matt Reeves speaks to a group about reconstruction of South Yard buildings used by the Enslaved Community. *Photo by Drew Precious, TMF.*

A striking view of Montpelier central area, showing the House and South Yard buildings of the Enslaved Community in late afternoon. *Photo by Kenneth Garrett, TMF.*

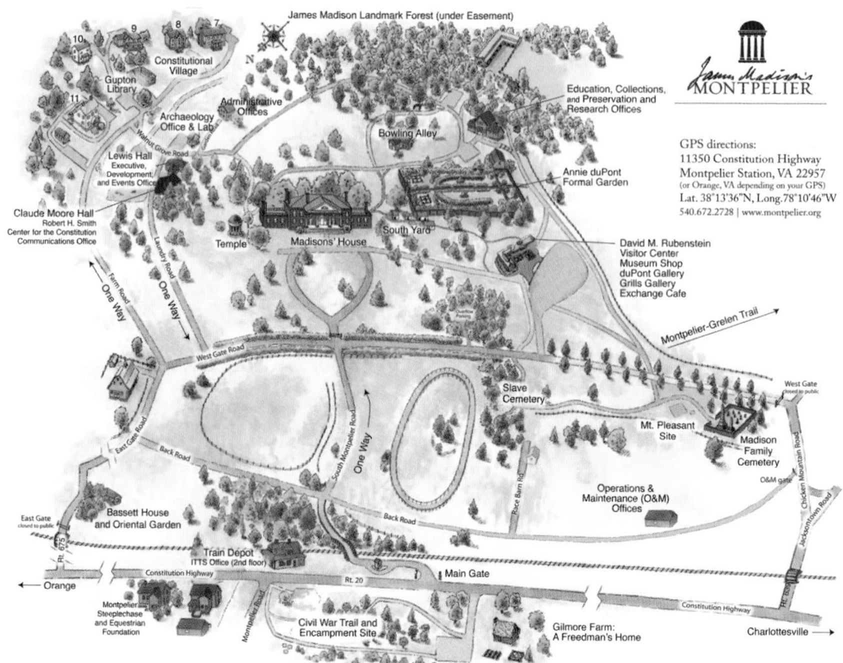

Map of Montpelier in 2018. *TMF.*

Archaeology in former Madison tobacco fields continues in The Montpelier Foundation's third decade. *Photo by Kenton Rowe, TMF.*

Mr. Smith made a $1 million gift to provide much of the construction funding.[51] By making a generous gift of a similar magnitude, Joe Grills, my successor as Board chair, and his wife, Marge, were granted naming rights to the building. They chose to honor me and my wife by having it designated William and Peyton Lewis Hall.[52]

Annual Constitution Day Claude Moore Lecture. In 2007, Montpelier's celebration of Constitution Day (September 17, the day of the signing in 1787) featured a lecture on the importance of Constitutional education by Dr. John J. Patrick, professor emeritus of education at Indiana University.[53] It was held in a tent near the newly completed Lewis Hall. Following the lecture, Mike presented four teachers with Montpelier's Excellence in Constitutional Education Awards. The several hundred guests then moved to Lewis Hall for its official opening. Mr. Smith, accompanied by family members, concluded the ceremony with the traditional ribbon cutting. The Claude Moore Foundation's funding began its annual support of a lecture that would become a highlight of Montpelier's Constitution Day celebration. Subsequent to Dr. Patrick's inaugural Claude Moore Lecture, the speakers have included renowned biographer Jon Meacham and Pulitzer Prize–winning syndicated columnist George Will. Acclaimed journalists Cokie Roberts, Diane Rehm and Roger Mudd participated as moderators in several years when the lecture was in a panel format. Since 2008, the lecture has been held most years in Washington, D.C., in the auditorium of the National Archives. Every year it was a standing-room-only event.[54]

Five-Year Teaching Goal Achieved. By 2007, the Center's programs had dramatically grown in number and scope. In addition to achieving a national reputation, the Center created the education program that we had envisioned for the Madison monument. Among the programs offered:

- Montpelier Weekend Seminars
- One-Day In-Service Retreats
- Half-Day On-Location School Programs
- Weeklong Summer Institutes
- Individualized Constitutional Weekend Seminars
- *We the People* Seminars and Competitions
- Ad Hoc Constitutional Programs

In 2007 alone, a total of 679 people participated in the Center's seminars. About 400 were teachers enrolled in Constitutional seminar programs of one to four days in length. The Center had greatly exceeded its original goal of providing Constitution education to 1,000 teachers within five years. And new activities continued to be added. That year they included a trial program, "Lessons for Leaders," for the staff of the National Association of Independent Schools, which was organized in connection with Branchwater Leadership Resources, and a meeting of 25 high school seniors who were part of a Congressional Youth Forum.[55]

The Constitutional Village. The Center's campus became a true Constitutional Village with the opening of Lewis Hall and renovation completion of the five early twentieth-century houses. Lewis Hall had a large lecture room; a dining room that could accommodate about 50 people; a kitchen; a large common area for informal discussions; and offices on two floors, including an office suite for Montpelier's president.[56] Four of the houses together would accommodate 20 people. Each house had bedrooms with private baths, a living room for small group conversations and a modest kitchen space. As mentioned previously, one of the houses was modified to create a library (later known as Gupton Library, based

Classroom in Lewis Hall with Center director Dr. Will Harris educating teachers on the Constitution. *Photo by John Strader, TMF.*

on a generous gift by Bruce and Jacqueline Gupton). The library's initial collection was thousands of volumes donated by Madison scholar and board member Dr. Ralph Ketcham. His contribution was reminiscent—albeit on a smaller scale and without compensation—of what Thomas Jefferson made to the Library of Congress. The appearance of the Village's landscape had been significantly enhanced over time and through many changes, as had a number of internal features.

Division of Leadership Roles. In 2007, the Constitution Center Committee decided the Center's growth had reached the point where its leadership responsibilities should be divided. As the executive director, Dr. Will Harris had been responsible for managing all aspects of the Center's operations. His principal role had been to serve as faculty for Weekend Seminars and almost all other on-site Constitutional seminars. In consultation with Dr. Harris, the committee determined that the Center needed both an executive director and an academic director. Dr. Harris would become academic director (a title later changed to principal scholar) with teaching and program content responsibilities. The executive director would have the overall management role.[57] After an extensive search, Dr. Sean O'Brien was extended an offer for the position and shortly thereafter accepted. Most recently, he had been executive director of the Sorenson Institute for Political Leadership, a nonprofit focused on providing education and training for mid-career public service–minded Virginians and candidates for public office.[58]

Planning for the Future. Also in 2007, encouraged by Robert H. Smith, the Foundation's Board and the Center's staff began an intensive review of the Center's mission. At the conclusion, a more ambitious program was proposed. Under the proposal, the Center would continue to be heavily focused on educators with responsibility for teaching children. However, its programs would be broadened to target a range of professions engaged with the nation's public life. As proposed in the Center's operations plan in 2002, they would include legislators, police officers, journalists and congressional staff. In addition, existing programs would be offered to schools in an increased number of states. Also envisioned were the establishment of a national network of faculty scholars and creation of a premier website on the Constitution to provide educational materials to a wide audience. To increase scholars' involvement in Center programs, the proposal recommended creation of a National Advisory Board.[59]

Proposed Major Expansion of the Center. Recognizing that the proposal to expand the Center should be part of Montpelier-wide planning, Mr. Smith provided funding for a comprehensive study to be conducted during 2008.[60] After months of discussion and development of plans for the entire site, the Board reached a decision that the Foundation would seek funding for a significantly expanded Center. Included would be creation of an educational and housing complex that would accommodate dozens of participants at the same time. Projected costs of the new facilities and required associated endowment were in excess of $20 million. Mr. Smith committed $10 million for the Center expansion, which was to be matched by other donors.[61] The new facilities would require demolition of a large farm barn from the duPont era that was in such poor condition that no adaptive reuse was possible. Salvageable materials from the wooden structure would be stored for use in the Center's new facilities or other Montpelier construction.[62]

Center Expansion Plans Are Abandoned. Despite several years of Board chair Joe Grills's dedicated leadership and commitment, efforts to raise the funding match were unsuccessful. As a consequence, the Board concluded that proceeding further would not be prudent. In retrospect, it is my judgment that undertaking the major construction that was planned, a decision in which I had participated, would have proved to be a monumental mistake. We dodged a bullet. Operational costs would almost certainly have been far too great to sustain on an ongoing basis. Programs for teachers had required, and still do require, substantial scholarship funding. Endowment revenue and donations would likely have been woefully inadequate. The dramatic increase nationally in web-based learning and offerings also contributed to making the successful establishment of such a major program too speculative. Indeed, the Center itself had been investigating creation of a series of online courses on Constitution topics (which it later decided to do). (See chapter 11 for more details on the expansion plans.)

Center Collaboration with Brookings. In 2008, in an example of what future programmatic expansion would look like, the Center began discussions with the Washington, D.C.–based Brookings Institution on collaborating to develop a program of seminars for journalists. The seminars would provide an introduction to Constitutional theory and address policy research Brookings had conducted. After terms for the collaboration were agreed upon, Mr. Smith committed the necessary funding for a five-year period.[63]

Essential Role of Robert H. Smith. The significance of Robert H. Smith's philanthropy and commitment to Madison and Constitutional education at Montpelier cannot be overstated. From the original planning for establishment of the Center through the next decade of programs and planned expansion, Mr. Smith was a hands-on, farsighted leader. After having told Mike and others of us that he did not support "start-ups," he participated in every Center development to ensure that it would grow and become a highly regarded institution. He insisted that Mike meet with him on a regular basis to discuss the Center's activities and future plans. This was his way of making certain that our promised progress was being made. Recounting his contributions that are catalogued in this book demonstrates why we felt, and continue to feel, so indebted to him for his support:

- Gift of $1 million, his first, which included $200,000 for renovating two houses that became part of the Constitutional Village (the balance was for an easement to protect the Landmark Forest)
- Initial commitment of $6 million for the Center for the Constitution, which included $4 million for endowment, $1 million for five years of operations and $1 million for housing and infrastructure
- Contribution of $1 million for renovation of a brick stable to create the Center's academic building (Lewis Hall)
- Donation of $1.5 million to assist in meeting the match required for an NEH 3-for-1 challenge
- Funding for preparation of a site-wide master plan, including development of the design of facilities for an expanded Center education and housing complex
- Five-year commitment for funding collaboration of the Center and the Brookings Institution
- Commitment of $10 million for expanding the Center (which ultimately could not be matched, but led to support from the Robert H. Smith Foundation after his death for other Center programs)
- Ongoing valuable advice on Constitutional education and building the Center's capability

Before he died, Mr. Smith agreed to the Foundation naming the Center "The Robert H. Smith Center for the Constitution at James Madison's Montpelier." No more fitting honor at Montpelier could be possible. In chapter 13, I briefly discuss the Center's growth and new directions in the Foundation's second decade.

9

VISITOR CENTER AND WILLIAM DUPONT GALLERY CONSTRUCTION—2002–2007

ARRIVAL AT MONTPELIER NOW SUITABLE FOR MADISONS' WELCOME

Development of plans for the new Visitor Center began in earnest once we received the Potters' $3 million commitment in 2002. Like erection of other Madison monument pillars—the restored House, the Center for the Constitution and the Gateway entry—construction of the Visitor Center project was a complicated multiyear endeavor.[1] But working together, the Board, staff and outside advisors designed and built an architecturally inspiring complex with spaces meeting the needs of visitors and the Foundation. It was opened to the public in early 2007.

This chapter reviews the journey with all its challenges and important decisions. The diverse experience of the Building Committee's members would prove valuable for shepherding the project. The chair, Bitsy Waters, had a background in planning, historic preservation and group leadership. Lou Potter was an architect and historic preservation leader. Benny Sedwick was a builder and business leader. Pete Anderson was an architect who had served as architect for the University of Virginia.[2] Throughout the process, the committee, with Bitsy taking the lead, made many presentations and held numerous meetings to discuss design with the Board, staff and duPont family representatives.

Site Selection

Logical Choice. Deciding where the Visitor Center complex should be located was the threshold determination to be made. The projected size of its footprint had increased dramatically—from the 4,000 to 6,000 square feet initially conceived to 15,000—when the Foundation agreed to build the William duPont Gallery next to the Visitor Center. The Board and staff believed that the best location would be the former site of the duPont pool and tennis courts, which were adjacent to the visitor parking area.[3] Two major advantages of the site were that the archaeology in most of the area already had been seriously disturbed and the complex would be within easy walking distance of the House. Also, views of the Blue Ridge Mountains would be similar to the spectacular ones from the House's portico. Bitsy expressed some concern about the location, however. She wanted to ensure that the complex "would fit in the landscape" and that the trees between the House and the site would obscure the new structures.[4]

Archaeological Investigation. Before the siting decision could be finalized, the location had to be thoroughly surveyed and analyzed for its archaeological interest.[5] The archaeology team, led by Matt Reeves, understandably devoted the greatest attention to areas that appeared not to have been disturbed. Finding no archaeology of concern in their investigation, they concluded the site would be acceptable for a complex of the size proposed—if great care was taken in positioning the buildings.[6] Later, however, their investigation of the areas proposed for parking and an entry road identified a major problem. In evaluating a configuration that would create a dramatic approach to the Visitor Center, the team determined there were major undisturbed areas of archaeological significance that should be avoided.[7] The areas included the former sites of field slave cabins and a tobacco barn that provided evidence of extensive Madison farming.[8] These discoveries prompted the team to design a less dramatic entryway and the associated parking areas. This site turned out to be the Madisons' main farm complex—an area containing over a dozen buildings. The site's importance led to the Foundation receiving two National Endowment for Humanities grants and $2 million of outside funding. The site's location is within view of and walking distance of the Visitor Center, thereby providing unique opportunities for interpreting the scope of Montpelier as an American founder's farm.[9]

Board Archaeology Policy. The Visitor Center siting issues were the first that required the Board to establish a policy, albeit an unwritten one, regarding archaeology stewardship. The guiding principle, which both Board and staff strongly supported, was that archaeology protection would be central to deciding whether an area would be suitable for new construction and, if archaeology might be affected, that area would first be completely excavated by the archaeology team—or avoided for future study, as the Board decided in the case of the Visitor Center entryway, which led to preserving an important site of a Madison-era complex.

DESIGN OF THE VISITOR CENTER COMPLEX

Basic Design Features. The Building Committee's deliberations over design of the complex began in late 2002. Interior elements to be included in both buildings were already known. The Visitor Center's spaces would be devoted to visitor orientation, a gift shop, a theater, public restrooms, limited food service and administrative support. Initially, visitors' admission fees would be collected at a self-standing kiosk at the site's entrance; later, fee collection was moved to the Visitor Center (see chapter 5). The Will Settlement amendment determined the nature and approximate size of the William duPont Gallery's spaces—that is, a great room at least as large as the duPont drawing and morning rooms, an interpretive space telling the duPont story at Montpelier, and the re-creation of Mrs. Scott's art deco Red Room.

Architect Selection. The committee's first design decision was selecting the architect. The process began with Mike Quinn and his staff preparing and circulating a request for qualifications.[10] Based on the responses, the committee identified five applicants for interviews. Each committee member, as well as Mike, took the lead in interviewing representatives of one of the five.[11] After completing and sharing the results of interviews and undertaking extensive background reviews, the committee chose a collaboration of two firms to provide the full array of architectural services: Richmond-based Glave & Holmes and Alexandria-based Bartzen & Ball. Early in the project discussions, Maynard Ball became the lead representative for the two firms. Montpelier's successful relationship with Maynard resulted in his subsequently being routinely selected for important design and master-planning projects.[12] (See, for example, the master plan and Lewis Hall projects described in chapter 8.)

Early Deliberations. Beginning in early 2003, the committee devoted considerable time to the project. It held two meetings with the architects that spring focused on the buildings' architectural elements and "overall character and feel."[13] Divergent views emerged among committee members and several donors about the exteriors' architectural character. The principal issue was whether the buildings' architecture should be similar to that of the House. After extensive discussion, the committee reached a consensus that the exteriors should have a different design; specifically, the buildings should not have white columns and other Georgian features.

Background for Design. To flesh out the architects' understanding of the buildings' intended uses, Glave & Holmes prepared three separate questionnaires for committee members and Montpelier staff to complete on the entry/orientation space, the gift shop and the William duPont Gallery.[14] To further inform the thinking of the committee and architects, they toured several visitor centers that were examples of a range of architectural designs, interior floor plans and function organizations.[15] During this time, the archaeology team completed its site survey. By mid-2003, the committee and architects were ready to focus on developing a schematic design.[16]

Initial Project Report. In October, Bitsy reported to the Board that the committee had made progress in resolving issues related to the "sizing of spaces, their relationships, infrastructure requirements, visitor circulation patterns, and the setting in the landscape." Central to their decisions was the judgment that, to accommodate visitation projected by the end of the next decade, the Center would need to be designed "to handle about 120,000 visitors annually, with growth [potentially] to 200,000 visitors."[17] Board members, however, expected that visitation at some point might increase sufficiently to require construction of a new visitor center elsewhere on the property.

Threshold Design Decisions. Over the next year and a half, the pace of work increased. There was more general agreement on design elements as the architects' preparation of drafts, and sessions for reviewing them, proceeded. To comport with archaeological restrictions and create the requisite interior spaces, the two buildings would be situated differently in the landscape. For arriving visitors, the Visitor Center would be on the left, next to the route to the House. They would instinctively start their visit there after parking in the adjoining parking area. The William duPont Gallery would be on the right, with its front entrance facing a large open lawn next to a courtyard between the buildings. A footpath to the Gallery from the formal garden would provide visitors direct access at the conclusion of their visit. The Gallery would be sited farther from the parking area than the Visitor Center. There would be an approximately 75-foot walkway to the Gallery entrance centered on the side facing the parking area. A café-like food service area, together with restrooms at each end, would create a corridor connecting the rear of the two facilities. This space and the outdoor courtyard would be able to accommodate dozens of visitors. An effort, ultimately successful, would be made to save and incorporate a several-hundred-years-old Norway spruce as part of the courtyard.

Visitor Center Design. The multipurpose Visitor Center would be designed with these features:

- More than half the space would be devoted to its reception area and gift shop (expected to be—and which has been—a significant revenue source). The inspiration for this area's design would be the architecture of duPont period barns.[18] It would have a louvered-appearing ceiling. The pitched roof would have a clerestory (windows in the roof) incorporated.
- To the left of the gift shop would be a 70-seat state-of-the-art theater for showing a brief film to orient visitors and educate them about James Madison. Later, at the Board's request, it was named the Alan and Louise Potter Theater, to recognize the Potters' essential financial contribution to the Center's construction (see chapter 5).[19]
- Adjacent to the theater would be a gallery providing a temperature- and humidity-controlled, museum-quality environment in which to display Madison artifacts and other valuable objects (later named the Joe and Marge Grills Gallery, in recognition of their $1 million gift).[20]
- The area between the Potter Theater and the Grills Gallery would be flexible enough for a portion of it to be used for educational exhibits as well.
- Outside, close to an exit from the Potter Theater, a small garden funded by the Potters would be created as a memorial to one of their sons.[21]

William duPont Gallery Design. The Gallery would provide a setting more formal than the Visitor Center. In addition to honoring the duPonts' life at Montpelier, it would be an impressive venue for lectures, dinners, concerts and receptions (see chapter 6).

- In the lobby, a large interpretive space would tell the history of the William duPont family at Montpelier through the use of exhibit panels, personal artifacts and photos.[22] A life-size portrait of Mrs. Annie duPont would be featured. To add design interest, a cupola would be built into the Gallery's pitched roof.
- To the right would be the great room/salon. Its design and decoration would reflect that of the duPont morning and drawing rooms. The décor would include two ornate marble fireplace surrounds, mirrors, Italian sconces and an exquisite chandelier—all relocated from the duPont drawing and morning rooms. Original duPont furniture, including an upright grand piano (beautifully restored thanks to a gift from Martha duPont) and a sofa and chairs, would be further representative of the William duPonts' residency.[23] In the center of the plaster ceiling would be a molded medallion, identical in appearance to the one in the Mansion's drawing room that encircled the duPont chandelier.[24] The Foundation later commissioned a rug that had a design influenced by the ceiling's features and covered almost the entire floor.
- To the left of the Gallery entry, Mrs. Scott's art deco Red Room would be carefully reinstalled, with all of the room's furnishings and equestrian memorabilia placed exactly as they had been at the time of her death. Every component that could be removed from the Mansion, even the chrome molding around the edge of the shelves and the star-based design on the ceiling, had been preserved for reinstallation. Because of its poor condition after having been moved, the ceiling design ultimately had to be re-created.

Architectural Details. The complex would not have a predominant architectural style.

- The one-story buildings would be constructed with handmade brick like the House. The front wall of the Visitor Center and café would largely consist of windows of treated glass.

- Originally, the architects proposed that the roofing material be copper, but because that metal's price was escalating rapidly, zinc would be used instead.
- Consistent with the Building Committee's consensus that the complex not seem to compete with the restored House, a small portico outside the entrance to the Gallery would have brick piers, not white columns.
- The buildings would have state-of-the-art mechanical systems. The costly geothermal heating and cooling system would ensure there would be no noise or visual intrusion.
- Storage capability on-site would be limited; a basement storage area, as proposed by some, would be determined not to be cost-justified. Maintaining extensive inventory was believed unnecessary and unwise.
- The buildings would use the same Marioff mist system as was used in the Madison home to provide the same minimal-water fire control system to protect as much as possible the artifacts in the Visitor Center and the duPont Gallery.

Final Design Decisions. In late 2004 and early 2005, committee members worked with the architects to finalize the buildings' designs.[25] Among the decisions they made were these:

- The Visitor Center's entry would be "enclosed by glass with columns."
- On the outside front wall, in a space that visitors could see as they came from the parking area, three large stone panels would be engraved and placed to recognize significant donors to Montpelier's comprehensive fundraising campaign (the "Donors Wall").
- To provide lighting in the courtyard area, lamps would be placed on poles, and steps and walkways would be lit at ground level.
- To achieve symmetry in the appearance of windows and doors, the height of both would be the same.

Design Wrap-Up. The architects began preparation of construction drawings as the last design details were agreed on.

- The goal was to obtain final design approval by April 2005, with construction completed by the end of May 2006.[26]
- The buildings' construction cost was projected to be $5.9 million, with the total cost for the project being $8.6 million.
- The final design received overwhelming Board and staff support.[27]

Financing the Cost of Construction

Need for Funding. Once the Orange County court issued the order amending the Will Settlement, the Foundation was legally obligated to open the Visitor Center complex by the time the restored House was opened to the public (also see chapter 6). This was expected to occur in 2007. Thus, construction would need to start by mid-2005. The projected cost of $8.6 million was almost three times the amount estimated in 2001 to construct the Visitor Center as a single facility. A fundraising goal of $8 million for the complex was included in the $60 million comprehensive campaign begun in 2003.[28] But by early 2004, it had become clear that securing donors interested in making major gifts sufficient to finance the building of the complex would almost certainly be impossible—even if the entire $3 million Potter gift were to be devoted to the project—and definitely not in time to begin construction in 2005.

Financing Options. Identifying a feasible funding option became our highest priority. We deemed bank financing unacceptable, even if available, because of the high interest rate that would be imposed. Board member Walter Craigie suggested issuance of tax-exempt bonds as a potential vehicle. In pursuit of this avenue, the Board's Finance Committee in early 2004 met in Richmond with tax-exempt bond experts from the firm of Morgan, Keegan & Co., a leading Virginia underwriter of nonprofit and municipal bond offerings, and Hunton & Williams, a highly regarded law firm that represented clients on bond issuances. The principal representative for Morgan Keegan was Jim Johnson and for Hunton & Williams, John O'Neill. They provided an overview of the few options for obtaining project financing. Quickly, it became clear that tax-exempt bonds would be the only realistic choice. The interest rate payable on bonds for which interest is not tax-exempt would be too high—as it would be for bank financing—and would create too great an ongoing financial burden.[29]

Consideration of Tax-Exempt Bonds. Following the meeting with Johnson and O'Neill, Finance Committee chair Joe Grills and Walter Craigie reported to the Board's Executive Committee at its March 26, 2004 meeting on the procedure for approval and issuance of tax-exempt bonds. They recommended that the Board explore the possibility of industrial revenue bonds issued through the Economic Development Authority of Orange County. After discussion of the obvious benefits, as well as potential risks, the Executive Committee approved moving forward.[30] The principal benefit would be that the Foundation could obtain funding as soon as needed and repay it over time at the lowest interest rate possible. Thereafter, Joe took the lead over many months representing the Foundation's interests and, in so doing, dealing with the extraordinary complexities of securing bond approval and issuance. Walter recused himself because he was a senior consultant with Morgan Keegan.[31] At Joe's request, I provided a legal review of the numerous documents required to complete the process.

Retention of Bond Advisors. Joe asked Jim Johnson and John O'Neill to attend the May 7 meeting of the full Board of Directors to present an overview of bond financing and specifically to address issuance of tax-exempt bonds.[32] Johnson made a detailed presentation and provided directors with a lengthy paper titled "Overview of Financing Alternatives."[33] At the presentation's conclusion, directors expressed their appreciation, and Johnson and O'Neill departed. Joe then briefly reviewed their experience and references. Following that, the Board approved formally retaining their firms to pursue tax-exempt bond financing.[34]

Bond Application and Approval Process. Prior to filing its application with the County Development Authority, the Foundation would need to analyze its past and projected future fundraising and finalize the amount of project funding needed. After the application was filed, Morgan Keegan would solicit a letter of credit from financial institutions, a requirement for the approval and issuance of bonds. The letter of credit provides security to bond purchasers that payments of principal and interest will be made. After the advisors negotiated the best terms possible, the Board, if it found the terms acceptable, would approve the letter of credit. This would be the approach followed for review and approval of the many other required documents.[35]

Obtaining a Letter of Credit. Over the next few months, we faced a major hurdle in attempting to obtain the requisite letter of credit.[36] The Foundation's brief fundraising history, its limited liquid assets and the National Trust's ownership of the site were an impediment to getting it at an acceptable cost from a financial institution. Finally, our team determined that we must ask the Trust to act as guarantor.[37] To seek Trust support, we had a meeting with its leadership in Washington, D.C. On October 3, the Trust's board approved guaranteeing up to $10 million.[38] Its approval was predicated on a number of conditions to assure that the Foundation would continue to follow sound financial practices.

The National Trust's Essential Role. Without the Trust's guaranty, the Foundation could not have proceeded with construction of the Visitor Center complex. Because the Will Settlement amendment required that the duPont Gallery be opened by the time the restored House was opened, absence of adequate funding for the complex would have meant that opening the House would not have been possible until Visitor Center funding was obtained and construction completed. Such a delay would have resulted in us violating our agreement with the Mellon executors to open the House by the end of 2007. Restoration had begun in late 2003 on our belief/hope that funding for the complex could be obtained soon enough to complete construction in 2007. Returning the Madisons to Montpelier had required our taking the risk.

Board Approval of Bond Issuance. After the Trust agreed to be the guarantor, the Foundation Board at its November 5 meeting approved a bond issuance of between $8.9 million and $9.2 million. Of that amount, $7.5 million would be for the Visitor Center complex and $950,000 for the Gateway project. Also, an amount would be available for payment of bond issuance costs and the first two years' interest.[39] Most of the Potters' $3 million gift, which was unrestricted, would be placed in a Board-designated endowment. At the Executive Committee's December 20 meeting, Joe Grills announced that $9.1 million in bonds had been successfully issued. The 30-year, interest-only bond was issued through Wachovia Bank with a variable rate that then translated to 1.69 percent.[40] To limit the risk of interest increasing, the Foundation executed a swap through Lehman Brothers that fixed the interest rate at 2.9 percent for five years. The bond proceeds were deposited with a trustee for use during the project.

The Trust's Conditions for Acting as Guarantor. At its November meeting, the Board also had considered, and approved, details related to the guaranty agreement with the National Trust. The Trust required the Foundation (1) to achieve and maintain increases in its unencumbered financial assets on a schedule, which would reach $9.1 million in 2009, and (2) to raise $5 million annually to achieve our $60 million goal of the fundraising campaign by the same year. In addition, the endowment the Trust held for Montpelier's benefit would continue to be held and managed by it for the bond's duration. If the Foundation were to default, the Trust could use endowment income to make bond payments.[41]

Limited Fund for Bond Retirement. The Trust's guaranty, in effect, required the Foundation to take steps to create a $9.1 million endowment that would be designated for payment of the bond principal. But the Foundation did not create a separate fund of that size by 2009, or subsequently. One action we had already taken did partially satisfy the $9.1 million commitment: placing $2 million of the $3 million Potter gift in endowment. The principal reason the Foundation never created a fund to cover bond retirement was that difficulties existed every year in raising sufficient funds just for ongoing operations. Admission fees, gift shop sales and endowment have typically provided less than half the Foundation's annual revenues. Donor contributions were—and will continue to be—the largest revenue source. Despite the imperative to cover Montpelier's operational needs, we still should have given a higher priority to attempting to build a fund for bond retirement. Even though such a fund could not realistically have been created by 2009, a plan for allocating a specified amount over a longer period would have eased the financial burden on future Boards.

Rolling Over Bond Issuances. At the time of the Foundation's bond offering, nonprofits often "rolled over" bond issues; in other words, they retired them through successive issuances of bonds. This practice was in lieu of actually paying them off, at maturity or earlier, from endowment or other funding sources. Financially, pursuing a rollover strategy was a wise decision. The rate of return nonprofits could typically earn on endowment investments was greater than rates they paid on tax-exempt bonds. But the soundness of this approach depended on continuance of two conditions: (1) the option of rolling over bonds being available and (2) the rate of return on the nonprofit's investments being greater than the bond interest rate. Unfortunately, the rolling-over option would eventually be foreclosed after Wells Fargo acquired Wachovia. In response to the 2008 financial crisis, Wells Fargo in 2013 required that the Foundation enter into a loan arrangement that would provide a schedule for payment of the $9.1 million bond principal. This demand would impose a major burden on us as principal payments became due.

Construction of the Visitor Center Complex

Management of Construction. With the complex's design virtually completed and funding secured, the Building Committee's focus shifted to overseeing construction. In early 2005, Mike and committee member Benny Sedwick took the lead in identifying contractor candidates with the requisite experience. After preparing the scope of work, they invited four firms to bid. Three submitted proposals. Benny and staff interviewed the firms and, after reviewing their experience and references, recommended selection of Westport Corporation.[42] Located in Ashburn, Virginia, Westport was led by its president Stephen Mullaney, who agreed to play an active role in managing construction. With the committee's concurrence, Mike had chosen Scott Little to handle project management and provide staff oversight.[43] Scott's principal role, working with Westport, would be to ensure that the contractor would meet design and budgetary constraints.

Construction Contract. As his first major task, Scott negotiated a draft "Stipulated Sum Contract" with Westport. Reflecting the architects' cost estimates, the contract called for a total construction cost of $5.9 million, resulting in an aggregate project cost of $8.59 million. Following a presentation of the contract's terms, the Board tentatively approved the contract. Final approval authority was delegated to Mike, Benny and me.[44]

Groundbreaking Ceremony. A groundbreaking ceremony was held on May 20, Dolley Madison's birthday, with Mike as emcee. Attendees had lunch in Montpelier's formal garden following the ceremony. These are highlights of the occasion:

- Noting the significance of the date for the groundbreaking, Mike said that Dolley, "the ever-ageless woman," had been universally acclaimed for her "grace and hospitality." These qualities had been the inspiration for her to be the first given "the title 'First Lady,'" a designation that later was routinely applied to wives of U.S. presidents.

- Dolley, Mike added, had been "the perfect complement to the genius of her husband."
- Turning to the ceremony's purpose, Mike said that in "a single groundbreaking [the Foundation is] taking a major step in achieving our two most important goals," namely, "preserving and telling Montpelier's great history, and serving those who devote the time to come to Montpelier to experience that history." He then briefly commented on the architects' model of the buildings, described the interiors and mentioned the roles that both the Visitor Center and the William duPont Gallery would play in meeting the two goals.
- Mike next introduced numerous individuals important in Montpelier's recent history, including many duPont family members. At Mike's request, Mrs. Jean Ellen duPont Shehan made a few remarks about the planned Gallery construction and her beloved aunt, Mrs. Marion duPont Scott.
- While emphasizing the exceptional contributions of the Building Committee members and architectural team, Mike gave special recognition to Bitsy Waters for her outstanding leadership.[45]
- Mike then called on Bitsy, Lou and Alan Potter, Delegate Ed Scott, Mrs. Shehan, Martha duPont and the Trust's Jim Vaughan to perform the ceremonial groundbreaking.

Construction Completion. The complex was constructed with only limited changes made to the approved design. By the end of summer 2006, construction was essentially complete. The final cost was approximately 2–3 percent over budget (an amount between $200,000 and $300,000).[46] The Building Committee commended Scott Little and Steve Mullaney for their excellent project management. Westport was particularly effective in ensuring that subcontractors didn't increase costs over their original estimates. To prepare the complex for occupancy, our House construction team devoted the latter half of 2006 and early 2007 to reinstalling the Red Room, and our curators installed exhibits cases and artifacts, while the Westport team finished outfitting the gift shop and performing myriad other details.[47] After overcoming delays in securing approval of the fire suppression system, we obtained the Certificate of Occupancy in January 2007.[48]

Groundbreaking of the Visitor Center and William duPont Gallery emceed by Mike Quinn, showing Bitsy Waters, Lou and Alan Potter and Mrs. Jean Ellen Shehan (*center*). *TMF.*

Visitor Center and William duPont Gallery as planned and constructed. *Photo by Maxwell MacKenzie, TMF.*

The Visitor Center/William duPont Gallery Opening

Opening on James Madison's Birthday. The grand opening ceremony for the Visitor Center and William duPont Gallery was held on March 16, 2007, the 256th anniversary of James Madison's birth. Recounting the extraordinary progress achieved at Montpelier, Mike summarized the major developments that had occurred since the Foundation assumed management responsibility in 2000. He also described interior features of the complex being celebrated. At Mike's request, Mrs. Jean Ellen Shehan made a few remarks and described her fondness for Montpelier, the home of her aunt Marion duPont Scott.

Ribbon cutting for Visitor Center complex opening showing Mrs. Shehan, Joe Grills and Lou Potter taking the principal roles. *TMF.*

Recognition of Key Supporters and Participants. Mike devoted much of the ceremony to introducing and recognizing the many people who had been instrumental in Montpelier's progress. Focusing on the complex's construction, he stressed the essential role of Lou and Alan Potter in making the lead gift and the importance of Joe and Marge Grills's major gift. Among others recognized were Mrs. Shehan and her son, Jamie McConnell, as well as other members of the duPont family. On behalf of the duPont family, Jamie had led negotiations of the essential amendment of the Will Settlement (see chapter 6). Acknowledged as well were the Board's Building Committee, architects and contractor for their extraordinary work in designing and constructing the impressive complex. Dignitaries present included former governor Gerald L. Baliles, Delegate Ed Scott and Orange County officials key to the bond financing.[49]

Ribbon Cutting. As the Marine Corps Band began to play background music, Mike welcomed "Mr. Madison and his visitors"—George Washington, Thomas Jefferson and James Monroe. When it was time to cut the ribbon, Mike asked Mrs. Shehan, Alan and Lou Potter and Joe and Marge Grills to do the honors, using the oversized scissors that had been obtained for the task. Joining them were Bitsy Waters, other Foundation directors, Mr. Madison and his friends and a number of other invited guests.[50]

10

PROGRAM HIGHLIGHTS—2002–2008

THE MADISONS AND LIFE AT MONTPELIER

During the time the Foundation undertook the transformative projects and programs described in chapters 6 through 9, the staff continued to build and improve complementary programs that play a critical role in educating visitors. This chapter discusses five programs: (1) visitor tours, (2) archaeology, (3) the enslaved community, (4) special events and (5) interiors research and furnishing. These programs are important, and in some cases essential, to providing visitors the educational experience that is a central part of Montpelier's being a national monument to Madison and the enslaved community. The chapter concludes with recognition of directors who were elected and strengthened the Board in the 2003–08 period.

Visitor Tours

Madison Education. For most visitors to Montpelier, guided tours of the House provide the principal opportunity for them to learn about the lives of the Madisons. And yet, during the Foundation's entire first decade, there was a factor that complicated our offering tours focused on the Madisons; namely, the house was not the Madisons' House. Rather, it was either the intact duPont Mansion or the mansion in various stages of demolition or restoration. As a partial offset to this obstacle, the guides' interpretation of the Madisons' life was aided from 1998 to 2001 by *Discovering Madison* exhibits (also see chapter 2), from 2001 to 2003 by 250th Madison birthday exhibits and room changes (also see chapter 5) and from 2003 to 2008 by ongoing House restoration activities supplemented by an introduction to the site in a modified construction trailer (on the path to the House) and by the Pony Barn exhibits (also see chapter 7).

Outstanding Guides. Despite the chaos involved in the house's transition, visitors uniformly expressed strong, positive views about Montpelier tours. Visitation more than doubled in the first decade, reaching approximately 80,000 annually by 2008.[1] A number of factors contributed to tours being so well received. First and foremost was—and still is—the priority given to providing a high-quality experience. As director of education, Elizabeth "Beth" Dowling Taylor worked intensively after joining the staff in 1999 to build and educate a strong, committed cadre of guides. Montpelier also has been especially successful in attracting guides with both a desire to gain knowledge about the Madisons and the capacity to present this information in a coherent, interesting fashion. Beth instituted a tradition of giving guides in-depth training and education about not just the Madisons, but Montpelier's programs as well.[2] As an example of their commitment, as House restoration proceeded, guides devoted time virtually daily to learning about what had been discovered so that they could share the information in tours.

Updated Interpretive Plans. Another key part of providing excellent tours was the development and ongoing revision of an interpretive plan for guides. On a room-by-room basis, the plan lays out biographical and historical information, as well as material on Montpelier activities and programs, that guides can shape into a narrative for visitors' tours. Decisions on which information to present in a tour are left to the guides. The plan has been regularly revised to reflect Montpelier's changing circumstances, not just in the House, but also on other parts of the property. Beth was instrumental during much of the first decade in overseeing this effort.[3] Other staff leaders, as well as Board members, also participated in reviewing and commenting on interpretive plan drafts.

Other Educational Opportunities. To supplement guided House tours, the staff offered a film on James Madison's life, new topical exhibits and thematic tours. For example, an exhibit was installed in the Education Center in 2003 to celebrate the 200th anniversary of the Louisiana Purchase and

Lewis and Clark expedition.[4] In 2004, an in-depth exhibit, *James Madison, Architect of the Constitution and the Bill of Rights*, was added (also see chapter 7).[5] Among the thematic tours offered were ones on the House's restoration, Montpelier's enslaved community, the James Madison Landmark Forest, the Gilmore Cabin and nearby Civil War encampments.[6]

Student Tours. A major emphasis also has been placed on student group tours. These were organized under the direction of Christian Cotz, the talented student-education coordinator. Later, he would become director of education and visitor engagement. Each year, 3,000 to 4,000 students visit for tours that have been both popular and educational. In 2004, for example, among the special programs offered were "Madison at Home" (with role-playing by students); "Digging Up the Past" (involving archaeological investigation); "No Press Allowed" (a reenactment of the 1787 Constitutional Convention in Philadelphia) and "In-Service to Madison" (focusing on life of the enslaved). The next year, new interpretive history programs were added at the Gilmore Cabin and at the Hands-On Restoration Tent set up near the House.[7]

Post-Restoration Planning. In 2005, the staff began developing an interpretive plan to be used for the House once restoration was completed. The three main topics to be addressed were James Madison, Montpelier and the Constitution. Through an iterative process, the staff and Board also chose a range of subtopics. The House would be restored to the 1820s period, but the plan would cover all of Madison's life, including his contributions to founding the nation.[8]

Archaeology

Historical Role. Archaeology has been integral to gaining an understanding of the Madisons' life at home. Much of the archaeological investigation activity during the 2002–08 period was a crucial part of the major building projects described in chapters 5 through 9.

The Trust's Site Investigation. From the time the Trust acquired Montpelier, a priority was placed on archaeology. Indeed, an important site investigation began prior to the Foundation's assumption of management responsibility.[9] In 1997, the Trust's staff under the leadership of Lynne Lewis, then the director of archaeology, began investigating Mount Pleasant, the homeplace that James Madison's grandparents had relocated to in 1732. This continued after Dr. Matthew "Matt" Reeves became director of archaeology in 2000. Montpelier staff and James Madison University Field School students investigated the site through 2003, greatly aided by a metal detector survey in 2000. Their discoveries included determining the configuration of the Mount Pleasant house and detached kitchen, numerous artifacts and trash deposits. They also did preliminary surface investigation of the Madison Family Cemetery, which adjoined the homeplace. The Mount Pleasant house was demolished in the 1760s after Madison's father had built the first phase of the Montpelier House. The free-standing kitchen burned to the ground around 1800.[10]

Talented Leadership. In its early years, the Foundation had limited funding for archaeology, except what was included in budgets for major construction and restoration projects. This began to change after Matt Reeves was named director (also see chapter 4).[11] The charismatic director, through persuasive oral and written advocacy, has been able to attract funding for a continuing stream of important investigations. These have contributed significantly to opportunities for showing the material culture in use during the Madisons' life. For example, preliminary site work done by Matt and his team convinced potential donors to fund an in-depth exploration of (1) the enslaved community in the South Yard (to the right of, and close to, the House); (2) the Enslaved Cemetery (near the Visitor Center); and (3) tobacco barns and enslaved fieldworker cabins (farther away from the front of the Visitor Center complex). In this investigation, they identified the locations of barns and cabins on more than fifteen undisturbed acres. This discovery is the only example of an undisturbed complex of enslaved fieldworkers in Virginia. Matt also successfully led the effort to obtain funding for investigating the Gilmore Cabin site and nearby Civil War encampments. Discoveries included nine Confederate Civil War camps containing "more than 1,200 hut features, nine troop support sites and a military road."[12] All of this was in addition to their major project work.

Archaeology director Matt Reeves, in his familiar role, explaining the team's work. *Photo by Drew Precious, TMF.*

A Capable Team. In large part due to Matt's expertise and infectious personality, Montpelier has attracted many capable staff and volunteers and built a highly regarded archaeology team with impressive university credentials.[13] Among the volunteers since 1995 has been Cynthia Reusche from the Chicago area. After a decade of volunteering, Cindy was asked to join the Foundation Board and became a leader in her new role on archaeological, site management and museum program issues.[14] She also has supported Montpelier by making major financial gifts.

Montpelier's Enslaved Descendants

The Enslaved People's Indispensable Role. From the outset, the Foundation emphasized the importance of recognizing that Montpelier's slaves were responsible for every facet of the Madison plantation's operations. Our initial formal recognition of their contributions occurred at the first Madison Slave Commemoration Gathering in 2001 (see chapter 5). Rebecca Gilmore Coleman, a descendant of former Montpelier slave George Gilmore, was a leader in organizing that gathering and every successive program for descendants of the enslaved to honor their ancestors.[15] She also was president and founder of the Orange County African American Historical Society.

Gilmore Cabin Investigations. The 2001 Gathering featured progress in restoring the home George Gilmore built on the Montpelier property he leased, and ultimately purchased, following emancipation (see chapter 5). A steering committee made up of Gilmore descendants and scholars created in 2002 guided the restoration. By 2005, improvements to the Gilmore Cabin had been completed sufficiently to open it to the public in a joint ceremony with the Orange County African American Historical Society. Mike Quinn promised Rebecca Gilmore Coleman that the Foundation would keep the cabin located on Route 20 open to visitors. This commitment was instrumental to building a long-term relationship between Montpelier and the local African American community. Following the opening of the cabin in 2005, the Gilmore family descendants donated the four-acre property to Montpelier.[16] That same year, a team from the SUNY Potsdam Field School conducted archaeological excavations around the site. They determined that, before building the cabin, the Gilmores had lived in a structure on the property similar to ones in a nearby Civil

War encampment. Some materials from that structure, which had been built with remnants from the encampment, were used in building the Gilmore Cabin.[17] Investigations on the Gilmore property also unearthed a variety of artifacts, including "beads, buttons, safety pins and other sewing items."[18] This suggests that Mrs. Gilmore did extensive seamstress work in their home.

The Second Descendants Reunion. Working with Mrs. Coleman, the Montpelier staff's goal was to hold a second, more inclusive reunion. Together they assembled an expanded record of descendants. The culmination of their planning was the Montpelier Slave Descendants Reunion held June 8–10, 2007. Descendants from across the nation attended and participated in programs on genealogical research and in events honoring African Americans who lived at Montpelier.[19] A highlight of the three-day reunion was a conversation between the renowned historian Dr. John Hope Franklin and Pulitzer Prize–winner Roger Wilkins. Dr. Franklin was professor emeritus of history at Duke University and was deemed the "father of African American history." Mr. Wilkins was the Clarence J. Robinson Professor of History and American Culture

Several of the leading participants in the 2007 Enslaved Descendants Reunion: *(from left)* Rebecca Gilmore Coleman, Professor John Hope Franklin, Mike Quinn and Lisa Cantor. *Photo by Jenn Smith, TMF.*

Professor Roger Wilkins, a Foundation Board member, speaking at the 2007 Reunion. *Photo by Jenn Smith, TMF.*

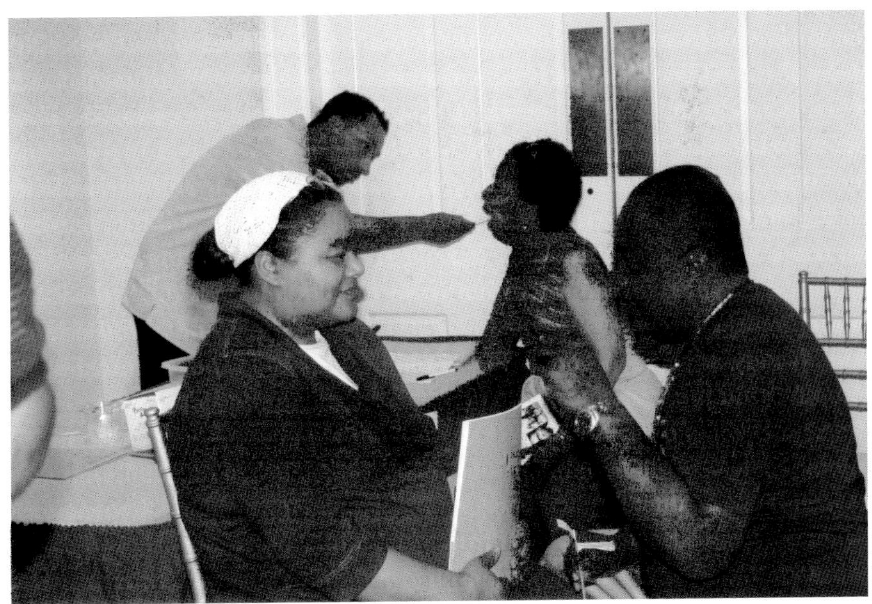

DNA testing to determine ancestry at the 2007 Reunion. *Photo by Jenn Smith, TMF.*

at George Mason University and a former U.S. assistant attorney general for civil rights (and a Foundation Board member).[20] When Roger joined the Board—after receiving much encouragement over many months from Mike and me—he told us that a major factor in his decision was his view that Montpelier had done a better job than other historic sites in presenting to visitors the reality and legacy of slavery. In his book *Jefferson's Pillow: The Founding Fathers and the Dilemma of Black Patriotism*, Roger also explained his particular interest in Madison as a founding father. "People often ask why I like James Madison so, bookish and boring as he seems to have been." Among qualities Roger mentioned were: Madison was the "founder most obsessed with ensuring that the country would 'long endure.'" While he was "devoted to rights and to the aura of freedom," Madison "was a good part of the glue that kept the new contraption from flying apart in its early stages, as well as the principal author of the machinery that kept it running over the long haul." He also pointed out that "Madison was brilliant, a consummate analyst and strategist, a fine writer, and one of the most exceptional legislators this country has ever known."[21]

Paul Jennings Research. Playing a major role in organizing the slave descendants reunions, Beth Taylor developed a friendship with many of them. A particularly close relationship evolved with Paul Jennings's descendants. Jennings had served Madison during the presidential years and was with him when he died on June 28, 1836.[22] He also was responsible—with the urgent encouragement of Dolley Madison—for removing from the White House the iconic Gilbert Stuart portrait of George Washington just before the British burned the executive mansion in 1814. His memoir, *A Colored Man's Reminiscences of James Madison*, has been called the first memoir by a White House staffer.[23] Based on much research with family members and other sources, Beth later wrote the well-received biography *A Slave in the White House: Paul Jennings and the Madisons*. In her research, she discovered an extremely rare photograph of Jennings.[24]

SPECIAL EVENTS

Each year, numerous special events are held at Montpelier. They have typically attracted 40,000 to 50,000 visitors (until the coronavirus pandemic).[25] Some events contribute materially to the Foundation's education mission. Others offer local visitors an experience that furthers

Montpelier's maintaining the good-neighbor reputation that Mrs. Scott had fostered.

James Madison's Birthday. To recognize Madison's birthday, a ceremony is held each year on March 16 at the Madison Family Cemetery. It begins with a Marine Corps detail presenting a presidential wreath. Wreaths are then presented by numerous other organizations. This is followed by remarks of a prominent speaker.[26] For example, in 2005, Hunter Rawlings, president emeritus of Cornell University and Foundation Board member, presented remarks on the importance of Madison's legacy. Madison's birthday also has been the day chosen for announcing certain important developments at Montpelier. Among them was the 2007 opening of the Visitor Center/ duPont Gallery.

Dolley Madison's Birthday. In 2006, the Dolley Madison Legacy Luncheon was inaugurated to honor Mrs. Madison each year on a Tuesday close to her birthday (May 20). It provides a forum for a guest speaker on a topic that is believed to have been of interest to her. Carolyn Quinn was the inspiration for this event. Her attention to detail ensured the luncheon would be a special occasion Dolley would have appreciated (fine linen and silver, flower arrangements on every table). The event continues to be held in a huge tent on the back lawn, the venue for many of Dolley's parties. With Carolyn's guiding hand, a committee co-chaired by Marge Grills and Peyton Lewis each year handled planning for the luncheon. From the beginning, greatly surpassing initial expectations, the luncheon was sold out and a source of significant revenue for House furnishings. The first speaker was nationally respected journalist Cokie Roberts, author of *Founding Mothers*.[27] Other speakers have included well-known authors, curators and garden designers.

Constitution Day. Each year on September 17, Montpelier celebrates the signing of the Constitution on that day in 1787. In a 2007 Constitution Day ceremony, Lewis Hall, the Center for the Constitution's newly renovated academic building, was opened (see chapter 8). In 2008, Montpelier held two events to mark the date. Celebration of the restored House's opening was held on the signing date (see chapter 12). Several days later, nationally syndicated columnist George Will spoke on "The Madison Persuasion Today," in the Montpelier Room of the Madison Building of the Library of Congress in Washington, D.C.[28]

Aerial view of the annual Montpelier Steeplechase, held since the 1920s. *Photo by Abbie Lucas, TMF.*

Montpelier Hunt Races. Continuing the tradition Mrs. Scott started, the Montpelier Steeplechase and Equestrian Foundation, a subsidiary of The Montpelier Foundation, annually holds a day of hunt races and tailgate parties on the first Saturday in November. The races typically attract between 15,000–20,000 paying attendees. Throughout the time the Foundation has operated Montpelier, the capable, successful leaders of the event have been its chair Charlie Seilheimer and treasurer Jamie McConnell.[29] The steeplechase foundation reimburses the Foundation for the costs of maintaining the steeplechase course and each year makes a financial contribution. Jamie McConnell's mother, duPont heir Mrs. Jean Ellen Shehan, established and regularly made donations to an endowment for the races.

Other Special Events. Additional functions became a customary part of the events schedule as well. These include the Wine Festival in May, in partnership with the Orange County Chamber of Commerce, as well as the Fall Fiber Festival and Sheep Dog Trials. For many years, the Orange County Fair was held on the property. Various activities also have been, and are, presented as "Evenings at Montpelier." Among them have been lectures by authors and scholars on recently published books on Madison or other founding period topics, summer family barbecues reminiscent of ones Dolley held on the back lawn and an autumn reenactment of the 1788 debate between James Madison and Patrick Henry at the Virginia convention on ratification of the Constitution.[30]

Interiors Research and Furnishing

Furnishings Research. The Foundation faced a major challenge to present the Madisons' home as it was in their lifetime. The furnishings and art, as well as the House itself, were sold in the 1840s.[31] Montpelier curator Lee Langston-Harrison and her staff successfully obtained a number of pieces—some by purchase, but mostly on loan—to display in 2001 during the 250th Madison birthday celebration (see chapter 5). But the emphasis in the next few years was on collections research and building a digital record. From hundreds of repositories, staff culled all manuscripts related to Madison, Orange County, Montpelier and the plantation's enslaved community, resulting in a catalogue of more than 30,000 documentary references. Using a relational database, the team was able to connect these historical documents with places, people and extant and conjectural objects that provided great detail on how the Madisons lived at Montpelier, particularly during Madison's retirement.[32] The database became an important tool in ensuring accuracy and authenticity in the site's exhibitions and interpretation and in assisting in furnishing the House's interiors.[33]

Expert Advice. To provide expert review of Montpelier's collections and acquisitions, Mike assembled in 2004 a Furnishings and Interpretation Advisory Committee consisting of curators from peer organizations.[34] He also built a team of talented staff and consultants. In 2005, in anticipation of the restoration's completion, he retained Susan Borchardt, formerly curator at Gunston Hall, George Mason's home, to provide furnishings oversight. She took the lead in creating the research design for the team's furnishings investigation.[35] Conover Hunt, the leading authority for more than 30 years on the Madisons' furnishings, also was retained.[36] Tom Chapman, an assistant in our archaeology department, was reassigned to be a research archivist.[37] Alison Deeds, an assistant curator, became the staff leader working on furnishing plans.[38]

Furnishings Authenticity. Montpelier's advisors insisted, with Board and staff concurrence, that the high degree of authenticity reflected in the House restoration be maintained in furnishing it. Absence of an inventory of Madison furnishings, except one for the dining room, meant that correspondence to and from Madison family and visitors would be the principal source for determining how rooms were decorated. Other information sources would include merchants' bills, newspaper articles and estate settlements. The advisors proposed that a plan initially be developed for furnishing four of the House's 22 rooms: the drawing room, the dining room, Madison's study and one of his mother's rooms. Vignettes would be set up in other rooms to assist in meeting interpretive goals.[39]

The Refurnishing Plan. The team realized that, notwithstanding extensive prior efforts, an ambitious research undertaking would still be necessary to gain an "understanding of the Madisons, their sense of style, their use of the home, and the household belongings they owned." To this end, an interiors research and refurnishing plan was developed in 2007 to (1) identify and review records and (2) examine and determine the provenance of nearly 400 objects identified as having a Madison connection. To achieve efficiency in accessing research, the team relied heavily on the powerful relational database system that had been acquired. Once the research and refurnishing plan was developed, the team used it to provide the justification for a funding proposal. The plan called for two years of research, with furnishing the House to start within three years after research was begun.[40] The budget was $1.45 million for research and $5 million for furnishing (replicating wallpaper, draperies and rugs; and acquiring furnishings and artwork). In support of the plan, the Mellon Estate executors approved $250,000 for research in 2007 and also 2008 but made our obtaining significant donations from others a condition of their funding.[41]

Furnishings Timing. The House could be furnished only to a limited extent until after the opening, planned for 2008. The Mesick team estimated it could take as long as a year for internal climate control to become stable enough for installing wallpaper and certain furnishings and painting walls. Staff knew it would probably never be possible for pieces with Madison provenance to be acquired to furnish even the four rooms. Thus, it would be necessary to use period pieces and possibly reproductions, based on the results of furnishings research.

New Directors—2003–2008

The Foundation's Board was strengthened during this period by the election of nine new members and two ex officio members.[42] They were Nancy Campbell and Bill Remington (2003); Martha duPont and Irenee duPont II (2003, ex officio); Roger Wilkins, Florence "Flossie" Fowlkes and Elinor Farquhar (2006); Gregory "Greg" May, John Sponski and Cynthia "Cindy" Reusche (2007); and Steve McLean (2008). See appendix A for their biographical sketches.

Contributing to the impressive array of programs and events at Montpelier from 2002 through 2008 was a cadre of dedicated people—from guides to staff to advisors and donors. Their commitment was critical to achieving the monument to Madison envisioned by the founding Board members.

11

LEADERSHIP, FUNDRAISING AND PLANNING

CRUCIAL CAPABILITIES FOR TRANSFORMING MONTPELIER

Throughout the book, I have identified three forces in particular that underlay The Montpelier Foundation's success. Two of them–leadership and fundraising–were consistently in evidence. They are the principal focus of this chapter. The third force–planning–was most apparent in undertaking the major projects discussed in chapters 6 through 9. But planning also was a focus intermittently on a more macro basis, which I address here.

Leadership

The founding Board and staff team that serendipitously came together has been generously acknowledged for its role in transforming Montpelier into a nationally significant historic site—a "monument" to James Madison. As I said in the prologue, the founders shared an inspiration that derived from the belief that education centered on Madison's life and legacies would contribute materially and importantly to a civil society and functioning democracy. We also felt strongly that Montpelier was uniquely positioned to create an institution for that education. This section is a tribute to the principal founders and to the exceptional oversight of financial management. (In the Foundation's second decade, it received a

$10 million gift from David M. Rubenstein that supported momentous actions to recognize enslaved families, resulting in Montpelier now also being a monument to its enslaved community.)

Principal Founders

1. **Michael Quinn**

   From the time Mike became chief executive officer in 1999, he focused with laser-like intensity on pursuing initiatives for Montpelier to become the national monument to Madison. His prior experience in historic preservation and museum management well equipped him to provide the necessary ambitious, creative leadership. As the history recounted in this book shows, Mike was the inspiration and leader of every major project and initiative during his tenure as CEO. Numerous Board and staff members, outside advisors and other contributors also played key roles. But in my view, Mike was most important to the realization of our vision of Montpelier as a national monument. At a celebration of Mike's contributions when he resigned to become chief executive of the proposed Museum of the American Revolution in Philadelphia, the accolades about his leadership made it clear that his importance was widely recognized.

2. **William Lewis**

   In presenting the story about Montpelier's transformation, this book also describes the leading roles played by founding directors Joe Grills, Lou Potter, Bitsy Waters and me. In serving as Board chair, my background leading nonprofit, corporate and legal groups was certainly useful. As it turned out, though, my decades of negotiations focused on achieving "win-win" results proved to be the most valuable experience I brought to the position. Particularly satisfying to me were reaching agreements for (1) the Foundation to manage Montpelier with unprecedented autonomy, (2) amendment of the Will Settlement so that the House could be restored and (3) the Mellon Estate's funding for restoration. I lacked a typically essential strength for the chair of a new nonprofit—experience raising significant donations. Fortunately for us, the Foundation's vision consistently attracted talented Board members who could contribute this and other important complementary skills.

3. Joe Grills

With his history in high-level finance and investment and university fundraising, Joe's expertise and judgment resulted in his immediately becoming a Foundation leader. Shortly after joining the Board, he was elected vice chair. Joe's emphasis on organization and focus on details were an integral part of everything he did. His invaluable oversight of the Foundation's financial health is described later, on page 166, under "Financial Management." Along with Mike and me, Joe participated in our important negotiations and sensitive meetings. His extensive experience on boards of leading pension and investment funds and investment committees expanded Montpelier's national exposure to potential advisors and major donors. Joe played a key role also as the Board's ambassador in the local community. Moreover, he and Marge have been multimillion-dollar donors who have supported a broad range of key initiatives.

4. Louise Potter

Lou's dedication to Montpelier becoming a successful historic site predated both Joe's and my involvement by a decade. As a trustee of the National Trust and member of the Montpelier Property Council, she had for years placed a priority on introducing potential donors to Montpelier, while it was still very much a duPont estate. Her efforts led to the one large individual donation made in the 1990s: Clayton and Anna Timmons's gift of $450,000 to renovate the Pony Barn to educate children about Madison's contributions. Of enduring consequence, she and her husband, Alan, also introduced philanthropist Robert H. Smith to the site. This association later led to Mr. Smith's donating more than $10 million, primarily for establishing and building the Center for the Constitution. The Potters have been among the largest of Montpelier's multimillion-dollar donors. Their major gifts have included contributions to the Visitor Center complex, to several donor challenges and, most recently, to Claude Moore Hall, which opened in 2017 in the Constitutional Village. Notably, as a Building Committee member, Lou never insisted on adherence to her personal views in advising on construction of the Visitor Center complex, despite her being the largest contributor to it. She has continued to be an ambassador for Montpelier in every place she has lived—Northern Virginia, Florida, West Virginia and Piedmont Virginia. Her enthusiasm and commitment are infectious and have led to major financial contributions from many other donors. With a distinguished background as an architect and nonprofit leader, she also has been an insightful Board member and emerita.

5. Elizabeth Waters

Bitsy's background in historic preservation, professional organizing and facilitating of groups and community service (including as mayor of Charlottesville) complemented her natural talents for playing a leadership role. This was particularly evident in her skill in analyzing the most complex matters and making thoughtful judgments and decisions. She was routinely called on whenever the Board needed a director to organize and lead a group to consider a challenging issue. In chairing the Building Committee, she devoted extraordinary energy and time to oversight of the design of the Visitor Center complex, the new entryway (Gateway) and Lewis Hall, as well as to each of the master planning initiatives. These are covered in depth in this and preceding chapters. On every initiative she guided, her leadership was central to the Foundation's achieving results that were uniformly recognized to be exceptional.

6. Board Leadership Change

In November 2006, after serving as Board chair for eight years, I felt it was time to elect a new chair. Establishing Montpelier as a monument to Madison was on a certain path. I was the first of the leadership team to hand off a key role but continued to be an active Board member for six more years and remained on the Governance Committee for an additional five. When Joe succeeded me as chair, he and Bitsy made laudatory comments about me that were equally applicable to all the founding directors and Mike: Montpelier "would not be where [it is] today" without us; each of us can be thought to be a Foundation "founding" father or mother; our "fingerprints are all over this place to the great benefit of Montpelier and all of us."[1]

Attempting to properly recognize the specific contributions of each founding director would be impossible—but the history presented here is a good place to start. As conveyed in this book, Board member contributions have been a hallmark of the progress made at Montpelier. In addition, our ongoing ability to attract talented staff at all levels, who likewise played significant roles, was necessary for designing and carrying out each of the Foundation's projects and programs. As I pointed out in chapter 3, the collegiality engendered among the Board and staff members was possibly the most important ingredient.

Financial Management

When the Foundation assumed responsibility for Montpelier in 2000, the number of staff was small (see chapter 4). A limited budget, together with Montpelier's rural location, initially made it difficult to build a staff with significant relevant experience for key senior roles. This situation made it critical for Board members to play a staff-like role in overseeing certain responsibilities, particularly with respect to financial oversight.

Joe Grills was the dominant force on financial matters throughout his time on the Board. His background in finance and investments made him ideal. Joe served as chair of the Finance Committee from 2000 until he became Board chair in late 2006. During that span of time, he held a committee meeting at least once before each Board and Executive Committee meeting, generally a total of seven or eight times a year. After personally reviewing financial information before meetings, he raised issues with staff that showed his detailed understanding of the Foundation's financial status and prospects.

Each year, Joe participated extensively in preparing the next year's budget. His advice was invaluable to the young Foundation in maintaining a stable financial condition. In 2005, based on Joe's proposal, the Board approved development of a long-range financial plan to guide future stewardship as the Foundation budget grew. To ensure compliance with sound accounting principles, he also took the lead in selecting auditors and consulted with them when they prepared their year-end audit (encompassing a $10 million–plus budget by 2007).[2] Needless to say, Joe's leadership was reassuring to the Board and Mike.

One staff person and two Board members, in particular, aided Joe in dealing with the Foundation's finances. Sherida Hawthorne was hired in 1999 and became director of the financial department. Over time, Sherida gained experience that allowed Joe to reduce somewhat the time he devoted to financial oversight. When Walter Craigie and David Gibson joined the Board, they accepted membership on the Finance Committee and, employing their strong financial expertise, together became an important part of the oversight team. When Joe was elected Board chair, David succeeded him as committee chair. Like Joe, he made a major time commitment to providing high-quality financial oversight. Montpelier's growth during the 2000s placed unusually heavy demands on the Finance Committee. The need was ongoing for its scrutiny of the risks associated with undertaking costly projects and programs before they were submitted for Board consideration and approval.

Fundraising

After we entered into a 75-year lease with the Trust, perhaps the most daunting challenge we faced was securing the financial resources needed to pursue our ambitious vision. Fortunately, the vision excited donors and, in a remarkably short period, led to major donations to fund transformative projects and programs. Many of those donations have already been reviewed in discussing specific projects (see chapters 5 through 9). Some fundraising highlights not previously described are reviewed here.

Early National Trust Support

Prior to the Foundation's creation, National Trust president Dick Moe took the lead, beginning in the early 1990s, in raising funding to keep the property open to the public and make infrastructure improvements. The Trust provided more than $3.5 million for infrastructure projects in its first decade of ownership and approximately $400,000 each year for operations during the time it managed the site.[3] As shown throughout the book, Dick continued to assist in material ways after the Foundation assumed responsibility for the site in 2000. Of particular importance to the management transition, his advocacy to Congress for issuance of a Dolley Madison Commemorative Coin resulted in $3 million for Montpelier, mostly for endowment.[4] This funding contributed to the Board's becoming cautiously optimistic about prospects for operating on a sound financial footing.

Virginia Legislature Support

Similarly important was Walter Craigie's advocacy—increasingly with Mike's support—for significant funding from the Virginia legislature. In the early 2000s, the legislature made grants that annually ranged from $200,000 to $500,000, which provided funds otherwise difficult-to-raise for staff salaries and other basic expenses.[5] This funding ended in the mid-2000s, as it did for all nonprofits in the Commonwealth. Montpelier had been the envy of other Virginia nonprofits because of our success in obtaining levels of legislative support greater than theirs. This funding loss, together with the Trust's ending its commitment for annual support in 2003 (see chapter 4), resulted in an overall reduction of between $600,000 and $700,000. Later, partially offsetting this reduction were annual "restoration grant" payments. After obtaining a special legislative authorization, grant payments to Montpelier were made in lieu of Virginia rehabilitation tax credits for the House's restoration. Walter and Mike took the lead in seeking the necessary legislation, but determined that they needed the professional assistance of a lobbyist and a law firm. Charles Guthridge and Hunton & Williams, respectively, were retained for these roles. The restoration grant payments over a decade totaled about $4.6 million.[6] In addition, under Virginia's historic preservation legislation, the Foundation sold tax credits for $271,000 in connection with renovation of Lewis Hall (see chapter 8).[7]

Madison Cabinet

We organized the Madison Cabinet in 1999 as our first new initiative to provide a significant source of annual giving. Members would include individual, corporate and foundation donors. Patterned on leadership donor groups of other organizations, the required membership contribution each year was $5,000. Benefits consisted of (1) unlimited admission to the house for members and their guests and (2) a two-day weekend event that included a black-tie dinner with a major speaker, workshops with staff on current programs, a business meeting and, in some years, a brunch at a member's historic home.[8] Speakers have included Chief Justice William H. Rehnquist (for Madison's 250th birthday), Justice Sandra Day O'Connor, renowned biographer David

McCullough, leading historian Gordon Wood and the PBS *NewsHour* anchor Jim Lehrer.[9] Joe and Marge Grills contributed funding of $25,000 for each of the first five Cabinet dinners. This donation included the cost of the Foundation's share of the 250th birthday dinner. Cabinet members who funded subsequent dinners included Jim and Alice Turner, Gerry and Betty Lowrie and Lou and Al Potter. Each year, members have provided the Foundation with a substantial source of revenue. Membership increased quickly; within several years, there were more than 100 Madison Cabinet members.

American Legacy Campaign

We recognized that an obvious important step for tackling funding needs in the early years was for us to create a Development Committee to provide assistance and direction to the single full-time staff person responsible for fundraising. Alan Potter offered to serve as the initial committee chair. Members included most of the Board and the steeplechase foundation chair. The committee quickly concluded that planning should begin for a fundraising campaign to secure funds both for major projects and for ongoing operations.

Retaining a consultant to assess the Foundation's prospects and provide advice on structuring a comprehensive campaign seemed essential. Thus, in 2003 the Board retained Peter Kellogg of the Kellogg Organization, a nationally known and respected expert in the field of fundraising. After conducting extensive interviews with Board members and other potential donors, Kellogg prepared a feasibility study and issued a report outlining the challenges and opportunities of a comprehensive campaign.[10] Absence of a large base of donor prospects would obviously present a particularly formidable challenge. Another weakness was the lack of a strong staff team to manage the campaign. Of course, the Mellon Estate executors' authorization to use $2 million of the estate's gift to hire a development team would dramatically bolster fundraising capability.[11] To provide staff leadership, later that year Mike recruited Joseph Taylor, vice president for development at Albany Law School, to serve in the same role for Montpelier.[12]

Offsetting the fundraising shortcomings were the phenomenal commitments of $20 million by the Mellon Estate for restoration;

$1 million by the federal government's Save the Treasures program, also for restoration; $6 million by Robert H. Smith for the Center for the Constitution; and $3 million by Lou and Al Potter for the Visitor Center. These leadership gifts would ensure an inspiring kickoff for the campaign. Together with the commitments, Kellogg predicted, our vision for Montpelier would generate enthusiasm that would lead to sizable donations from Board members, other individual prospects and foundations.

After a year in a "quiet phase," the American Legacy Campaign was launched on November 6, 2004. Board member Hunter Rawlings, president emeritus of Cornell University, agreed to be chair.[13] Having the advantage of his extensive fundraising experience, Hunter spearheaded an amazingly successful campaign. We also had other key campaign leaders with a history of raising funds for educational institutions and/or foundations. They were Al Potter, vice chair for leadership gifts; Peter Rice, vice chair for annual giving; and Walter Craigie, vice chair for planned giving. As the Foundation's chief executive, Mike had the heaviest burden—directing the campaign. Most Board members participated in some way to help make it a success. Providing staff support to Mike were Joseph Taylor and his successor Kimberly Skelly, who joined the team in 2007.

When the campaign was launched, we had received commitments totaling $36.4 million. Our goal was $60 million:

$29 million for restoring and furnishing the House
$15 million for the Center for the Constitution
$8 million for the Visitor Center and duPont Gallery
$2.5 million for the new entryway to the property
("Gateway" project)
$5.5 million for five years of stewardship support[14]

The campaign ultimately secured leadership gifts (those of $500,000 or more) from numerous individuals and foundations. Among them, in addition to the ones previously mentioned, were Nancy Woodson Spire Foundation, Joseph and Robert Cornell Foundation, Crean Foundation, Fidelity Foundation, Joe and Marge Grills, Bruce and Jacqueline Gupton and Clayton and Anna Timmons.[15]

The paths to the leadership gifts varied. For example, the Crean Foundation's commitment was a direct result of Johnny Crean coming for a single visit to Montpelier and then, a year later, without being solicited, making a gift of $1 million through his foundation. Dick Moe initially introduced the Nancy Woodson Spire Foundation. After receiving background information on the Center for the Constitution from Mike, the foundation developed an ongoing relationship with Montpelier and has made numerous leadership-level gifts over a number of years. The Guptons' interest in the Center led to their leadership gift and the naming of its library in their honor.[16] The Fidelity Foundation's gift was the result of the efforts of Glen Moreno, the Fidelity director and senior executive who had chaired the Montpelier Property Council and devoted significant time and energy to the planning for establishment of The Montpelier Foundation.

Late in the campaign, Mike and Carolyn Quinn met Joseph and Robert Cornell Foundation trustee Richard Ader and his wife, Tessa, at a dinner party held to assist in raising funds to acquire the original Flemish painting *Pan, Youths and Nymphs*, which had hung in the Madisons' drawing room (see chapter 12). Mary Howard, wife of Board member A.E. Dick Howard, had suggested that the Aders be invited. Montpelier traced the painting's chain of ownership from Dolley's list of paintings, to its inclusion in her estate, to its then-current owner in Amsterdam. A leading supporter of nonprofits in the Charlottesville area, the Joseph and Robert Cornell Foundation supported purchase of the painting and, in future years, made numerous other significant leadership gifts.[17] Richard and Tessa Ader and later co-trustee Joseph Erdman and his wife, Rosemary, became important Montpelier friends and donors.

In 2007, the Campaign Committee decided it would conclude the campaign in 2008, when completion of the House's restoration would be celebrated. It was confident that the $60 million fundraising goal would be achieved by that time. The committee realized, though, that one or more of the individual campaign targets would not be met (see, for example, Visitor Center costs in chapter 9).

National Trust Historic Sites Support

The Trust's Historic Sites program contributed support (usually on a matching basis) for many infrastructure projects that assisted in maintaining and improving Montpelier buildings. The Trust's financial support under the program has been in excess of $1 million during the period since the Foundation assumed management of Montpelier in 2000.[18]

Major Gifts and Annual Giving

With the $2 million of the Mellon Estate gift used for development, the greatest emphasis was initially on annual giving and major gifts to address short-term needs and build a donor base. We spelled out our strategy for fundraising in the American Legacy Campaign prospectus.[19] The dramatic increase in Foundation contributions that made the campaign a success underlined the value of the expanded staff. In 2005 and subsequent years, recognizing the long-term importance of vehicles for planned giving, the Foundation added a panoply of options to strengthen fundraising. Among them were charitable gift annuities, remainder trusts and lead trusts, as well as straightforward will bequests.[20]

Planning

The strategic plan that the founding directors developed in 1999, while not used as a formal blueprint, nonetheless produced initiatives reflecting a shared vision (also see chapter 3). When Mike became CEO in the fall of that year, we gained the leadership to convert the elements of that vision into compelling projects and programs to present to potential donors. What unexpectedly followed was the rapid ability to undertake and fund the highest priority projects. In the first few years, these projects became the components of a de facto plan guiding the actions of the Board and staff.

By 2003, however, there was increasing recognition among Board members that we needed to devote attention more systematically to preparing plans to assist in shaping the Foundation's future. One of the most important would be a master plan for Montpelier's 2,650 acres, with its more than 100 buildings. With a master plan in place, we could proceed with more confidence in making short-, medium- and long-term program and building decisions. A plan that required a similar priority was a financial plan that was developed by the Finance Committee (see

"Financial Management" earlier in this chapter). This section discusses the master plan and an interpretive plan for the restored House (see chapter 10). To provide guidance for preparation of a site-wide strategic plan, our goals for future actions are outlined in appendix B.

Master Plan

1. Elements of the Site Plan

Under Bitsy Waters's leadership, the Board's Building Committee began preliminary discussions in 2003 on development of a master plan.[21] For the next four years, work continued on a relatively sustained basis, with the full Board receiving regular updates and some directors participating in Board and staff workshops. At the November 2005 Board meeting, having reached a consensus on the master plan's scope and the staffing for it, Bitsy reported that work had begun on the plan's three elements: "1) documenting existing land uses and resources, 2) identifying projected staff and space needs and 3) mapping a growth plan to accommodate these space needs."[22]

Because Montpelier's archaeology department had developed sophisticated mapping expertise, one of the senior archaeologists, Tom Chapman, was tasked with handling the first element. He prepared maps that included an "overview land use map that identifie[d] general zones of land use, detailed maps of each zone, and the supporting information on all facilities and other resources within each zone."[23] Having had experience working with databases, Tom also undertook the time-consuming—and valuable—task of preparing and regularly updating, in tabular form, a detailed listing of every one of Montpelier's buildings. For each, he identified its condition; its needs for maintenance or repair, or a recommendation for demolition; the projected cost of recommended work; a priority ranking for carrying out the work; and a proposed schedule. The uses for this comprehensive building assessment were many.[24] For example, when staff unexpectedly identified the presence of mold in a number of buildings that were in active use, Tom was able to prioritize the remediation.

Mike took the lead in identifying staff and space needs. The initial focus would be on the Center for the Constitution and administrative zones because they had "the greatest growth pressures."[25] Space was needed for the following: additional senior staff offices; office and storage for the curator and storage for furniture; offices, lab, library and equipment for archaeological stewardship; storage and presentation of artifacts; and improved storage for Montpelier's extensive inventory of farm equipment. In locating space for grounds maintenance equipment, it was necessary to take into account the ability to move it without disrupting traffic.[26] In general, it was expected that these space needs would be accommodated in repurposed existing buildings. The one major exception would be a new building for storage of equipment and materials. It could be located outside the 814-acre "core" area because it need not be readily accessible to management.[27]

Maynard Ball of Bartzen & Ball was assigned the lead role in mapping a growth plan. He was tasked with addressing issues such as whether the Center for the Constitution and administrative zones would be "adequate for growth, or need to be moved."[28] One option discussed was whether either the Center or administrative facilities should be moved to the area on Route 20 where the duPont store, formerly used as the visitor center, was located. Ultimately, the committee decided to retain the Center in the Constitutional Village and renovate the nearby brick carriage house/stable as an academic building (later named Lewis Hall). The executive offices would be located, at least temporarily, in Lewis Hall—where they still are located (see chapter 8).

We identified these key growth principles to be embodied in the master plan:

- No new construction would be allowed in the viewshed of the House.
- Other "conservation zones" receiving a high level of protection would include the Madison Family and Enslaved Cemeteries, James Madison Landmark Forest, Constitutional Village, Annie Rogers duPont Garden, Gilmore Cabin and the surrounding farm, Confederate encampment area and steeplechase course.
- Adaptive reuse of existing buildings would be the preferred option for expansion.
- Use of best stewardship practices to protect archaeology would be mandatory both for already disturbed and undisturbed portions of the landscape.[29]

We recognized that some buildings were in such poor condition that a future decision would likely be made to demolish them. In fact, a decision was reached to stop leasing the houses on Tagg's Island, because of their advanced deterioration, lack of infrastructure and poor potential for reuse.[30]

2. **Consideration of Expansion of Center for the Constitution**

Having concluded that the location of the Center for the Constitution should not be changed, our focus shifted to whether its educational capacity could, and should, be significantly expanded in the relatively short term. Robert H. Smith provided funding to support preparation of the master plan with an eye to the Center's expansion.[31] Accordingly, in mapping the growth plan, Maynard first focused on the potential for expanding the Center. In late 2008, he concluded that the "current general location could accommodate the Center growing to…as many as 150 to 200 participants."[32] He recommended the Farm Barn complex as the "preferred site" for its growth and proposed a first phase of expansion that would "accommodate 50 to 75 participants." The complex was located a short distance from the existing housing for Center participants and just across a small pond from the Lewis Hall academic building. He also concluded that Lewis Hall could "evolve over time to accommodate programs" near the House. Among his conclusions on other growth possibilities was one related to the duPont farm store complex on Route 20. He said that it might be an appropriate location for a "visitation and on-site programs increase."[33]

In considering expansion of the Center, the question was raised as to whether the large Farm Barn could be repurposed to be part of the additional facilities. After extensive analysis, the Board and staff, relying heavily on Maynard's analysis, concluded that the barn must be deconstructed in its entirety due to its condition. The barn had not been used for many years. No funding had been available to support its maintenance, and it had been seriously compromised. No part of it appeared usable. Even its foundation could not support new construction because its loose stone construction had no footings. Nonetheless, the Trust and the local preservation community raised serious concerns about no adaptive reuse being planned for the barn. As a consequence, a meeting was held with their representatives to review that decision. In the meeting, Mike stressed policies and actions that demonstrated the Foundation's preservation ethic. He particularly focused on the great extent to which buildings had been renovated for new uses, even where demolition and new construction would have been a less costly option. Maynard presented an in-depth analysis of the barn's condition, after which meeting participants walked to the barn to view its structure and condition. We decided that to recycle at least some of the barn's material, potentially reusable wood would be carefully removed for use in the new Center facility. After follow-up conversations and our exchange of correspondence with them, the Trust and preservation representatives indicated that they would not actively oppose our proposal.[34]

As discussed in chapter 8, with financial support from Mr. Smith, the Foundation subsequently retained Bartzen & Ball to prepare full-scale design and elevation drawings of facilities that, in phases, could accommodate the Center growth envisioned for the Farm Barn complex area.[35] With a first increment of Mr. Smith's $10 million challenge match, we moved forward with deconstructing the Farm Barn in preparation for building the new facility.[36] When it was later determined that raising funding for the match was not possible, the expansion project was not pursued further. Mr. Smith's generous and much appreciated challenge may have unintentionally overridden our usual sound judgment. The one clear benefit of Mr. Smith's challenge, at least in my opinion, was that removal of the Farm Barn significantly improved the appearance and safety of the Constitutional Village. The Center for the Constitution, of which the Village is a part, is now named for Robert H. Smith. Very sadly, during the time the initiative was being pursued, Mr. Smith died.[37] Under the leadership of his daughter, Michelle Smith, the Robert H. Smith Foundation continued to be a major donor in support of the Center's programs.

3. Scenic Easement

In developing the master plan, a significant consideration was whether a scenic conservation easement should be placed on a portion of the 2,650 acres. Obviously, an easement could greatly circumscribe the Foundation's future actions. A conservation easement's purpose is, first and foremost, to restrict actions at the "eased" property. But its specific terms would determine the extent to which property decisions would be affected. Under a typical easement provision, the owner's ability to "subdivide" the eased property is limited—for example, permitting only one division per 100 acres. It was understood that this type of limitation would not be relevant for much of Montpelier. No easement would be placed on the 814-acre "core" (location of the House and surrounding area) because it was already subject to express limitations on its transfer under the Will Settlement.

The Board was committed, and it expected future boards also to be committed, to maintaining the integrity of Montpelier property. Thus, we believed that there was little need for an easement. However, from shortly after the Foundation's assumption of responsibility, the Piedmont Environmental Council (PEC), a Virginia nonprofit devoted to protecting the rural character of central Virginia, encouraged the Board to put an easement on significant portions of the site. PEC asserted that Montpelier's doing so would have the ancillary benefit of encouraging nearby owners to put an easement on their property and thereby restrict its subdivision as well.[38]

From our standpoint, the greatest concern was that an easement's terms not restrict the Foundation's ability to undertake programmatic initiatives involving new or modified construction. Despite our reservations, we agreed to consider the development of an easement—as long as Montpelier would have an unfettered ability to engage in "mission-related activities." In a letter dated April 12, 2002, to address our concern—without which negotiation of an easement would not have begun—PEC said that "the eased portions would permit the construction of mission-related structures."[39] Another key commitment reflected in the letter was that the Foundation would receive payment of the easement's fair market value.

PEC posited that negotiation of terms of an easement deed could be done in a matter of months.[40] We recognized that this projection was highly unrealistic. However, we did not expect that discussions would continue, as happened, off and on for a period of more than seven years. PEC was not willing to agree, after all, to an unqualified provision that would allow "construction of mission-related structures." The Foundation and PEC both had doubts at various times about whether agreement could be reached on (1) the tracts of land to be put under easement and (2) terms acceptable to the Foundation for it to have sufficient flexibility to use the land.[41]

Through persistence, the organizations ultimately agreed to an easement being established on four parcels and on the restrictions to be imposed on each. The parcels and associated acreage were Chicken

Mountain (237.86 acres), East Woods (202.74 acres), Gilmore Cabin and Freedman's Farm (16 acres) and Civil War Encampments (260.38 acres). Chicken Mountain and East Woods are heavily forested areas at the rear of Montpelier and adjoin the James Madison Landmark Forest. The Virginia Outdoors Foundation co-holds the easements with PEC on these two parcels.[42] The other two parcels were located on the north side of Route 20. The Virginia Department of Historic Resources co-holds the easements on them. PEC had indicated early in the negotiations that it could raise $1.95 million to acquire easements and believed this amount would represent a reasonable determination of the easements' fair market value.[43] Although the Foundation consultant retained to estimate valuation concluded that the market value was somewhat higher, the Board decided that it should accept the amount PEC was prepared to offer, and it approved the easement terms. Payment would be made to the Trust (the legal owner of the property) and added to the endowment held by the Trust that is restricted to Montpelier.

As lead negotiator for the Foundation, Mike effectively represented our interests throughout the long process. As an advisor to Mike, Frank Thomas, a highly regarded lawyer with offices in the town of Orange, provided many hours of pro bono advice during that entire period. His creativity, experience and knowledge of easements were essential to working out terms acceptable to Mike and the Board. Tom Mayes, who represented the Trust's interests, also provided valuable legal advice. His participation ensured that the easement terms would be acceptable to the Trust before it executed the deed. The principal PEC negotiator was John "Jeep" Moore, the staff member then responsible for the region in which Montpelier is located. Also participating on an ongoing basis for PEC, John "Jack" Snyder, a resident in the Chicken Mountain Road area, contributed a significant portion of the amount paid for the easements.

Interpretive Plan

Throughout the period the House's restoration was under way, the staff devoted significant attention to developing an interpretive plan for presenting Montpelier to the public after it was completed. Having determined the three main topics for it—James Madison, Montpelier and the Constitution—the staff settled in general on basic themes to be covered under each of the topics. But the plan continued to be a work in progress as the time came closer for opening the House. The essence of the plan's themes is reflected in the following text from a draft paper titled "Over-Arching Themes."[44]

- Topic: James Madison

  Theme: Known as the Father of the Constitution in his own lifetime, James Madison was the chief architect of the Constitution and the Bill of Rights. Madison's creative and penetrating mind blended an astute understanding of political theory with profound insight into human nature and practical matters. Socially reserved in large groups, but "full of anecdote" in small ones, Madison's personality was complemented by that of Dolley Madison, whose grace and charm inspired the title "First Lady."
- Topic: Montpelier

  Theme: The Montpelier plantation, supported by slave labor, was James Madison's lifelong home, where his character and beliefs were shaped. It was at Montpelier that Madison researched and developed his ideas on individual liberty, religious freedom and constitutional government. He modified and expanded the architecture and landscape of Montpelier to reflect his personal vision, and the home's interior reflects both his and Dolley Madison's style.
- Topic: The Constitution

  Theme: The Constitution, based on James Madison's theories and vision, created a federal union authorized by a sovereign people, with strong but limited national government and representative institutions that had no precedent in history. It has protected the liberties of its citizens for more than two centuries.

The staff also developed a series of suggested subthemes to be presented in venues in the House and in other venues elsewhere on the property.[45] As with the overarching themes, these continued to be adapted in the coming months and years. The Board's Education, Interpretation and Collections Committee worked with the staff in reviewing interpretive techniques and approaches.[46]

Board Establishment of Goals

As the Foundation approached the end of its first decade of operations, and in anticipation of the opening of the restored House, the Board began to develop in a more systematic way goals for its future actions—with some being short-term and others more ambitious long-term ones. Some of the goals have been discussed previously. The goals are set forth in appendix B.

Talented people, generous donors and assiduous planning contributed to transforming a dream into a reality: Montpelier had become a monument to James Madison. The achievement merited a proper celebration.

Opposite: Map of Montpelier in 2008. *TMF*.

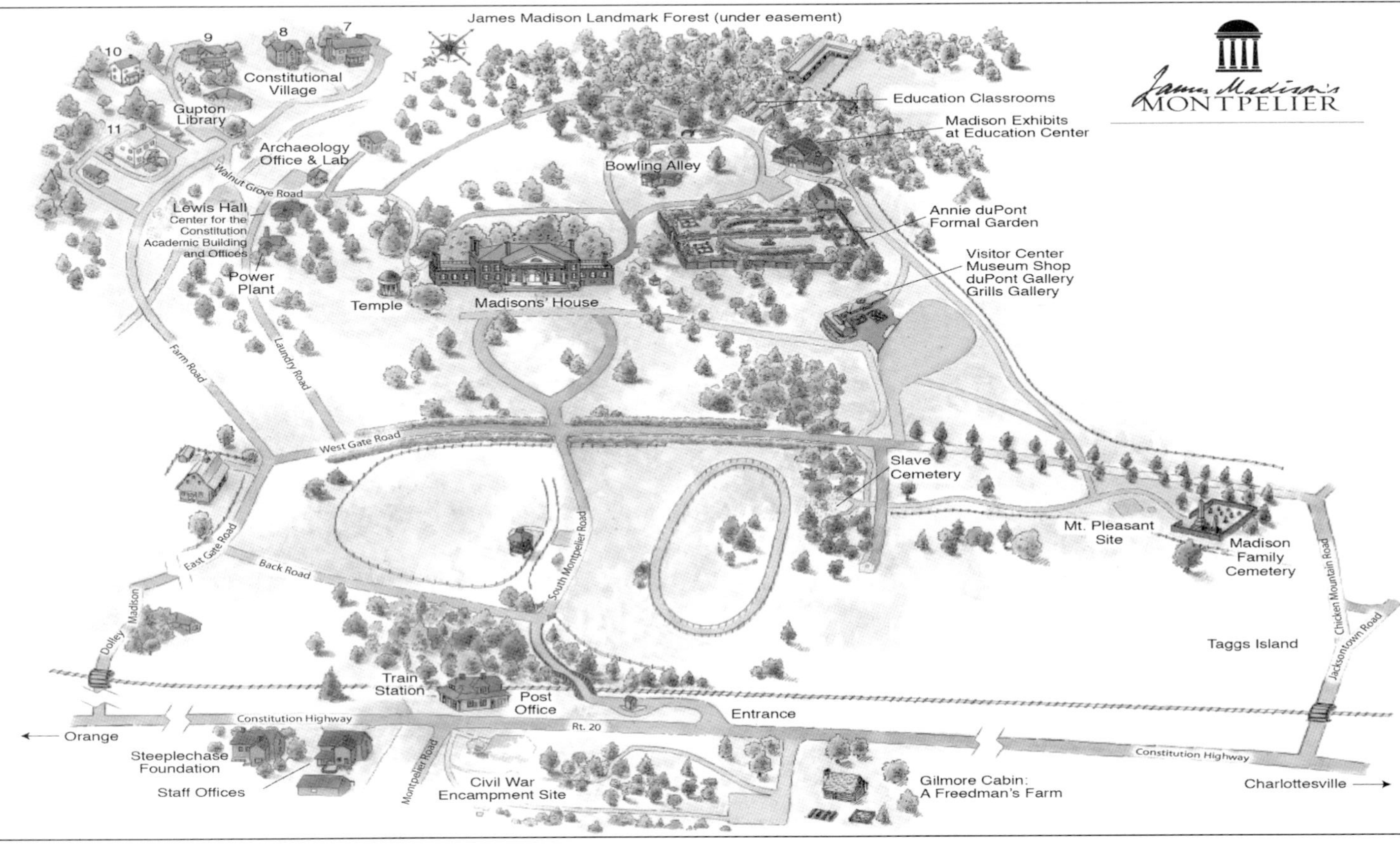
James Madison's Montpelier
James Madison Landmark Forest (under easement)
N
10
9
8
7
Constitutional Village
Gupton Library
11
Archaeology Office & Lab
Walnut Grove Road
Lewis Hall
Center for the Constitution
Academic Building and Offices
Power Plant
Temple
Madisons' House
Bowling Alley
Education Classrooms
Madison Exhibits at Education Center
Annie duPont Formal Garden
Visitor Center
Museum Shop
duPont Gallery
Grills Gallery
Farm Road
Laundry Road
West Gate Road
Slave Cemetery
Mt. Pleasant Site
Madison Family Cemetery
East Gate Road
Back Road
South Montpelier Road
Dolley Madison
Chicken Mountain Road
Jacksontown Road
Taggs Island
Train Station
Post Office
Entrance
Constitution Highway
Rt. 20
Orange
Steeplechase Foundation
Staff Offices
Montpelier Road
Civil War Encampment Site
Gilmore Cabin: A Freedman's Farm
Constitution Highway
Charlottesville

12

YEAR OF CELEBRATION OF MADISON MONUMENT—2008

THE IMPOSSIBLE DREAM REALIZED

The "National Restoration Celebration" on Constitution Day 2008 marked the culmination of a decade of major Foundation initiatives. Taken together, they transformed Montpelier into a national monument to James Madison. When the year began, the restoration team had to scramble to get the House ready for its official opening on September 17. Among the needed finishing touches: painting many rooms (using only paints with original formulations and colors), repairing and rehanging doors, cleaning original floorboards, restoring fences and lawns and archaeological excavation of the front yard (also see chapter 7).[1] As the restoration was wrapping up, the staff calculated some of the interesting statistics associated with the restoration:[2]

- $25 million was spent restoring the House
- 23,739 square feet of living space were removed from the duPont Mansion
- 1,921 tons of masonry rubble were removed (1,480 tons of brick, 270 tons of plaster and 171 tons of concrete)
- 377,600 hours of labor were devoted by skilled craftsmen and artisans
- 56,000 bricks, each hand-molded and sand-struck, replaced damaged ones

- 30,000 old-growth cypress roofing shingles were each hand-scalloped
- 90 tons of dry-mixed plaster, combined with 56 pounds of horsehair, were applied to Montpelier's interior walls
- 2,300-page feasibility study was developed that determined the House could be authentically restored (the prerequisite to undertaking restoration)
- 206,398 visitors had visited the restoration (through June 1, 2008)

For the opening to be the success that the historic restoration deserved, it was critical that it have the attention of national and local media. The first major national attention was a feature on *CBS Sunday Morning* on March 16, Madison's birthday. Correspondent Rita Braver and her team had spent two days at Montpelier in preparation for a segment that was seen by an estimated audience of 5.5 million.[3] About two dozen other journalists from national and local publications participated in a "media preview" in May, and later dozens of others expressed interest in the restoration.[4]

This chapter's focus is the celebration of the opening of the restored House. It also includes a discussion of three other notable actions in 2008 that previously were mentioned in less detail.

Day of Celebration

When September 17 arrived, James and Dolley Madison would have recognized the restored House as their home. And they would have appreciated the celebration of the five-year restoration in a style appropriate for its historic significance. More than 6,200 people came together on the front lawn to hear national speakers and observe the festivities marking the official completion of the architectural restoration. While baritone Eric Greene of the Virginia Opera Company sang "The Star-Spangled Banner," more than 2,600 local-area school children held aloft red, white and blue placards, creating a "living" American flag that was spread across Montpelier's front yard. The Old Guard Fife and Drum Corps (Third U.S.

Infantry Regiment) provided a moving musical introduction, and cadets from the Virginia Military Institute presented colors during the ceremony.[5]

Foundation president Mike Quinn welcomed visitors and dignitaries, and Jim Lehrer of the PBS *NewsHour* served as master of ceremonies. Speakers included Chief Justice John Roberts of the U.S. Supreme Court; Governor Tim Kaine; Congressman Eric Cantor, who held Madison's congressional seat; and Dick Moe, president of the National Trust for Historic Preservation. Raleigh Marshall, a descendant of Montpelier slave Paul Jennings, and Madison Iler, a descendant of Madison's sister Sarah, read aloud the Preamble to the U.S. Constitution.[6]

In his remarks, the Chief Justice said, "If you are looking for Madison's memorial, look around. Look at a free country governed by the rule of law."[7] Dick Moe said, "The soul of any historic place is the stories. The story of Montpelier is the centuries-long saga that embraces the frontier, the birth of a new nation, the Civil War, and the coming of a new age. It's a story of patriots and slaves, millionaires and jockeys, farmers and preservationists, and all the drama and drudgery of daily life. But mostly it's the story of James Madison, the most underappreciated but absolutely indispensable Founding Father."[8]

Celebration on Constitution Day in 2008 of the restored House's opening and Montpelier's transformation into a Monument to James Madison—in just 10 years—featuring thousands of local children creating a "Living Flag." *Photo by James Roney, TMF.*

Top: Ribbon being held by *(from left)* Beverly Carter, journalist/author Jim Lehrer, Bill Lewis (author), Joe Grills, Governor Tim Kaine, Chief Justice John Roberts, Dick Moe, Jean Ellen Shehan, Ted Terry and Lou Potter. The Estate of Paul Mellon donated almost all of the funding for the House's restoration. Estate executors Carter and Terry were responsible for the Estate's donation. *TMF*.

Bottom: Montpelier Board chair Joe Grills and Governor Tim Kaine cutting the ribbon with oversized scissors appropriate for the occasion. *Photo by Jen Fariello, TMF*.

The National Restoration Celebration activities on Montpelier's front lawn concluded with a ribbon-cutting by Governor Kaine and Foundation Board chair Joe Grills. Joining them and other speakers on the portico to assist were Mellon Estate executors Frederick Terry and Beverly Carter, duPont family member Jean Ellen Shehan, Senator Edd Houck, Delegate Ed Scott, Martha-Ann Alito (also present was Justice Samuel Alito of the

U.S. Supreme Court), Marge Grills, Foundation Board members Lou Potter, Bitsy Waters and me (now chair emeritus). I was looking quite wan due to surgery to address a staph infection resulting from a knee replacement but determined nonetheless to participate in this historic celebration.[9]

In reflecting on the restoration's completion, Mike Quinn said that the restored House, "even unfurnished," already "makes apparent James Madison's presence and creative mind" (but he noted that the next major project would be to furnish the home). "By restoring Madison's presence, it is our aim for Montpelier to take a leading role in teaching the ideas that make up the Constitution." By coming to Madison's newly restored home, visitors can "gain an understanding of the man who, more than any other individual, created the Constitution and gave us the enduring idea of the American nation." He then added, quoting Madison, "Knowledge will forever govern ignorance: And a people who mean to be their own Governors, must arm themselves with the power which knowledge gives."[10]

Gala Dinner for Donors

On the evening of the celebration, the Foundation feted major donors to the American Legacy Campaign with a formal dinner. The evening began with a tour of the restored House, including champagne served on the south wing's upper terrace, with its spectacular views of Virginia's Blue Ridge Mountains. Dinner was served out on the tented back lawn. The evening concluded with a visit from "Mr. and Mrs. Madison" and their good friend "Thomas Jefferson" and a performance of period music by soprano Amanda Balestrieri. The evening was made possible through the generosity of current and past Madison Cabinet co-chairs Gerald M. Lowrie and Betty Lowrie, Alan L. Potter and Louise B. Potter and Drs. Alice P. and U.G. "Jim" Turner III.[11]

At the end of 2008 when the American Legacy Campaign concluded, it was announced that contributions to the Campaign totaled $64.5 million.[12] The goal had been $60 million. Hunter Rawlings, chair of the Campaign Committee, said, "It has been gratifying to see so many rally to the vision of the invigorated Montpelier that is both one of the America's finest historic homes and a leader in teaching Madison's Constitutional legacy." He announced that the names of all those who contributed $25,000 or more would be engraved on a "Wall of Honor," permanent stone panels on the exterior of the Visitor Center.[13] Private donors (individuals, foundations

Mr. and Mrs. Madison's portraits in the Drawing Room of their newly restored home. *Photo by Jen Fariello, TMF.*

and corporations) contributing $500,000 or more, who would head the Wall's list, were as follows:[14]

- **Lead Donors**—Estate of Paul Mellon **($20,000,000+)** and Mr. and Mrs. Robert H. Smith **($10,000,000+)**
- **Benefactors ($2,500,000 and above)**—Alan L. and Louise B. Potter and Mr. and Mrs. Joe Grills
- **Leaders ($1,000,000 and above)**—Donna and John Crean and Family, Nancy Woodson Spire Foundation, Clayton and Anna Timmons and two anonymous donors
- **Patrons ($500,000 and above)**—The Joseph and Robert Cornell Memorial Foundation, O. Bruce and Jacqueline F. Gupton, Charina Endowment Fund and William R. Kenan, Jr. Charitable Trust
- **Public Fund Sources combined ($10,500,000)**—These included the Commonwealth of Virginia, the National Endowment for the Humanities, Save America's Treasures, U.S. Department of Transportation Enhancement Funds, National Scenic By-Ways and Virginia Department of Transportation

Lecture Concludes Celebration

The final official event in the Celebration was the second annual Claude Moore Lecture. It was held on September 22 in the Montpelier Room in the James Madison Building of the Library of Congress. Prior to the Claude Moore Lecture, Montpelier Board member David Gibson presented to the Library of Congress a photograph of the newly restored Madison home. It would replace the one showing the home prior to restoration that was then hanging next to the entrance of the Madison Building's Montpelier Room.

Nationally syndicated columnist George Will delivered the lecture on "The Madison Persuasion Today." His remarks focused on the U.S. presidency and how it has steadily grown from being the executive in charge of carrying out legislation Congress enacts into being the dominant official in national government and politics. Mr. Will said that Madison

> *conducted a revolution in democratic theory, an astonishing achievement. Before Madison…political philosophers…believed* [democracy] *would be possible…only if it were practiced in a small face-to-face society, something you can walk across in three hours…because that would be a society free of factions, which were thought to be the bane of popular government. Madison turned this on its head. He said what we want is a "saving" multiplicity of factions to produce this constant social churning and turmoil that would prevent the greater evil to which democracies are prey: stable, oppressive, tyrannical majorities.*[15]

As discussed in chapter 8, the lecture, which the Center for the Constitution had established, became an annual event in the nation's capital. Its purpose was "to enhance awareness of, and commitment to, civic responsibilities with a thoughtful discussion of the Constitution." David Gibson, as well as The Claude Moore Charitable Foundation, provided support for the 2008 lecture.[16]

Other Major 2008 Projects

While celebration of the restoration's completion was the dominant focus of 2008, there were several significant additional projects that were initiated or completed that year.

A New Archaeology Facility. Recognizing firsthand the need for a new archaeology lab—the result of her longtime participation in the digging—Board member Cindy Reusche made a lead donation that allowed Montpelier to house the lab in a "larger, more sophisticated facility." Based on her support, Montpelier was able to accept a gift of a used classroom trailer from James Madison University and convert it into an expanded lab that would "accommodate conservation work, storage of a teaching collection, classroom meetings and, eventually, programs for visitors." The new facility was added next to the existing archaeology office. Visitors to the 1,440-square-foot lab, with all its functions housed together, could see archaeologists "conserving metals, mending ceramics, cleaning artifacts from the lab, and processing soil samples."[17] The lab subsequently began to provide visitors with an opportunity to look through display cabinets housing the mended ceramic vessels and artifacts discovered in past excavations.

A New South Yard Dig. In summer 2008, Montpelier's archaeology team initiated a project that would ultimately be recognized as the first step in programs to appropriately educate the public about the critical

Archaeology in the South Yard, which led to confirmation that it was the location of the community of enslaved who worked in the Madisons' home. *TMF*.

role of Montpelier's enslaved. The team's focus was exploration of the South Yard, which is just to the right of the House (also see chapter 10.) A nineteenth-century insurance company map discovered in 2002 was used to guide its work. Dolley Madison insured the House and its outbuildings in 1837, a year after James Madison died. Referencing the map's significance, archaeology director Matt Reeves pointed out that the map "illustrated the size and extent of the South Yard, which contained two smoke houses and three residences—each a duplex for two slave families."[18] Excavation of the site over a number of years led to the buildings being reconstructed and becoming a significant part of a multimillion-dollar permanent exhibit on the enslaved community funded by philanthropist David M. Rubenstein (see chapter 14).

Archaeology Expedition Programs. In 2008, weeklong digs began for the public. Over 1,400 individuals have participated, which has provided a significant part of the archaeology department's annual budget. Involvement in these programs includes an opportunity to dig and learn how archaeology informs interpretation of slavery at Montpelier.[19]

Acquisition of an Important Madison-Owned Painting. In their research, Montpelier's curatorial team found numerous instances where the Madisons' visitors described the walls of the Montpelier drawing room "as being 'entirely covered' with paintings, some of which were 'quite large.'" Among the larger paintings was a seventeenth-century Dutch painting of a classical scene: *Pan, Youths and Nymphs*. The scene shows Pan, the half-goat, half-human creature of Greek mythology, and a group of youths and nymphs. It is attributed to the Dutch painter Gerrit van Honthorst. It is thought that Dolley Madison's son, John Payne Todd, purchased the painting in Europe when he accompanied a diplomatic delegation sent to Ghent in 1814.[20]

Montpelier's curatorial research team discovered the painting through impressive detective work. Research consultant Dr. Lance Humphreys saw the name of the painting on a document titled "List of Oil Paintings at Montpellier [*sic*]" that was made at some point after James Madison died in 1836. The list was apparently assembled in conjunction with Dolley's subsequent move to Washington, D.C. After her death in 1849, her executor, James C. McGuire, became the owner of the painting. The staff found an unbroken chain of ownership from McGuire to a Virginia family in Charlottesville. The painting was sold in 2004 to a private Dutch collector.

Three years later, the curatorial team rediscovered its location during their research in preparation for furnishing the House.[21] The Dutch owner then loaned it to Montpelier. After the Foundation purchased the painting, it became the first large Madison-owned work to be installed in the drawing room (also see chapter 13).

Montpelier, National Monument to James Madison

With the restoration of the Madisons' home, The Montpelier Foundation completed its first decade by achieving a critical step to transforming Montpelier into a national Monument to James Madison's life, legacy and contributions.[22] Restored to Madison's full vision, it "reflects the man whose intellect and political skill contributed the key innovative concepts that make the Constitution work and provided the leadership to bring about the Constitution's creation and ratification. The House serves the twin functions of preserving James Madison's legacy and educating Americans about his singular contribution to our nation and its Constitution."[23] Transforming Montpelier into an even more important and significant tribute to Madison and its enslaved community lay ahead for the Foundation in the next decade.

13

SECOND DECADE HIGHLIGHTS—2009–2016

MOST IMPORTANT WAS DAVID M. RUBENSTEIN'S GIFT THAT SUPPORTED PERMANENTLY TELLING THE STORY OF MONTPELIER'S ENSLAVED

Having surmounted seemingly impossible hurdles and accomplished the projects in just 10 years that resulted in Montpelier becoming a Madison monument, the Foundation principally devoted the next decade (2009–18) to growing and expanding its educational capabilities. The one major deficiency in Montpelier's infrastructure that remained was in establishing an appropriate permanent recognition of its enslaved community. In 2014, philanthropist David M. Rubenstein's $10 million commitment rectified the absence of funding to address this priority. His gift supported establishment of both a historic exhibition on the tragedy of slavery and the essential role of enslaved people in building Montpelier. It included reconstruction of housing and other buildings for the enslaved who worked in the Madisons' home. Now, Montpelier is properly recognized as a monument to its enslaved community, as well as to the life and legacy of James Madison.

This chapter presents highlights of some of the most significant of the Foundation's activities from 2009 to 2016, with prominent focus on Montpelier's enslaved community and House furnishing initiatives. Chapter 14 describes the opening in 2017 of *The Mere Distinction of Colour* exhibition and awards and other recognition that followed, as well as program highlights in 2018. Throughout the second decade, Montpelier continued to be guided by exceptionally talented leadership. In 2013, Kat Imhoff was chosen to be the Foundation's second CEO. Her first primary focus was working with Mr. Rubenstein in designing the multiple projects that his gift supported.

2009

Interior Furnishings. Initiating its project to restore the House's interior, the Foundation embarked on a "presidential detective story" to rediscover the Madisons' furnishings, style and décor. Using its furnishings plan as a template, the curatorial department began a "comprehensive research effort to understand, locate and provide context for Madison's furniture and decorative arts."[1] The furnishings project was led by Lynne Dakin Hastings, vice president for museum programs. Before joining Montpelier in 2009, Lynne was curator for historic interiors for the Colonial Williamsburg Foundation. She had also served on Montpelier's Interiors and Interpretations Committee.

Statue and Murals. Continuing his extraordinary generosity, Robert H. Smith commissioned the first statue of James and Dolley Madison together. Mr. Madison is seated on a bench reading a book, with Mrs. Madison standing behind him, her hand resting on his back while he points out a passage to her. Mr. Smith also commissioned two murals portraying key events in the Madisons' life. One shows James Madison introducing the Bill of Rights in Congress in 1789. The other depicts an iconic event during the War of 1812. In it, Mrs. Madison and enslaved manservant Paul Jennings are saving Gilbert Stuart's portrait of George Washington in 1814 before the British burned the White House.[2] President Madison was away at the time, having gone to determine the status of U.S. troops at the Battle of Bladensburg, becoming the first and, as of this writing, only president to be under fire on a battlefield while in office. (The Washington portrait by Stuart is now recognized as possibly the White House's most valuable holding.) To celebrate Jennings's role, director of education Beth Taylor arranged for his descendants to gather for a reunion at the White House.[3] She identified the descendants using the Jennings genealogy that she developed.

2010

In the Time of Segregation *Exhibit*. The Montpelier Train Station, which was built for William duPont Sr. in the early twentieth century, reflects the era of Jim Crow segregation, with its separate "white" and "colored" waiting rooms. After an extensive restoration of the two waiting rooms, an exhibit was created and installed: *The Montpelier Train Depot: In the Time of Segregation*. Its purpose is to teach visitors about the racial segregation that African Americans continued to face in Orange County and throughout Virginia after the Thirteenth Amendment abolished slavery. With the addition of this exhibit, an arc of the African American experience—from slavery through the freedman's era (depicted at the nearby Gilmore Cabin) to segregation—was represented at Montpelier. The restored depot was opened at an event attended by hundreds of guests that was jointly sponsored with the Orange County African American Historical Society.[4] The featured speaker was Emmy Award–winning journalist Juan Williams. The depot's exhibit is dedicated to Russell Coffin Childs, a former Montpelier projects director, whose friends and family supported its creation.[5]

Opening of *In the Time of Segregation* exhibit at the Montpelier Train Station, which had doors marked "white" and "colored." *Photo by John Strader, TMF.*

Montpelier Demonstration Forest. A one-mile loop trail was opened in April as "an outdoor teaching exhibit that shows how to manage a healthy, sustainable forest." At an event marking the opening, former U.S. senator John Warner encouraged guests to explore the "grandeur" of Montpelier's grounds and forests. Those walking the trail could learn from a map brochure and signs erected at four sites.[6]

Celebration of "Constitution Month." Expanding on its annual observance of Constitution Day, Montpelier held a number of educational events for Constitution Month in September. At the yearly Claude Moore Lecture at the National Archives, a distinguished panel discussed the results of the Center for the Constitution's national survey on knowledge about the Constitution. Mike Quinn was the moderator. The panelists were respected NPR news analyst Cokie Roberts, University of Baltimore law professor Michael Meyerson and Civic Education Center executive director Chuck Quigley.[7] The survey regrettably, but not surprisingly, found that a high percentage of Americans had limited knowledge and understanding of the Constitution (see chapter 8). To obtain ongoing snapshots, the Center for the Constitution instituted a national survey on the Constitution as a regular part of its work. Other activities in Constitution Month included Montpelier's first webcast, a lively discussion between "Mr. Madison" and "Mr. Jefferson" with 400 area schoolchildren present, a five-kilometer race and costumed student reenactors entertaining visitors with music, activities and games.[8]

2011

House Furnishings and Exhibits. Major strides were made this year in furnishing the interior of the House under the leadership of Megan "Meg" Kennedy, acting director of museum programs:

- The greatest progress was made in the drawing room and dining room. Drawing room features included reproduction wallpaper with a pomegranate design in crimson flocking; an original painting owned by the Madisons, *Pan, Youths and Nymphs*; replicas of other paintings that the Madisons hung in the room, which included portraits of the Virginia presidents, a landscape and a portrait of Dolley; and period

Furnished Drawing Room, looking from the east toward the House's front door. *TMF.*

furniture and games the Madisons were known to have.[9] The paintings were mounted in replicas of their original frames if they could be identified.

- The dining room was furnished with original sideboards and period furniture. The Madisons' entertaining in their retirement period was shown through life-size representations of notable guests seated at the dining table. Among the guests are Thomas Jefferson, Andrew Jackson, James Monroe and Marquis de Lafayette. Standing by is Madison's personal servant Paul Jennings.[10]
- Furnishings were added in a room adjacent to the dining room that Madison designed as a first-floor library, as well as in the library upstairs where he prepared for the Constitutional Convention.[11]
- In the cellar, an educational opportunity was created for visitors to learn about the slaves who worked in the House. Under the leadership of education programs director Christian Cotz, a multipart furnishing/interpretive exhibit was installed in the cellar kitchen in Dolley's Wing. It was very interactive and not only showed operation of the kitchen but also introduced

a number of the slaves who had been kitchen cooks and workers.[12] The cellar was the only semi-furnished space when the House first reopened.

Enslaved Living in the South Yard. Based on the plat in the 1837 insurance policy Dolley purchased and archaeology evidence that the staff developed, Montpelier began construction of six "timber frame ghost structures" to represent the enslaved community complex in the South Yard near the House. Included were three slave quarters, two smokehouses and a detached kitchen (also see chapter 12).[13] This was the first effort to present a physical demonstration of the living situation of Montpelier slaves who worked in the House. It was ultimately followed in 2017 by the full-scale re-creation of the complex as part of *The Mere Distinction of Colour* exhibition (see chapter 14).

2012

Center for the Constitution Developments. The Center continued to expand the number and types of its education programs about the Constitution. Recognizing the potential for online learning, the Center offered the second of a planned series of courses through a newly designed website. The first course, Introduction to the Constitution, was followed this year with one on the Bill of Rights. The Center also announced an app on the Bill of Rights.[14] In celebrating the 200th anniversary of the War of 1812, Montpelier emphasized that Madison's actions as commander-in-chief were consistent with the Constitution, in contrast to those of some later presidents (including Abraham Lincoln).[15] This was particularly significant given the challenges in successfully prosecuting the controversial, long-in-doubt war with Britain. The Center's leadership changed in the fall of 2011 when Douglas "Doug" Smith became its executive director and Foundation vice president.

Completion of the Interiors Research and Refurnishing Project. In 2012, continuing with the "presidential detective story" initiative, Montpelier's curatorial department completed its three-year project supported by the Mellon Estate to carry out research to assist in refurnishing and restoring the interior of the Madisons' home.[16] The guiding commitment was to achieve the "same level of accuracy and authenticity" in furnishing the House as in the architectural restoration (also see chapter 10). The progress of Montpelier's team of more than 75 historians, archaeologists and material culture and decorative arts scholars exceeded their initial expectations to such an extent that refurnishing could be accelerated.[17] Highlights of the team's work included the following:

- Development of a powerful research database encompassing nearly 30,000 Madison- and Montpelier-related documents, among which were "all known, extant documents written or received by James and Dolley Madison, James Madison Sr. and Nelly Madison, John Payne Todd (Dolley's son) and other close family members"
- Identification of 5,100 items associated with the Madisons that justified future study, a change to the initial plans to carefully study only the estimated 400 objects that were then known to have an association with the Madisons or Montpelier
- Identification of 1,400 titles in Madison's library, as well as the periodicals he subscribed to in his retirement[18]

Often, discoveries held promise whether they seemed significant or not. For example, a bit of bone excavated from a trash midden (dump) initially identified as a sewing bobbin was later determined to be a pawn piece from a nineteenth-century chess set.[19] Subsequently, Montpelier purchased an example of the chess set for the drawing room.

Executive Leadership Change. After serving as president and CEO for 12 years, Mike Quinn resigned to assume the same role at the Museum of the American Revolution in Philadelphia. His outstanding leadership has been discussed throughout the book, with a special tribute described in chapter 11. Greg May, who had succeeded Joe Grills as Board chair in late 2011, led a national search for Mike's successor through most of 2012. During that time, Sean O'Brien served as the Foundation's interim staff leader. Before being named Montpelier's chief operating officer and executive vice president in 2011, Sean was executive director of the Center for the Constitution.[20]

2013

Kat Imhoff, New President and CEO. After interviewing a number of outstanding CEO candidates, the Board's search committee recommended, and the Board unanimously supported, extending an offer to Katherine "Kat" Imhoff. Kat had a distinguished 30-year career in preservation, conservation and planning. Most recently, she had been state director for The Nature Conservancy in Montana. Prior to that, she served as vice president of the Thomas Jefferson Foundation, which owns and operates Monticello. Kat accepted the Board's offer and became president and CEO of the Foundation at the beginning of 2013.[21]

Field Slave Living Quarters Excavation. Continuing with its exploration of the Montpelier landscape, the archaeology team completed an 11-month excavation that identified the apparent footprint of housing for the enslaved who worked in Montpelier's fields. Among the discoveries were building foundations, glass, ceramics, nails and bones—all of which would contribute to learning how the enslaved lived. This was supported by a three-year research grant from the National Endowment for the Humanities. The Perry Foundation also was a major contributor to Montpelier's ongoing archaeology investigations.[22]

2014

David M. Rubenstein Gift. The most exciting development in the Foundation's second decade was the transformative initiative made possible by a $10 million gift commitment from philanthropist David M. Rubenstein.[23] The gift was designed in conversations over the course of a year with CEO Kat Imhoff. A brief plan for the gift is described below:

- Announced in the fall of 2014, Mr. Rubenstein's generous gift had two purposes: (1) reconstructing six structures adjacent to the House in the South Yard where domestic slaves lived and worked, as part of telling the story of the Montpelier Enslaved Community; and (2) completing the furnishing of the Madisons' home.[24]
- The South Yard work and related activities would build on the extensive investigation and research of Montpelier's

archaeology team over more than two decades (also see chapters 10 and 12). Also incorporated was the knowledge gained in past enslaved descendants' reunions and the two-day slavery interpretation workshop held earlier in 2014. Buildings to be reconstructed included three duplex slave quarters, two smokehouses and a detached kitchen. These would replace the South Yard "timber frames."[25]

In recognition of Mr. Rubenstein's gift, the Visitor Center was named the David M. Rubenstein Visitor Center for James Madison's Montpelier. The gift received extensive coverage, including articles in the *Washington Post*, member outlets of the Associated Press and international publications (e.g., the *Guardian*).[26]

Refurnishing of Madison's Library. Montpelier celebrated the opening of Madison's refurnished library earlier in the year on Presidents' Day (February 17). At the time of Madison's death, his library contained more than 4,000 volumes. Madison planned for his books to go to friends, family and institutions. He identified 431 for the University of Virginia, which were to be accompanied by a monetary bequest. Unfortunately, the books he gave to the University burned in a catastrophic Rotunda fire in 1895. The balance of his collection had been sold in 1854 at auction to settle debts of his stepson, John Payne Todd. Montpelier has not been able to locate any original Madison-owned volumes. Although there is no complete inventory, Montpelier staff identified the titles of about half of the books in Madison's library. With this research, substantial progress was made in locating and acquiring replacement volumes to re-create the library.[27]

Global Reach of the Center for the Constitution. The Center continued its effort to bring leaders from other nations to study constitution-making and building self-government. Since the Center's creation, hundreds of leaders from more than 65 nations had visited. Many of these visits had been in conjunction with partnerships Montpelier had established with the U.S. State Department and the Presidential Precinct coalition. The other members of the coalition are the University of Virginia, The College of William & Mary, Monticello, Morven and Highland. In 2014, with support from President Obama, the Presidential Precinct hosted the first of several six-week summer academic and leadership institutes for 25 young African leaders. Montpelier's Center for the Constitution worked with the leaders during one of those weeks. The focus was on building citizenship and "cultures of constitutionalism."[28]

Weekend Constitutional Seminars. The Center for the Constitution's extensive program of weekend seminars in 2014 featured these topics and teachers:[29]

- The Bill of Rights—Sue Leeson, senior justice of the Oregon Supreme Court, and Dr. Lynn Uzzell, scholar in residence at the Center
- The Presidency and the Constitution—Dr. Ben Kleinerman, associate professor of constitutional democracy at James Madison College at Michigan State University
- Suffrage in America—Dr. Alexander Keysaar, professor of history at Harvard University
- Slavery and the Constitution—Dr. Holt Merchant, professor emeritus of history, Washington and Lee University

2015

The Rubenstein Initiative Progress. The archaeology and curatorial teams took major steps this year to begin the work necessary to reconstruct six structures in the enslaved community complex in the South Yard and complete the refurnishing of the House.

- The staff removed the temporary timber-frame structures in the South Yard and continued excavation previously undertaken where the re-created structures would be built. Identifying a team to help develop an enslaved community exhibit in the House's cellar also moved forward.[30]
- The Madisons' principal bedchamber was furnished in mid-May shortly before the annual Dolley Madison Legacy Luncheon, a major supporter of the House's refurnishing. This achievement involved acquisition of several dozen pieces of furniture and objects, as well as installation of window coverings, carpeting and bed hangings. The boldness of the room's colors was consistent with wallpaper that had been discovered under several layers of paint.[31]

The Center for the Constitution Milestone Year. By early 2015, the programs of the Center had engaged more than 40,000 people during

Removal of "timber frames" and continued archaeological excavation in the South Yard in preparation for reconstruction of housing and other buildings used by the Enslaved Community near the Madisons' House. *TMF*.

its 12-year life. The Center had achieved its educational success through seminars, online courses and documents and events.[32] Highlights of 2015 included the following:

- The Center launched its Creation of the Constitution course, which integrated videos, podcasts and additional digital material. Staff also began video production of courses on slavery, the presidency, suffrage, law enforcement and the judiciary.[33]
- The Hewlett Foundation underwrote six Montpelier Summit weekend retreats for congressional staff and others involved in politics in Washington. About 25 attended each retreat. They participated in discussions on America's founding documents and principles as they apply to twenty-first-century life.[34]
- Among the Center's other programs was the "Dolley's Diplomacy: Inspiring Women's Leadership" conference, held at Montpelier in conjunction with several other organizations. Two dozen outstanding, well-known speakers participated. Among these were the nation's leading Dolley Madison expert,

the chancellor of the University of North Carolina, the president of the University of Virginia, a former U.S. secretary of labor, senior corporate executives and scholars. Foundation Board member Leigh Middleditch organized this conference for the Center, as well as a number of others that brought distinguished participants to Montpelier.[35]

Curator Becomes Head of Museum Programs. Upon completing an extensive search, Kat Imhoff named Elizabeth Chew to be vice president for museum programs. Elizabeth assumed responsibility for all facets of programs interpreting and studying the House and landscape. Her educational background in art history and time as curator at Monticello well equipped her for the role. Her other prior experiences included leading the opening of *The Paradox of Liberty: Thomas Jefferson and Slavery*, the first exhibition on slavery at the National Museum of African American History and Culture.

2016

The Rubenstein Initiative. The Montpelier staff made further progress this year in re-creating structures in the South Yard and in furnishing the House:[36]

- Construction of both of the duplex enslaved quarters moved toward completion. This included building their foundations, masonry work on chimneys, framing, roofing and adding siding. The construction team scheduled work on flooring and coating of the buildings for later in 2016 or early 2017.
- After conducting a study of period smokehouses, the team began and almost completed design and construction drawings for the two to be re-created in the South Yard. The archaeology team's work discovered evidence of an additional building used as a slave dwelling. The team also exposed the foundation of the South Yard kitchen. Throughout the area, it found significant amounts of ceramics and other artifacts.
- Progress also was made in completing the Enslaved Community exhibition, *The Mere Distinction of Colour*. The staff finished writing and laying out text and graphics for the static panels and solidified concepts for all the multimedia pieces.

- In the House, "Mother Madison's Best Room" and her dining room were furnished with period furniture and pieces having Madison provenance.

The Opening of Claude Moore Hall. After a four-year construction project in the former location of a collapsing duPont-era power plant, Claude Moore Hall opened in November 2016 to create an expansive structure next to Lewis Hall for the Center for the Constitution. The new space had two studios, a production room, conference facilities and staff offices. Claude Moore Hall provided a necessary digital component for the Center's programs and included a state-of-the art podcast booth. Before year's end, the Center aired its inaugural radio broadcast.[37]

Restoration of Madison's Temple. The iconic Temple, the only original Madison structure at Montpelier other than the House, had incurred much damage since its eighteenth-century construction. As with the House, it required a major project, albeit a much less extensive one, to address its problems and restore it to its initial condition and appearance. The dome, wood-shingle roof, brick piers and column bases needed substantial remediation, while the icehouse below the Temple was in relatively good condition. The restoration team carried out the work on the distinctive roof without losing any Madison-era framing materials. It accomplished

The iconic Temple, the only Madisonian structure other than the House. *Photo by Rick Seaman, TMF.*

this by using a creative method for attaching new swamp cypress shingles to the original framing. In the investigation to determine the roof's exact appearance, a surprising finding was made. The paint analysis showed that the shingles, which were a dark brown color, had originally been stained red. Staining was done after the new shingles' installation had time to stabilize.[38]

14

CELEBRATION OF MONTPELIER'S BECOMING A MONUMENT TO ENSLAVED COMMUNITY

PRESENTING HISTORY OF SLAVERY AS IT "MUST BE DONE EVERYWHERE"

From the time it was established, the Foundation emphasized the importance of (1) educating visitors about the critical role enslaved African Americans played at Montpelier and (2) including descendants of the enslaved as key partners. Indeed, in the month prior to its formal incorporation, one room in the duPont Mansion was devoted to exhibits titled *Plantation Life: The African American Community*. Descendants were particularly helpful in assembling research for telling the enslaved community story.

Among the activities focused on the enslaved that the Foundation undertook in the first decade and a half were (1) restoring the home of a Montpelier slave, (2) working with descendants to develop a registry of descendants, (3) holding two weekend Enslaved Descendants Reunions and (4) conducting extensive archaeology and research to discover slaves' housing and work activities. But the Foundation did not accomplish the more appropriate recognition that the enslaved deserved until David M. Rubenstein made his $10 million gift that supported creating *The Mere Distinction of Colour* permanent exhibition and reconstructing the dwellings and other buildings in the South Yard for the enslaved who worked in the Madisons' House. Completion of these actions occurred in 2017. Montpelier is now properly known as a "Monument to the Life and Legacy of James Madison and its Enslaved Community."

***The Opening of* The Mere Distinction of Colour *Permanent Exhibition*.** Montpelier's journey to effectively educate visitors about the human tragedy that slavery represented climaxed with creation of *The Mere Distinction of Colour* exhibition. The official opening was held on June 5, 2017. The exhibition's title was drawn from James Madison's words on June 6, 1787, at the Constitutional Convention, when he said that the "most oppressive dominion ever exercised by man over man" has occurred in "the most enlightened period of time" due to "*the mere distinction of colour*" (emphasis added). The archaeology investigation, research and collaboration with descendants of Montpelier's enslaved people required to create this award-winning exhibition was carried out over two decades. But the extraordinarily generous gift of David M. Rubenstein and the leadership of Foundation CEO Kat Imhoff provided the essential elements to bring the program to fruition. The exhibition included not only the re-creation and interpretation of the six structures of the domestic slave community near the House but also highly professional video and interactive presentations throughout the

The Mere Distinction of Colour permanent exhibition is opened by philanthropist David M. Rubenstein, the donor responsible for funding it. On the far right on the dais is Montpelier CEO Kat Imhoff. *Photo by Jen Fariello, TMF.*

Listening at the exhibition opening are *(from right)* enslaved descendants Margaret Jordan, a Montpelier Board member, and Rebecca Gilmore Coleman; and speakers Professor Hasan Jeffries and Professor Ed Ayres. *Photo by Jen Fariello, TMF.*

Aerial view of reconstructed South Yard buildings of the Enslaved Community. *TMF.*

House's cellar. The exhibition was the dominant highlight not just of 2017, but of the Foundation's entire second decade.[1] (In my view, it should be visited and thoughtfully considered by every American for decades to come.)

Visitor Reaction and Press Coverage of the Exhibition. One visitor's response to *The Mere Distinction of Colour* exhibition provides an excellent summation of its quality and importance:

> *The tone, content and visitor experience were perfect and set a standard for interpreting this most difficult of subjects. The balance between emotional impact and history, theater and substance was just right. The courage to include a strong statement about the legacy of slavery today and the wisdom to include the voice of the descendants provided a tangible contemporary relevance that is missing in other interpretive efforts.*

Reflecting the exhibition's importance, 12 media outlets (including the *Washington Post*, NPR, Buzzfeed and the PBS *NewsHour*) came to cover it, 64 articles were published about it, and there were 548 media mentions about the opening.[2]

***Awards for* The Mere Distinction of Colour.** The exhibition quickly began to receive numerous major honors. Among the awards reflecting prestigious recognition were these:[3]

- Award of Merit, presented by the American Association for State and Local History (AASLH) for excellence in history programs, projects and people, when compared with similar activities nationwide.
- HIP (History in Progress) Award, given at the discretion of the AASLH awards committee to 5 percent or less of the winners of the Award of Merit for "a project that is highly inspirational, exhibits exceptional scholarship, and/or is exceedingly entrepreneurial in terms of funding, partnerships, or collaborations, creative problem solving, or unusual project design and inclusiveness."
- Outstanding Public History Project Award, presented by the National Council on Public History (NCPH) for work completed within the previous year that contributes to a broader public reflection and appreciation of the past or that serves as a model

of professional public history practice. The award specifically recognized the contributions of two Montpelier senior staff, Elizabeth Chew and Christian Cotz.

- American Alliance of Museums MUSE Awards (two awards), presented to institutions and independent producers who use digital media and celebrate scholarship, community, innovation, creativity, education and inclusiveness.

A Glowing Review of the Exhibit. Following the selection of *The Mere Distinction of Colour* exhibit for its 2018 award, the NCPH published an eight-page review in its periodical, *The Public Historian.* The article recognized the difficulties in "presenting a more accurate, troubling and complicated history of slavery in America" than had been done in the past, and it commended the Foundation's Board and staff for proving that "not only can this be done, but that it must be done everywhere." The review further asserted that the Montpelier site "should serve as a model for how historic sites can flip preconceived narratives, interpret African American life beyond the Civil War and explain the ramifications of the oppressive racial hierarchy that may have developed 400 years ago but has serious implications for African Americans today."[4]

Display in one of the South Yard duplexes in *The Mere Distinction of Colour* exhibition. *Photo by Drew Precious, TMF.*

Other Significant Developments in 2018

House Furnishing Almost Complete. Progress continued in achieving the other objective of Mr. Rubenstein's gift: furnishing the House. This was done under the guidance of Teresa Teixera, leader of the museum programs' collections department.

- A major change was made in presenting the large upstairs bedchamber, which previously had been interpreted as the Madisons' master bedroom. Based on more recent research, the bedroom seems to have been the "best guest chamber," and changes were made to so present it.
- Two other rooms were furnished for the first time: the bedroom of John Payne Todd, Dolley Madison's son, interpreted in a manner to show his carelessness; and a guest chamber with four low-post bedsteads to accommodate the Madisons' frequent overnight visitors.
- Among the other changes was the addition of copies of Old Master paintings in the South Passage (between the drawing room and Mother Madison's Best Room). Using this passage as a gallery hall was possibly a result of John Payne Todd's having observed the practice in Europe.[5]

National Summit on Teaching Slavery. Over a three-day period in February, nearly 50 leading academics, public historians and descendant community advocates convened at Montpelier to develop new guidelines for how cultural institutions and historic sites teach and interpret slavery by engaging descendant communities. The summit was a partnership between Montpelier and the National Trust's African American Cultural Heritage Action Fund. It was the first interdisciplinary effort to formulate a model for best practices in descendant engagement and built on the success of engagement in the creation of *The Mere Distinction of Colour* exhibition. Institutions participating with the summit scholars included Mount Vernon, Monticello, Southern Poverty Law Center, Whitney Plantation and the National Civil Rights Museum (Memphis). The summit's model guidelines were written up and published as a report titled *Engaging Descendant Communities in the Interpretation of Slavery at Museums and Historic Sites: A Rubric of Best Practices Established by the National Summit on Teaching Slavery.*[6]

Selection of Chief Advancement Officer and Executive Vice President. After a national search, Douglas "Doug" Trout was chosen to assume the Foundation's number-two staff position. Immediately prior to coming to Montpelier, he was executive director of the University of Virginia's Miller Center Foundation. Before that, he was director of the Graduate Fellowship program for the University's Jefferson Scholars Foundation.[7]

Rediscovering Madison's Planted Landscape. An extensive archaeology investigation was conducted to discover two areas of plantings that flank the House. Madison's interest was to frame the House so as to focus the eye on the front of it and away from the work areas. Clumps of black locust, cherry and aspen trees created a South Grove, which obscured the view of the enslaved community of the House servants. Archaeology was carried out to locate a double row of pine trees that once ran from the iconic Temple and the House's portico.[8]

Doubling of Montpelier Conservation Easement. With generous support from the Mars Family Conservation Fund, Montpelier was able to add approximately 1,000 acres to the site's conservation easements. Of the total 2,650 acres, 915 acres previously had been subject to easements (see chapter 11).[9]

Opposite: Map of Montpelier in 2018. *TMF*.

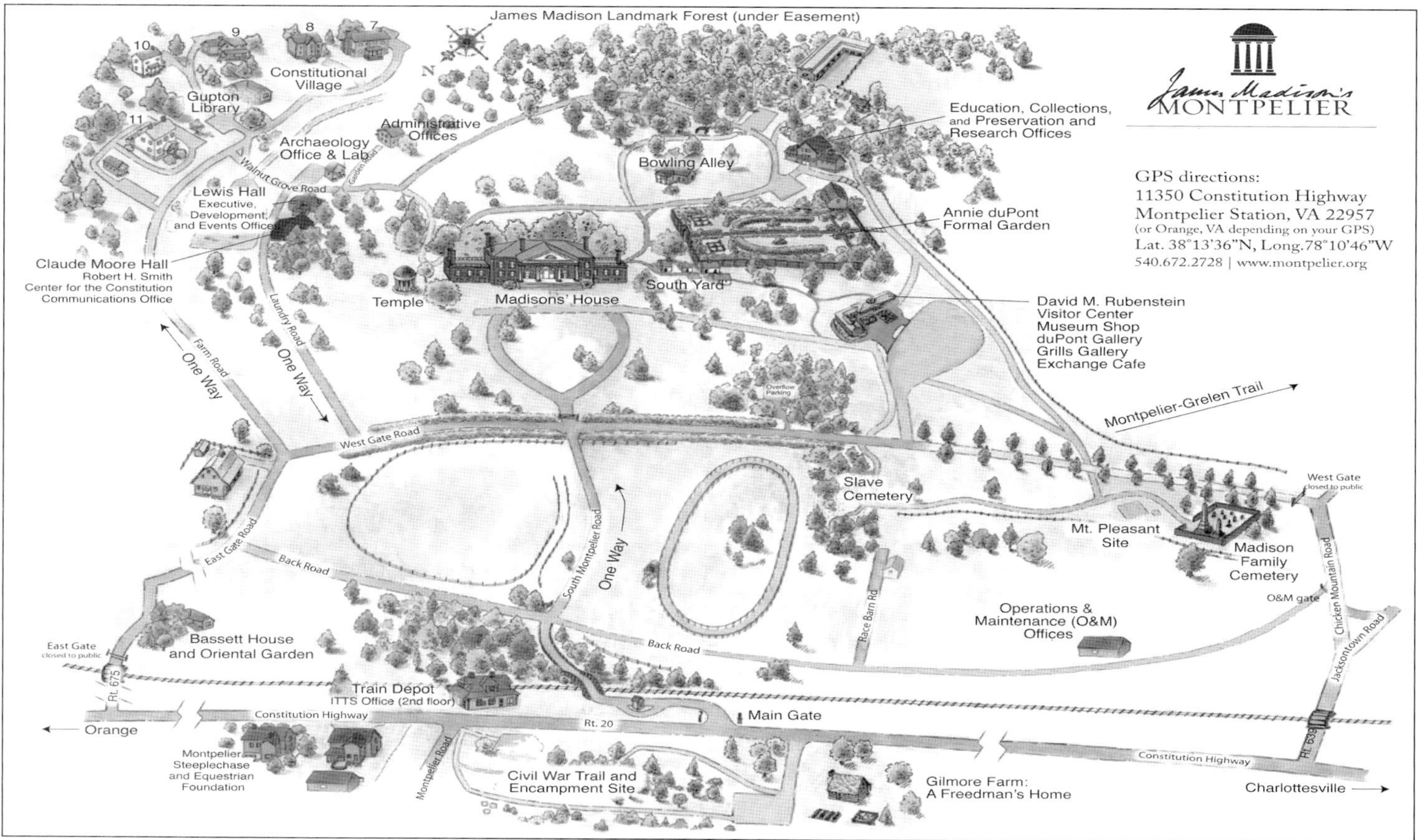
James Madison Landmark Forest (under Easement)
James Madison's
MONTPELIER
GPS directions:
11350 Constitution Highway
Montpelier Station, VA 22957
(or Orange, VA depending on your GPS)
Lat. 38°13'36"N, Long.78°10'46"W
540.672.2728 | www.montpelier.org
N
10
9
8
7
11
Constitutional Village
Gupton Library
Administrative Offices
Archaeology Office & Lab
Garden Road
Walnut Grove Road
Lewis Hall
Executive, Development, and Events Office
Claude Moore Hall
Robert H. Smith Center for the Constitution
Communications Office
Education, Collections, and Preservation and Research Offices
Bowling Alley
Annie duPont Formal Garden
Temple
Madisons' House
South Yard
David M. Rubenstein Visitor Center
Museum Shop
duPont Gallery
Grills Gallery
Exchange Cafe
Farm Road
One Way
Laundry Road
One Way
Overflow Parking
Montpelier-Grelen Trail
West Gate Road
West Gate
closed to public
Slave Cemetery
Mt. Pleasant Site
Madison Family Cemetery
South Montpelier Road
One Way
East Gate Road
Back Road
Back Road
Race Barn Rd
Operations & Maintenance (O&M) Offices
O&M gate
Chicken Mountain Road
Jacksontown Road
East Gate
closed to public
Bassett House and Oriental Garden
Train Depot
ITTS Office (2nd floor)
Rt. 675
Orange
Constitution Highway
Rt. 20
Main Gate
Constitution Highway
Rt. 639
Charlottesville
Montpelier Steeplechase and Equestrian Foundation
Montpelier Road
Civil War Trail and Encampment Site
Gilmore Farm: A Freedman's Home

EPILOGUE

CONTINUED BUILDING ON THE FOUNDERS' DREAM

In its first decade, The Montpelier Foundation achieved the founding directors' "impossible" dream of transforming Montpelier into a monument to James Madison—and realized our guiding mission that Montpelier would become a national resource of historic significance for education about the life and legacy of Madison and his essential role in creating the nation's founding documents. When we organized the Foundation in 1998, the dream was just that. Realizing it in the first decade was beyond the hopes of even the most optimistic of us. But astonishingly, we celebrated achievement of the dream during the Foundation's 10-year anniversary.

The dominant focus of the second decade was to recognize the essential role of Montpelier's enslaved in building the site and creating the environment critical to James Madison's making his many contributions to the nation. With the establishment of the award-winning exhibition on slavery in Montpelier's cellar—the domain of the house slaves—and reconstruction of their adjacent housing and ancillary structures, Montpelier now fully provides the historic setting for understanding the life and times of James Madison and educating the public about the U.S. Constitution. Montpelier has now been transformed into a monument to the life and legacy of Madison and to its Enslaved Community.

In the third decade, the Foundation continued to build and increase its programs on the Madisons, the Constitution, the enslaved and the Montpelier landscape. Its extensive archaeology has expanded

James Madison's Montpelier in 2018, the restored House and reconstructed South Yard buildings of the Enslaved Community. *Photo by Aaron Watson, TMF.*

understanding about the areas where the enslaved people worked on parts of the plantation both near and distant from the House. The location of a circa 1750 house, which was built before the Montpelier House and in which Madison lived as a young child, is being reconstructed based on archaeology of the area where the House slaves later lived and worked. Much is also being learned about the Madisons' tobacco fields and barns, blacksmith shop and site of the overseer's house. In late 2019, Kat Imhoff resigned after seven successful years as CEO and joined the Piedmont Environmental Council to serve as a senior consultant.

With the hiring of Roy F. Young II early in 2020, the Foundation continued its notable track record of attracting talented, experienced CEOs. Roy previously held leadership positions at a number of other institutions, including George Washington's Mount Vernon and the Winterthur Museum in Delaware. He joined Montpelier just as the coronavirus pandemic caused Montpelier, like other historic sites, to dramatically curtail its onsite operations available to visitors. House tours were halted completely for a while but resumed later in the year when the site returned to normal operations on a phased basis. Archaeologists returned to the field in June 2020, and curtailment of Montpelier visitation was relaxed significantly by early 2021.

During the time the site could not operate in its normal mode, the staff was able to create an extensive ongoing program of online lectures on Constitution and Madison subjects, virtual teacher seminars and book talks on a broad range of relevant topics, as well as continue to work with Board members, enslaved descendants and national and local organizations. In significant respects, the online offerings were more extensive and broad-based than would have been possible to create and make available during a period of normal operations. Also, the staff and Board developed a detailed 18-month strategic plan for enhanced operations.

Of particular long-term significance, Montpelier established "The Constitution Initiative" in the spring of 2021 to provide the ongoing central focus for the site. The heart of the initiative is the adoption every year of an annual theme around which extensive site-wide programming will be created. The inaugural theme chosen was *Race and the U.S. Constitution.* In June, to emphasize the significance of Montpelier's enslaved, the Foundation's Board revised its bylaws to create a goal of one-half the Board being directors recommended by the Montpelier Descendants Committee.

Current and future generations of Foundation staff and directors will be able to build on the successes that occurred in a period of just slightly more than two decades. By continuing to expand the scope of Montpelier's programs and gain a large national audience for education critical to sustaining a strong American democracy and civil society, they will be perpetuating a monumental legacy.

ACKNOWLEDGEMENTS

Telling the story of Montpelier's transformation seemed important for numerous reasons. But the encouragement of others was the most critical factor in my decision to write the book. Most supportive were my wife, Peyton, and fellow founding colleagues of The Montpelier Foundation: Mike Quinn, Joe Grills, Bitsy Waters and Lou Potter. Also, Kat Imhoff, the Foundation's CEO and president during most of its second decade, was supportive throughout her tenure. Kat's successor, Roy Young, continued to ensure that I would receive support from Montpelier's staff.

The person who first encouraged me to write a work on Madison and Montpelier was Ralph Ketcham. Since its publication in 1971, his biography of Madison has been recognized to be the preeminent treatment of Madison's life. For more than a decade, I had discussions with Ralph about my interest in writing a biography on some aspect of Madison's life. Ralph was unfailingly enthusiastic and regularly asked me about my current thinking when we were at Foundation Board meetings and at other times. David Mattern of UVA's Madison Papers Project also was encouraging and continued to be helpful by responding to requests for Madison research. Ralph and I both hoped that as Montpelier's transformation evolved, one ancillary result would be that recognized founding period authors would devote more attention to Madison and his contributions. Happily, this did occur. So, I discontinued my consideration of attempting to make a biographical contribution. Also, as the monument increasingly became a reality, the encouragement of others began to turn my thoughts to writing this Montpelier history. Ralph added his support and concurred with views being expressed about the value of my writing this book. Regrettably, Ralph died before my research and writing had reached the point where I could share my work with this wonderful man.

My research began with assembling the extensive Montpelier files I had maintained in my home and law offices. The files covered in depth the Foundation's first decade and most of the second. I had copies of memos, correspondence, Board and Executive Committee meeting minutes, annual reports, other reports on all of the projects undertaken, newsletters, draft and final agreements on major actions and many other miscellaneous papers. This, together with my firsthand knowledge, gave me much of the material necessary to review in preparation for writing the Montpelier transformation story.

Numerous other sources were helpful and, in many cases, essential. Joe Grills, Board vice chair and later chair, loaned me his extensive Montpelier files, which, in particular, supplemented mine on financial issues. Bitsy Waters gave me copies of her Building Committee summaries, with details in them not readily available elsewhere. Mike Quinn provided 12 single-spaced pages of his recollections about his time as Montpelier's president. Files in Montpelier's archives contained many documents to supplement my files and numerous documents from other sources. Kat Imhoff generously directed her staff to be responsive to my requests for documents and photographs. Her deputy, Sean O'Brien, made many of Mike's files available electronically. Elizabeth Ladner of the curatorial staff and Jeni Spencer of the communications staff reviewed files and provided me specific categories of documents I requested. Meg Kennedy, formerly of the museum programs staff, offered helpful insights regarding development of Montpelier's research database.

At my request, Mike Quinn carefully reviewed every chapter. This contribution was invaluable. He provided numerous suggestions on the Foundation's first 14 years. They included possible additions and elaborations, rephrasing of certain points in the text, preparation of drafts of several paragraphs and minor editing. He also raised questions about accuracy in a few places, causing me to undertake additional research to test our recollections or interpretations of the written record. In short, while not changing the overall content, Mike's contributions were many and of high quality. Also, I appreciated his repeated positive statements about depth of coverage and quality of writing as he reviewed each chapter. His words provided me a high degree of reassurance about the book's substance.

Where I have relied on his suggestions, I have included a citation to the emails transmitting them. The book is highly laudable of Mike's leadership, but he made no suggestions that affected any point relating to that. I am solely responsible for the book's content.

Montpelier's director of restoration, John Jeanes, twice reviewed the sections discussing the House's restoration to ensure that they comported with the work performed and issues faced. Architectural historian Mark Wenger, principal investigator in studying the feasibility of restoring the House and later the architect's lead representative on the project, reviewed the final version of the restoration chapters and suggested a number of helpful additions that were included. Mike Quinn's review provided a further level of comfort of that discussion. These reviews of the restoration chapters were particularly important because much of the detail was in the memories of those involved. They helped assure the accuracy of many aspects of the project's description that could not be obtained fully from the overview and itemized listing of the work detailed in the feasibility study report.

Kat Imhoff's assistance included a helpful review of the period during her tenure as CEO, which is covered in chapters 13 and 14. She suggested that I include several additional programs and that I elaborate on programs I had referenced. Elizabeth Chew, executive vice president and chief curator, provided expert advice on *The Mere Distinction of Colour* exhibition. With support from Elizabeth and later CEO Roy Young, Jeni Spencer located photos that I requested and suggested others for inclusion. She also helped me in organizing them and worked with the publishing team as decisions were made on incorporating images in the book. Her assistance was, in a word, essential. Using her talents as a graphic designer, Jeni worked with Tom Chapman—formerly an archaeological assistant who had developed many maps for the site—in preparing the book's three maps of Montpelier. Tom also provided helpful history on Montpelier as a public site in the early period.

Two reviewers of the almost-final version of the manuscript were director of archaeology Matt Reeves and the National Trust's legal counsel, Tom Mayes. Matt reviewed the descriptions of all of the archaeological projects and provided valuable insights and details to supplement the book's narrative. Tom thoughtfully read the entire manuscript. His relatively few comments related to issues involving the Trust and a few questions about appropriate terminology.

Mike's secretary Pat Mahanes and, later, executive assistant Ellen Wessel were always gracious in responding to my numerous and frequent requests, providing me with many of the documents that I ultimately relied on in my research. Their assistance greatly reduced the time required for me to accumulate written factual support.

In addition to being a supportive voice, Peyton Lewis served as my editor, enabling me to take advantage of her extensive experience as an author. Her editorial suggestions and questions were useful and improved the flow of the narrative. Based on the recommendation of a friend, I had the good fortune to retain Margaret "Peggy" Mucklo to be the copy editor for detailed review and advice on the manuscript. Her assistance was essential for producing the book for publication. It included everything from general advice on my first draft to detailed comments on both the content and style of the many subsequent drafts of the entire manuscript, to editing and incorporating endnotes and preparing the index. This assistance continued until the manuscript was in a form for me to submit for publication. After I submitted my book proposal to The History Press, Kate Jenkins, the acquisition editor, provided much appreciated, outstanding guidance on an ongoing basis from the time my proposal was accepted to the time the book was released.

Appendix A

NEW FOUNDATION DIRECTORS 2003–2008

In 2003, Nancy Campbell and Bill Remington joined the Board. Martha duPont and Irenee duPont II were selected to be ex officio members.[1]

- Nancy Campbell had engaged extensively in civic activities, a number of which involved historic preservation. She previously served as chair of the National Trust for Historic Preservation and chaired its successful $105 million comprehensive fundraising campaign. She had served in numerous other leadership roles, including as chair of the Preservation League of New York, as a commissioner on the Connecticut Historical Commission, as a member of the White House Millennium Committee to Save America's Treasures and as a trustee of Hollins University. Nancy also was a leader in encouraging the National Trust to support creation of the Foundation for the purpose of its assuming responsibility for Montpelier. In 2014, Nancy completed the usual maximum of three terms on the Foundation Board. At the Governance Committee's request, she agreed to being nominated for an additional term and serve as Board chair from 2014 to 2018. Up to that time, election to a fourth term had been reserved for founding directors. Upon completing her term as chair, she was asked to and agreed to continue on the Executive Committee in her role as chair emerita. Throughout Nancy's Board service, she served as an ambassador for the Foundation, extending its reputation among the nation's community of historic preservation and decorative arts nonprofit organizations. She also played an important role as an expert in connection with acquisition of decorative arts and furnishing of the House. As Board chair, she distinguished herself with her leadership and in making thoughtful presentations to donors and other groups.

- Bill Remington held numerous posts in insurance sales and management across the United States in a 31-year career with Johnson & Higgins. He also provided management consulting to London-based Royal/Sun Alliance Insurance Company. As discussed in Chapter 8, Bill was a key leader in organizing and overseeing the Foundation's Center for the Constitution.
- Martha Verge duPont and her son, H.E. Irenee duPont II, served as ex officio Board members, representing the family of William duPont Sr., who had acquired Montpelier in 1901. As discussed in chapter 6, Mrs. duPont was instrumental in working with the Foundation to amend the Will Settlement so that the House could be restored. The amendment called for construction of the William duPont Gallery to honor the duPont family.

In 2006, Roger Wilkins, Florence "Flossie" Fowlkes and Elinor Farquhar joined the Board.

- Roger Wilkins was a civil rights champion in government and journalism.[2] After an early career as a welfare lawyer in Cleveland, Ohio, and an international lawyer in New York City, he moved to the Washington, D.C. area to become a special assistant to the administrator of the U.S. Agency for International Development. President Johnson selected Roger to lead the federal Community Relations Service. This role also vested him with the title of assistant attorney general. Later he joined the Ford Foundation, where he was responsible for awarding funding to address inner-city problems. Then, as a journalist for the *Washington Post*, he was on the team awarded a Pulitzer Prize for its Watergate coverage.[3] When he joined the Foundation Board, he was a professor of history at George Mason University in Arlington, Virginia. Throughout his Board service, he served as an advisor on programs that recognized the indispensable role of the enslaved and dealt with post-Madison civil rights–related activities at Montpelier. (See the discussion in chapter 10 of his lead role in the 2007 Enslaved Community Descendants Reunion.)

- Flossie Fowlkes had been active in a number of civic and conservation organizations and served on the boards of the Children's Hearing and Speech Center, the McLean School of Maryland and the Women's Committee of the Corcoran Gallery. She served as chair of the Foundation's Museum Programs Committee and played a leadership role in connection with furnishing the House after its restoration.
- Elinor Farquhar had held a number of leadership positions in arts and historic preservation organizations. She served on the boards of the National Trust for Historic Preservation, the Corcoran Gallery (as chair) and the Roosevelt Institution. While on the Foundation Board, she served as co-chair of the Madison Cabinet and was a leader in building philanthropy programs.

Three new directors joined the Board in 2007: Gregory "Greg" May, John Sponski and Cynthia "Cindy" Reusche.

- Greg May was a partner in the Washington, D.C. office of Freshfields Bruckhaus Deringer and a member of the firm's governing council. His tax law practice focused on cross-border corporate transactions, structured finance and financial products. After graduating from law school, Greg clerked for a federal appellate court judge and then for Justice Lewis Powell of the U.S. Supreme Court. He had been a trustee of the Historic Alexandria Foundation and the Friends of Carlyle House Historic Park. Greg served as chair of the Foundation from 2011 until 2014. Prior to holding that position, Greg was chair of the Board's strategic planning task force and the Museum Programs Committee, on which he brought to bear his extensive expertise in decorative arts.
- John Sponski was active in a number of community organizations and formerly was an executive vice president of Bank of America. When David Gibson stepped down as chair

of the Board's Finance Committee, John agreed to assume this important responsibility. In that role, like prior Committee chairs, he devoted an extraordinary amount of time to effectively overseeing the Foundation's budget and ensuring maintenance of financial stability.

- Cindy Reusche had a career in financial management. She was an active volunteer in various roles, including the advisory board for public humanities at Brown University, where she received her undergraduate degree in American studies. She was a board member and president of the Women's Board for the University of Chicago Cancer Research Foundation and was active as a volunteer for various other organizations. Cindy's decade-plus of active participation in the Foundation's archaeology program and her substantial financial support for it are discussed in chapter 12. In 2007, Cindy became chair of the Foundation's Site Preservation and Management Committee, the successor to the Building Committee, and devoted substantial time and energy to oversight of Montpelier's buildings and landscape.

Stephen "Steve" McLean joined the Board in 2008. He is a founder and principal of McLean Faulconer Inc., a prominent real estate firm based in Charlottesville, Virginia, that specializes in farms and estates. He has been active in a number of organizations in Charlottesville, including an advisory group for the University of Virginia's Medical Center. Steve served as chair of the Foundation's Marketing Committee. He also played an active role on a Board land use task force to consider possible uses of portions of the Montpelier landscape.

Appendix B

BOARD ESTABLISHMENT OF GOALS

As the goals the Foundation developed in 2007 make clear, despite Montpelier having truly become a monument to Madison, achieving the Foundation's expansive vision would mean continuing to undertake a broad array of important initiatives.[1] And, as evidenced by the remarkable achievements in the succeeding decade, the Foundation was able to expand and achieve its objective to become a monument to Madison and to the enslaved community (see chapters 13 and 14).

House Restoration. The focus here was on finishing the architectural restoration and preparing to open the restored House. In addition to carrying out the final construction-related projects, this included completing the planning for the opening celebration and developing an estimate of the cost for operation of the House (including utilities, staffing and maintenance).

House Interior. The most important goals for the House's interior were obvious: undertake the already planned research and then furnish at least a significant portion of the House. Doing so would involve the following:

- Continuing with the intensive documentary research phase
- Accurately furnishing the drawing room and dining room, although interpreting them would not be possible until the research was largely completed (the estimated cost in 2007 was $1.5 to $2.0 million, primarily for object research and furnishings acquisition)

- In the interim, presenting the drawing room and dining room as being "in process," with possibly some pictures hung and some furniture added, but no installation of carpets and other key decorative features
- Interpreting a number of other rooms (with the priorities being Madison's study, Mother Madison's parlor, Madison's library and the Madisons' bedroom), using vignettes to convey an interpretive message that would suggest room use
- Setting a goal of announcing the opening of exhibits in the House on September 17, 2010 (in other words, two years after the House's official opening)

Other Curatorial Priorities. The curatorial focus extended to interior spaces beyond the House. These were the planned activities:

- Maintaining and rotating the exhibits in the Joe and Marge Grills Gallery, together with the necessary monitoring of conditions and cleaning
- Maintaining the exhibits in the duPont Gallery and doing some rotation of the artifacts
- Modifying the dining room and drawing room exhibits in the Pony Barn (Education Center) to address flaws and create an "experimental" interpretation—or close them
- Moving the Pony Barn furnishings to the House or to storage elsewhere by the end of 2009
- Deciding the fate of the *Madison: Architect of the Constitution and Bill of Rights* exhibit in the Pony Barn
- Developing exhibits for the Montpelier Train Station lobby

Archaeology. Continuing the tradition established over the Foundation's first decade, perhaps the most ambitious goals were those of the archaeology department. The principal focus was on the "House grounds precinct" (also called the historic core). The long-term goal would be to fully restore all features, both landscape and buildings, to be as they were when the Madisons lived there. The immediate goals would consist of the following:

- For the front of the House, determining the configuration of the road, paths and fences and plantings to enable the creation of a "coherent" front yard by September 2008

- For the back of the House, determining the configuration of paths to enable creation of a coherent backyard by September 2008
- For the South Yard, conducting archaeology sufficient to permit "ghosting" of enslaved community structures and possible reconstruction
- Developing and conducting projects for the Madison farm complex (in the area of the Visitor Center) and the Gilmore farm (with possible reconstruction of a work building and well structure)
- Surveying and/or excavating the Civil War encampment and other on-site Civil War features
- Coordinating with forestry management experts to avoid damage to important archaeological sites

Interpretation/Education. The heart of the Montpelier experience for most visitors would always involve the interpretation and education programs. For that reason, the Board set these goals:

- Continuing the refining and updating of the interpretive plan
- Developing a documentary video for the Alan and Louise Potter Theater by 2010
- Considering new interpretive approaches (such as costumed-character interpreters, horse-drawn wagon, mobile audio guides versus human guides)
- Developing a forestry interpretive program (possibly with walking trails)
- Considering expansion of the Gilmore farm program, including additional buildings, farming operations and farm animals
- Exploring the possibility of preparing additional monograph publications

Research/Archives. The Board also recognized that protecting Montpelier records should be given a high priority. This would include creating two systems:

- A research library as a repository for data from documentary research obtained in the interiors furnishing project, as well as research and data from the House restoration and other projects

- An archive for the Foundation, with a key part being organizing storage of other internal records

Center for the Constitution. The Center was in a state of transition due to its change of leadership. As a consequence, the succinctly stated goal for the Center was to continue preparation of a master plan for future development and implementation that would address these elements:

- Future expansion of audiences for programs
- Establishment of a broad curriculum of online courses
- Improvement and possible reconfiguration of roads
- Construction and adaptive reuse of buildings

Forestry. The Forestry Subcommittee had embarked earlier on developing a comprehensive forestry program. Thus, the forestry goal was to complete preparation of the program.

Finance/Administration. The human infrastructure goals included upgrading capabilities in two areas:

- Technology, including adding a new fiber optic network (estimated 2007 cost was $100,000) and more on-staff resources
- Human resources, including conducting regularly scheduled performance evaluations and other good practices

Site Stewardship. The goals for sound stewardship were challenging to set in a realistic manner, given the extensiveness of the site, the number of buildings (about 125) and the massive potential cost of addressing many of the issues. The goals that were set included these items:

- Considering the need to improve and/or replace some housing for staff
- Making needed improvements to Bassett House, the residence of the CEO, and its iconic Oriental Garden
- Identifying and removing buildings with no historical significance and no foreseeable reuse
- Beginning more maintenance and repair of leased barns
- Considering the future of residences on the south side of the property, including water and sewer issues

- Making major improvements to roads and to the transportation system in general

Most Urgently Needed Facilities. Notwithstanding the existence of the many buildings on the property, the Board recognized that several spaces were urgently needed:

- A new storage facility with at least 20,000 square feet of space to provide storage for duPont Mansion artifacts, archaeological items and curatorial items, as well as to provide a facilities workshop (for carpentry, paint and supplies)
- An archaeological facility with a combined lab and office capable of becoming a featured location for visitation, with the most likely location being near the Pony Barn
- Space for administrative staff offices and records

Appendix C

NEW DIRECTORS AND EMERITI—2009–2018

2010. Joining the Board were Arthur H. Bryant Jr., banking executive and community leader; Dr. Eugene W. Hickok, retired professor of political science and law, with service as U.S. deputy secretary of education (elected Board chair in 2020); Dennis A. Kernahan, executive in financial and technology sectors (elected Board chair in 2018); Stephanie K. Meeks, president and CEO, National Trust for Historic Preservation; and Leigh B. Middleditch Jr., senior lawyer, community leader and recipient of numerous major awards—with extensive experience founding nonprofits and chairing and serving on boards and advisory groups of university, law association, state government and community organizations.

2011. Joining the Board were Patricia "Trish" Crowe, president of a land trust, an artist and founder of an artists' network; Roger H. Mudd, retired award-winning journalist, national television network correspondent and history documentary host; Ella D. Strubel, formerly a senior public relations executive for a national firm, national television networks and other major corporations—and founder and managing director of a greeting card company and the recipient of numerous honors; and G. Edward "Ted" White, an award-winning law professor.

2012. Joining the Board was Jack N. Rakove, professor of history and American studies, Pulitzer Prize–winning author and eminent national scholar on James Madison and the Constitution.

2013. Joining the Board were Robert A. Leath, museum curator and collections and research executive; John F. Macon II, retired senior wealth management executive for a national bank and a Madison family descendant; and Frank Qiu, co-founder of a global enterprise for decorative products for home and garden and a nationally recognized entrepreneur.

2014. Joining the Board were Dennis M. Campbell, former headmaster of Woodberry Forest School, dean of the Divinity School and professor of theology at Duke University, member and chair of boards of institutions and recipient of numerous honors and awards; Margaret H. Jordan, senior executive for Texas health care systems, board member of numerous major institutions, former director of the Federal Reserve Bank of Dallas and recipient of numerous awards (also a direct descendant of Paul Jennings, President Madison's enslaved manservant); and Alan Taylor, Thomas Jefferson Foundation professor of history at the University of Virginia, two-time Pulitzer Prize–winning author and nationally recognized expert on colonial America and the early U.S. republic.

2015. Joining the Board was Linda C. Gibson, a certified public accountant with a career in public accounting, previously business officer for the College Foundation for the University of Virginia and co-recipient of the University's Miller Center exemplary leadership award.

2016. Joining the Board were John B. Adams Jr., chair emeritus of The Martin Agency, after a career of 43 years leading that top-10 advertising agency; David T. Dreier, former Member of Congress from California, venture capital fund partner and board advisor to technology firms; and Paul W. Edmondson, chief legal officer and general counsel for more than 20 years of Montpelier's owner, the National Trust for Historic Preservation (later elected Trust president and CEO).

2017. Joining the Board were Francois L. Baird, founder and chair of Baird's CMC Ltd., an international communications management consultancy, Baird's US LLC and Calbridge (Pty) Ltd., consulting internationally on issues, communication and strategy to clients around the world; and Stacy Zolt Hara, Midwest director of Edelman's Transformation Communications office, who has nearly 20 years of experience in advising on reputation, public affairs and communications.

2018. Joining the Board were Frank B. Atkinson, senior advisor of McGuireWoods Consulting LLC, for which he was principal founder, and partner of McGuireWoods LLP—also an author, lecturer and previously a senior federal and state official; Pamela F. Edmonds, leader in nonprofit, community and church activities; and Benjamin Brewster, formerly managing director and portfolio manager at Silvercrest Asset Management Group LLC and principal and founding partner at Heritage Financial Management LLC.

Directors Emeriti. Elizabeth B. Waters (2007); Ralph Ketcham and Peter G. Rice (2009); David E. Gibson, Richard Moe and H.B. Sedwick III (2010); Arthur J. Collias, Walter W. Craigie, Joe Grills (chair emeritus), A.E. Dick Howard, Louise B. Potter and Hunter R. Rawlings III (2011); William H. Lewis (chair emeritus), William C. Remington and Margaret B. Rhoads (2012); Gregory May (chair emeritus) (2014); and John J. Sponski (2017).

NOTES

Prologue

1. The Library of Congress refers to its James Madison Memorial Building as the "nation's only memorial" to James Madison.
2. Report of the Working Group of Montpelier, Presented to the Board of Trustees, National Trust for Historic Preservation, October 20, 1976, 4 [hereafter Working Group Report with page number].
3. Ibid.
4. Email from Michael Quinn to the author, William Lewis, November 27, 2018. [Hereafter, emails from Michael Quinn to the author that provide his comments and suggestions on, or related to, the manuscript of this book are cited as "M. Quinn," followed by the date sent.]
5. Last Will and Testament of Marion duPont Scott, February 6, 1975 [hereafter "Scott Will"], Article Two.
6. Opinion dated June 10, 1988, by Justice John Charles Thomas, Supreme Court of Virginia, in Henry E.I. duPont, et al. v. V.R. Shackelford, Jr., et al. (No. 850443), 2–3.
7. Agreement of Settlement and for the Entry of Decrees dated October 15, 1984, in Henry E.I. duPont, et al. v. V. R. Shackelford, Jr., individually and Executor of the Estate of Marion duPont Scott, et al., filed in Circuit Court of Orange County, Virginia (Decree entered on October 22, 1984), 7 [hereafter "Will Settlement" with page number].

8. Working Group Report, 3.
9. Will Settlement, 16.
10. Scott Will, Article Two.
11. Working Group Report, 3.
12. Ibid., 1–2.
13. Ibid., 11.
14. Ibid., 7–8.
15. Ibid., 11.
16. Ibid., 1.
17. Ibid., 2.
18. M. Quinn, November 27, 2018.

1. Montpelier in 1997

1. Gerald Strine, *Montpelier: The Recollections of Marion duPont Scott* (New York: Charles Scribner's Sons, 1976); Richard Guy Wilson and Sara A. Butler, *Buildings of Virginia: Tidewater and Piedmont* (New York: Oxford University Press, 2002), 130; M. Quinn, November 27, 2018.
2. From the 1920s to the 1960s, Charles Freeman Gillette designed numerous gardens for estates and public and private institutions in Virginia and the upper South. See George C. Longest, *Genius in the Garden: Charles F. Gillette and Landscape Architecture in Virginia* (Richmond: Library of Virginia, 1992) and Laura L. Hutchison, "'Kit' House Is a Hidden Treasure at Montpelier Bassett House," *Free Lance-Star* (Fredericksburg, VA), April 10, 2008, https://www.fredericksburg.com/special_sectiongarden_week/bassett-house-kit-house-is-a-hidden-treasure-at-montpelier/article_b931c0fb-33de-5878-8ff4-a014b919496b.html.
3. Emails and attachments from M. Wenger to W. Lewis, September 13–17, 2021.
4. C. Thomas Chapman, "James Madison's Grave—A Study in Contextual Analysis" (master's thesis, The College of William and Mary, 2005). Also see M. Quinn, November 27, 2018.
5. Evelyn Bence, ed., "James Madison's Montpelier: Home of the Father of the Constitution," The Montpelier Foundation, 2008. Also see M. Quinn, November 27, 2018.
6. Working Group Report, 4.
7. Ibid., 2–3.
8. Ibid., 3.

9. National Trust for Historic Preservation Press Release, announcing successful capital campaign, raising $28 million over $105 million target, March 6, 2003.
10. Working Group Report, 4.

2. A Perplexing Beginning—1998

1. The Montpelier Property Council Executive Committee members were Carolyn Sedwick, Peter Rice, Ed Jaenke, Les Williams, Watt Dunnington and Glen Moreno.
2. Note and Attachments from G. Moreno to R. Moe, National Trust for Historic Preservation (NTHP), January 22, 1998 [hereafter G. Moreno January 22, 1998 Note and Attachments] and telephone conversation with W. Lewis on same date.
3. Memo from W. Lewis to file, October 2, 1997.
4. Ibid.
5. G. Moreno January 22, 1998 Note and Attachments.
6. Ibid.
7. Memo from R. Moe to G. Moreno, March 11, 1998 [hereafter R. Moe, March 11, 1998 Memo].
8. Ibid.
9. Memo from G. Moreno to R. Moe, May 4, 1998 (by fax).
10. Memo from R. Moe to G. Moreno, May 13, 1998 (by fax).
11. NTHP paper, "Discovering Madison," Spring 1998.
12. *Discovering Montpelier*, Summer 1998, a newsletter for Friends of James Madison's Montpelier [hereafter *Discovering Montpelier*, with the issue date].
13. NTHP paper, "Discovering Madison," Spring 1998.
14. Certificate of Incorporation issued on July 31, 1998, by Virginia State Corporation Commission upon filing Articles of Incorporation of The Montpelier Foundation (TMF) [hereafter Articles of Incorporation].
15. Letter of R. Moe to G. Moreno, July 30, 1998.
16. Ibid.
17. Memo of G. Moreno to R. Moe, August 16, 1998.
18. Memo and attached History of NTHP/Foundation Discussions from K. Mullins to G. Moreno, September 21, 1998.
19. Letter from R. Moe to G. Moreno, September 23, 1998.
20. Memo from G. Moreno to R. Moe, September 29, 1998.
21. Memo from G. Moreno to Board of Directors, TMF, October 1, 1998.

22. Letter from R. Moe to G. Moreno, November 2, 1998.
23. Memo from W. Lewis to R. Moe, November 5, 1998.
24. Letter from R. Moe to W. Lewis, December 17, 1998.
25. Minutes of TMF Board of Directors Meeting, November 6, 1998 [hereafter Minutes with the applicable date]. No distinction in these notes shall be made between Minutes of the full TMF Board meetings and those of the Board's Executive Committee. In its meetings, the Executive Committee acts with the full authority of the entire Board.
26. Ibid.
27. Minutes, December 18, 1998. Also see Letter from W. Lewis to G. Moreno, October 7, 1999.
28. Memo and Attachment from P. Mahanes to TMF Board, January 29, 1999.
29. Minutes, August 14, 1998 (Approval of Bylaws).
30. Minutes, October 4, 1999.
31. Ibid.
32. Minutes, May 9, 2003.
33. Minutes, April 27, 2007.
34. Minutes, December 18, 1998.
35. Memo and Attachments from K. Mullins to W. Lewis, November 17, 1998.

3. Year of Foundation Organization—1999

1. "Madison, An Extraordinary Man; Montpelier, A Memorable Place: A Strategic Plan for the Next 10 Years," September 1999 [hereafter Strategic Plan 1999].
2. Strategic Plan 1999, Foreword–1.
3. Ibid., III–1.
4. Ibid., Contents.
5. Ibid., Summary, 1–5.
6. Statements of J. Grills, L. Potter, E. Waters and W. Lewis, in files of the author.
7. Memo and Attachments from K. Mullins to TMF, et al. (Debriefing Information), July 14, 1999 [hereafter Mullins Debriefing].
8. Holly C. Shulman, PhD, is a research professor at the University of Virginia. She coauthored *Dolley Madison: Her Life, Letters, and Legacy*, a historical biography for children (2002), and is editor of the Dolley Madison Digital Edition (accessible online at https://rotunda.upress.virginia.edu/dmde).

9. Montpelier Progress Report, July 1998–May 1999.
10. Promotional paper titled "The Madison Cabinet," fax dated March 25, 1999.
11. Mullins Debriefing.
12. Memo from K. Mullins to R. Moe and W. Lewis, May 18, 1999.
13. Memo from W. Lewis to Members of TMF Board, August 10, 1999.
14. Letter from M. Quinn to R. Moe, August 10, 1999.
15. Minutes, December 10, 1999.
16. Minutes, August 30, 1999.
17. Mullins Debriefing.
18. Minutes, December 10, 1999.
19. *Discovering Montpelier*, Fall 2000, 12.
20. Delegation Agreement between NTHP and TMF, February 1, 2000.
21. Memo from W. Lewis to C.H. Seilheimer Jr. and J.H.T. McConnell Jr., December 15, 2005.
22. Minutes, December 10, 1999.
23. M. Quinn, November 29, 2018, and W. Lewis reply, November 30, 1999.
24. Minutes, December 10, 1999.
25. Summaries of Board members' biographies are based primarily on Board member summaries contained in a Montpelier Foundation document dated 2014. The observations about their contributions are based on the author's fourteen years on the Board.
26. Hunter R. Rawlings III, Woodberry Forest Commencement Address, May 30, 1997.
27. Peggy Rhoads is descended from James Madison's sister, Sarah, and thus a collateral descendant.

4. Management Transferred to The Montpelier Foundation—2000

1. Memo from M. Quinn to B. Lewis, February 7, 2000 [hereafter Co-Stewardship Instructions].
2. Ibid.
3. Ibid.
4. Ibid.
5. Ibid.
6. Minutes, February 18, 2000.
7. Email from M. Quinn to W. Lewis and Attachment, March 1, 2000, and follow-up phone conversations.

8. Ibid.
9. Letter from W. Lewis to R. Moe, with attached drafts of co-stewardship agreements, April 25, 2000.
10. Email from M. Quinn to W. Lewis, May 18, 2000, with marked-up M. Quinn summary of TMF-NTHP discussions dated May 12, 2000.
11. Letter from W. Lewis to R. Moe, with attached revised drafts of co-stewardships, May 31, 2000.
12. Letter from R. Moe to W. Lewis, with attached letter from T. Mayes, NTHP, to W. Lewis, both dated July 25, 2000.
13. Ibid.
14. Letter from R. Moe to K. Mullins and W. Lewis, April 12, 1999, promising "high degree of autonomy."
15. The thirteen buildings for which a Trust objection to a material change to the building's exterior must be resolved, and their current use, are the following: (1) Montpelier Train Station (built in 1910, now restored to be an exhibit on segregation); (2) Montpelier Supply (Farm) Store (the exterior has been renovated, now used for offices); (3) Pony Barn (now the Education Center); (4) Brick Stable (carriage house) (renovated to be Lewis Hall, for use as a Center for the Constitution academic building and executive offices); (5) Arlington House and its outbuildings (used for archaeological volunteers); (6) Gilmore Cabin (built about 1870, restored to be an exhibit on the freedman's era); (7) Bassett House (residence of Foundation CEO); (8) Farm Barn (demolished due to its unstable condition and lack of adaptive use); (9) Schooling Barn (structurally stabilized and repaired, used for storage and staging area); (10) and (11) House numbers 7 and 8 (renovated and used as housing for Constitution Center participants); (12) one example of a Sears Barn to be selected by the Foundation (used in equestrian activities); (13) one example of a Montgomery Ward House selected by the Foundation (used for staff housing).
16. Executed Co-Stewardship Agreements between NTHP and TMF, dated September 16, 2000, effective October 1, 2000.
17. *Discovering Montpelier*, Spring 2001, 2.
18. Letter from W. Lewis to J. Billington, June 28, 2000.
19. Minutes, May 15, 2000.
20. *Discovering Montpelier*, Fall 2000, 7, 10.
21. Minutes, May 8, 2000. TEA-21 authorized highway, highway safety, transit and other surface transportation programs for the six-year period 1998–2003 (see https://www.fhwa.dot.gov/tea21/index.htm). John J.

"Butch" Davies III (D) was Culpeper's delegate to the Virginia General Assembly from 1992 to 2000.

22. Minutes, May 8, 2000.
23. Memo from M. Quinn to Board of Directors, TMF, October 23, 2000.
24. "Montpelier Donates Forest: Two Miles of Walking Trails in Woods Will Also Be Opened," *Richmond Times-Dispatch*, April 14, 2000.
25. FY 2000 Fundraising.
26. Minutes, January 12, 2001 (Resolution to Establish a Finance and Investment Committee).
27. Ralph Ketcham, *James Madison: A Biography* (New York: The Macmillan Co., 1971); paperback reprint (Charlottesville: The University Press of Virginia, 1990).
28. M. Quinn, November 29, 2018.
29. "Historic Garden Week: Homes and Gardens Across the Ages in Montpelier Hunt Country," *Orange County Review*, April 10, 2008.

5. Madison Monument Advances Toward Reality—2000–2002

1. Letter and Attachments from M. Quinn to R. Smith, February 13, 2002.
2. Minutes, February 9, 2001.
3. Update on the 250th Anniversary of the Birth of James Madison, July 2001 [hereafter Madison 250th Update], 2–3.
4. M. Quinn, November 29, 2018.
5. Madison 250th Update, 1; TMF 2001 Annual Report [hereafter 2001 Annual Report], 3.
6. The flute was made for Madison by Claude Laurent of Paris. Its silver joint is inscribed with Madison's name and title and the date the flute was made (1813). To listen to music from the flute and an interview with flutist Rob Turner, visit "Madison's Crystal Flute," National Public Radio, March 16, 2001, at www.npr.org/templates/story/story.php?storyid=1120053. To learn more about Laurent and the history of the Madison flute, see Dorie Kline, "Claude Laurent and the Madison Flute: Discoveries Through Archival Research," Library of Congress, at https://www.loc.gov/static/collections/dayton-c-miller-collection/images/klein-miller-flute-project-madison-report-summer-2015.pdf.
7. Madison 250th Update, 2.
8. Letter from Justice Sandra Day O'Connor to James Billington, Librarian of Congress, March 19, 2001.

9. Madison 250th Update, 4–5.
10. Ibid.
11. 2001 Annual Report, 4.
12. Virginia Civics Education Inc., a Virginia nonprofit, succeeded to the sponsorship responsibility for *We the People* in Virginia from the Foundation. John J. Sponski, a Foundation director emeritus who played a lead role in connection with Montpelier's management of the program, organized Virginia Civics.
13. Madison 250th Update, 6.
14. 2001 Annual Report, 4.
15. Report, Mellon Grant for Education (undated), 1.
16. Madison 250th Update, 5.
17. During the restoration of Montpelier, workers discovered a rodent's nest lodged in an upstairs wall that contained pieces of scarlet fabric, wallpaper and a note in James Madison's handwriting that read "Mother would." Peyton Lewis used that information to tell the story in a children's book of a mouse living at Montpelier during Lafayette's visit in 1824. Its title is *The Diary of Maggie: A Madison Mouse*; it is available at the Visitor Center for James Madison's Montpelier and at Amazon Books.
18. Memo from W. Lewis and M. Quinn to TMF Board of Directors, June 26, 2001.
19. M. Quinn, November 29, 2018.
20. Memo from W. Lewis and M. Quinn to TMF Board of Directors, June 26, 2001.
21. Ibid.
22. Ibid.
23. Letter and Attached Education and Restoration Feasibility Study Proposals from R. Moe and M. Quinn to F. Terry and B. Carter, August 8, 2001.
24. Memo from W. Lewis and M. Quinn to TMF Board of Directors, June 26, 2001.
25. Ibid.
26. Letter from R. Moe to M. Quinn, October 30, 2001, and Mellon Estate Restoration Feasibility Study and Education Agreement between F. Terry and B. Carter, as Paul Mellon Estate Executors, and NTHP and TMF, as of September 16, 2002 [hereafter Mellon Estate Restoration Feasibility Study and Education Agreement].
27. Letter and Attachments from M. Quinn to R. Smith, February 13, 2002.
28. Letter from R. Smith to M. Quinn, June 10, 2002.

29. Letter from R. Moe to M. Quinn, October 30, 2001, and Mellon Estate Restoration Feasibility Study and Education Agreement.
30. TMF Building Committee Meeting Summary, April 9, 2001.
31. Minutes, February 9, 2001.
32. TMF Building Committee Meeting Summary, April 9, 2001.
33. Montpelier Gateway Project Workshop Summary, May 16, 2001.
34. Memo from B. Waters to Building Committee Members, July 17, 2001.
35. TMF Building Committee Meeting Summary, April 9, 2001.
36. M. Quinn, December 1, 2018.
37. TMF Building Committee Meeting Summary, August 19, 2004.
38. Memo from P. Kapp, AIA, to Montpelier Building Committee, et al., December 14, 2001 [hereafter Kapp Memo].
39. The Montpelier Gateway Project Feasibility Study, July 13, 2001 (preliminary draft).
40. Kapp Memo.
41. Minutes, September 12, 2003.
42. After several years, the Foundation stopped its regular use of the booth. It was more efficient and created a more welcoming entry for visitors to have staff collect admission fees in the new Visitor Center.
43. Memo from M. Quinn to TMF Board of Directors, May 12, 2003.
44. Memo from M. Quinn to file, June 22, 2004.
45. TMF Building Committee Meeting Summary, August 19, 2004.
46. M. Quinn, January 27, 2019.
47. 2007 TMF Annual Report, 3.
48. Letter from A. Potter to M. Quinn, March 4, 2002.
49. Minutes, March 7, 2003.

6. Surmounting Restoration Hurdles—2001–2003

1. W. Brown Morton III, "Preserving Montpelier," paper submitted for The Madison Conference, June 26, 1989, 2.
2. Note from B. Morton to W. Dupont, April 18, 2002.
3. Working Group Report, 1.
4. James Madison's Montpelier Feasibility Study; Mesick, Cohen, Wilson, Baker Architects LLP, for TMF, July 17, 2002 [hereafter Feasibility Study], Introduction, 1.
5. The fabric of a building consists of all internal and external structural elements: floor, walls and roof; joinery (windows and doors and their

frames, sills and thresholds); fixtures, fittings and fasteners; claddings, coverings and coatings; openings, hidden/sealed spaces, cavities and gaps.

6. The CWF investigation was funded by a $1 million federal Save America's Treasures grant. *Discovering Montpelier*, Fall 2000, 7, 10.
7. Feasibility Study, Introduction, 1.
8. Ibid.
9. Statement of the Montpelier Restoration Advisory Committee, January 29, 2003. The members listed were on the committee at the conclusion of the restoration. During the course of the restoration, the following three people were also members: Willie Graham, Colonial Williamsburg Foundation, and William duPont and Barbara Campagna, National Trust architects. Email from J. Jeanes to W. Lewis, May 21, 2020.
10. Bryant Clark Green, Ann L. Miller, with Conover Hunt, "Restoring James and Dolley Madison's Montpelier," from *Building a President's House, The Construction of James Madison's Montpelier* (The Montpelier Foundation: 2007), 34. [The publication is part of a Monograph Series and is hereafter cited as Restoration Monograph, with page numbers.] The Restoration Monograph provides the most comprehensive summary that I have found of the history of the original construction and components of all three phases of the Madisons' House, as well as of the 2003–08 restoration. Support for much of the Feasibility Study section appearing in this chapter is contained in the Restoration Monograph.
11. Restoration Monograph, 5.
12. Ibid., 17–30.
13. Ibid., 2, 17–30.
14. M. Quinn, December 5, 2018. Also see Restoration Monograph, 17–30.
15. Restoration Monograph, 1–4 (Figure 1), 11–16.
16. Ibid., 1–9 (Figure 6).
17. Ibid., 7 (Figure 5), 11 (Figure 7), 22 (Figure 12).
18. Ibid., 34.
19. Ibid.
20. Email from J. Jeanes to W. Lewis, March 31, 2017 [hereafter J. Jeanes Email]. Director of restoration John Jeanes was asked to review a draft of portions of this book dealing with restoration of the House. His suggestions/corrections have been reflected. When a citation is to J. Jeanes Email, it is to indicate that he has reviewed the information and provided the information on which the statement in the book is made, or he has not indicated any issue with the statement as it appears in the text.

21. M. Quinn, December 5, 2018.
22. J. Jeanes Email.
23. M. Quinn, December 5, 2018. Also see email from M. Wenger to W. Lewis, together with marked copy of manuscript, September 10, 2021 [hereafter M. Wenger Email]. Architectural historian Mark Wenger, the principal investigator for the Montpelier House restoration, was asked to review the final version of the portions of this book dealing with House restoration. When a citation is to M. Wenger Email, it indicates that he has reviewed the information and provided information on which the statement in the book is made, or he has not indicated any issue with the statement as it appears in the text.
24. Restoration Monograph, 29; M. Quinn, January 27, 2019.
25. J. Jeanes Email. Also see M. Wenger Email.
26. Restoration Monograph, 34. Also see M. Wenger Email.
27. Feasibility Study, Organization, 1.
28. Ibid., Introduction, 1–2.
29. Restoration Monograph, 34.
30. The Digital Montpelier Project, 1, http://www.digitalmontpelier.org (click on "About").
31. Feasibility Study.
32. Ibid., Introduction, 2.
33. Ibid., Schedule, 1–2 and attachments.
34. Ibid., Introduction, 2.
35. Ibid., Cost Estimate, 1– 5.
36. Statement of the Montpelier Restoration Advisory Committee, January 29, 2003.
37. Memo and Attachments from M. Quinn to T. Terry and B. Carter, July 15, 2002 [hereafter Quinn July 2002 Memo].
38. Ibid.
39. Ibid.
40. Agreement between F. Terry and B. Carter, executors of Paul Mellon Estate, NTHP and TMF, dated as of September 30, 2002 [hereafter Mellon Estate Restoration Agreement].
41. Ibid.
42. Memo from M. Quinn to TMF Board of Directors, October 6, 2002.
43. Minutes, October 16, 2002.
44. Letter from W. Lewis to Mr. and Mrs. Henry E.I. duPont, October 2, 2001.
45. Ibid.

46. Memo from M. Quinn to W. Lewis, April 9, 2002. Also see M. Wenger Email.
47. Email from J. McConnell to M. Quinn and J. Grills, May 2, 2002.
48. See Memo and Attachments from M. Quinn to TMF Board of Directors, June 13, 2002. Also see Emails from M. Quinn to W. Lewis, December 5 and December 7, 2018.
49. Amendment to Agreement of Settlement, dated as of December 2002, between duPont signatories and NTHP, with concurrence of TMF [hereafter Amendment to Settlement Agreement].
50. Draft Amendment to Settlement Agreement (parties not listed), May 31, 2002.
51. Memo from M. Quinn to W. Lewis, June 25, 2002.
52. M. Quinn, May 15, 2020.
53. Memo and attached draft letter from Jean Ellen Shehan to M. Quinn, September 16, 2002.
54. Memo and attachments, including example letter, from M. Quinn to W. Lewis, et al., October 28, 2002.
55. See, for example, email from W. Porter to M. Quinn, et al., June 7, 2002, and email from J. Keith to W. Lewis, et al., June 22, 2002.
56. TMF, et al. v. Martha A.C.V. duPont et al., Petition to Modify Court-Approved Settlement Agreement, filed April 18, 2003 (Orange County [Va.] Cir. Ct.).
57. Order [TMF, et al. v. Martha A. C. V. DuPont et al.], August 18, 2003.

7. House Restored—2003–2008

1. Mellon Estate Restoration Agreement.
2. Feasibility Study, Summary of Project Schedule, July 17, 2002.
3. Amendment to Agreement of Settlement.
4. James Madison's Montpelier, Press Release, October 20, 2003 [hereafter October 2003 Press Release].
5. Philip Kennicott, "Madison's Makeover," *Washington Post*, August 13, 2006, Arts Section N1. Also see Minutes, December 12, 2003.
6. Email from J. Jeanes to W. Lewis, May 21, 2020. The percentage of the Mansion demolished was determined by comparing its square footage to the square footage of the House after restoration.
7. M. Quinn, December 7, 2018.
8. Feasibility Study, Introduction, 1. Also see Minutes, October 31, 2003.

9. Feasibility Study, Organization, 1.
10. Ibid., Schedule, 1.
11. See, for example, Memo from J. Jeanes to M. Quinn and W. Lewis, August 21, 2006.
12. See, for example, Minutes, Restoration Advisory Committee, July 20–21, 2005.
13. Feasibility Study, Organization, 1.
14. See, for example, Minutes, April 28, 2005.
15. M. Quinn, December 7, 2018.
16. Feasibility Study, Organization, 1.
17. M. Quinn, December 7, 2018.
18. See www.digitalmontpelier.org (click on "About").
19. Ibid.
20. 2004 Annual Report, 11; Minutes, June 24, 2005.
21. 2004 Annual Report, 11.
22. Restoration Monograph. See page iii for a biographical sketch of Ann Miller.
23. Minutes, March 26, 2004.
24. Ibid.
25. M. Quinn, December 7, 2018.
26. Feasibility Study, Project Directory, 2.
27. Minutes, March 26, 2004; Feasibility Study, Organization, 1.
28. Feasibility Study, Schedule, 1.
29. Amendment to Settlement Agreement.
30. M. Quinn, December 7, 2018.
31. Ibid.
32. Madison Exhibits in the Education Center, enclosed with October 2003 Press Release; Minutes, December 12, 2003.
33. Ibid.
34. Feasibility Study, Organization, 1.
35. See Minutes, May 7, 2004.
36. See Minutes, April 28, 2005.
37. M. Quinn, December 7, 2018
38. Feasibility Study, Schedule and Tasks.
39. J. Jeanes Email.
40. Ibid.
41. See 2006 Annual Report, 4.
42. M. Quinn, December 7, 2018.
43. Ibid.
44. Feasibility Study, Schedule and Tasks.

45. M. Quinn, December 7, 2018. Also see J. Jeanes Email.
46. M. Quinn, December 7, 2018.
47. Feasibility Study, Schedule and Tasks. Also see J. Jeanes Email.
48. 2004 Annual Report, 4.
49. 2006 Annual Report, 6. Also see M. Quinn, December 7, 2018, and J. Jeanes Email.
50. 2006 Annual Report, 6.
51. J. Jeanes Email.
52. 2005 Annual Report, 8.
53. Feasibility Study, Schedule and Tasks. As noted in the prologue, the National Trust's installation of the copper roof at a cost of about $1 million had been the most significant infrastructure project it had undertaken while managing Montpelier.
54. M. Quinn, December 7, 2018.
55. J. Jeanes Email.
56. Feasibility Study, Schedule and Tasks.
57. Feasibility Study, Schedule and Tasks. Also see M. Quinn, December 7, 2018, and J. Jeanes Email.
58. J. Jeanes Email.
59. Ibid.
60. Ibid. Also see M. Wenger Email.
61. 2006 Annual Report, 6.
62. J. Jeanes Email.
63. M. Quinn, December 7, 2018.
64. 2005 Annual Report, 8.
65. 2006 Annual Report, 6.
66. 2005 Annual Report, 8.
67. Feasibility Study, Tasks and Schedule.
68. 2007 Annual Report, 4. Also see M. Wenger Email.
69. Feasibility Study, Tasks and Schedule.
70. 2006 Annual Report, 4.
71. Feasibility Study, Tasks and Schedule.
72. J. Jeanes Email.
73. Ibid.
74. Feasibility Study, Tasks and Schedule.
75. Ibid.
76. 2006 Annual Report, 8.
77. Email and marked manuscript draft from Matthew Reeves to W. Lewis, September 22, 2021 [hereafter M. Reeves Email].

78. 2006 Annual Report, 8.
79. M. Quinn, December 7, 2018.
80. Feasibility Study, Tasks and Schedule.
81. Ibid. Also see J. Jeanes Email.
82. J. Jeanes Email.
83. Restoration Room description based on email from M. Quinn to W. Lewis, January 4, 2019, as well as author's observations.
84. Email from J. Jeanes to W. Lewis and attachment, May 20, 2020. Also see M. Quinn, June 26, 2020.
85. *Discovering Montpelier* 5, no. 1 (2008): 3.
86. M. Quinn, December 7, 2018.
87. *Discovering Montpelier* 5, no. 2 (2008): 2.
88. Click on "About" at www.digitalmontpelier.org.
89. Ibid.
90. M. Reeves Email.

8. Center for the Constitution—2002–2008

1. TMF undated paper titled "The Center for Constitutional Studies" [hereafter Center Plan], 1.
2. TMF undated paper titled "The Educational Mission of The Montpelier Foundation," 1.
3. "Recent Commentary" in TMF undated paper titled "Five Year Operations Plan," 1.
4. See, by way of example, Memo from R. Haltzel to File re Montpelier Project, May 16, 1994.
5. Center Plan, 1.
6. "TMF Report—Mellon Grant for Education," 1.
7. Ibid.
8. See, for example, 2004 Annual Report, 8.
9. TMF Press Package titled "Montpelier Center for Constitutional Studies," issued October 20, 2003.
10. Center Plan, 2. Also see M. Quinn, December 12, 2018.
11. Center Plan, "Five Year Budgets," 1.
12. Ibid., 2.
13. Memo from D. Kernahan, interim director, to Constitution Studies Committee, July 19, 2002 [hereafter Kernahan Memo].
14. Center Plan, "Five Year Objectives" [hereafter Five Year Objectives], 1.

15. Kernahan Memo, 1.
16. Five Year Objectives, 1.
17. Center Plan, "Five Year Operational Plan," 1.
18. Memo from W. Lewis to TMF Board re Committees for Montpelier's Center for the Constitution, October 11, 2005.
19. Center Plan, "Five Year Operational Plan," 1.
20. Minutes, March 7, 2003.
21. Minutes, May 9, 2003, 2.
22. Draft letter from W. Harris to R. Smith, Fall 2003.
23. Ibid.
24. Ibid.
25. See, for example, Montpelier Weekend Seminar Brochure, "Constitutionalism in America," Autumn 2005, and "Montpelier Texts in Constitutional Thought," March 2004.
26. 2004 Annual Report, 8.
27. 2006 Annual Report, 11.
28. See, for example 2004 Annual Report, 11.
29. Ibid. Also see M. Quinn, December 12, 2018.
30. Letter from M. Quinn to R. Smith dated October 14, 2004 [hereafter 2004 R. Smith Letter], 4.
31. 2004 Annual Report, 8.
32. See 2005 Annual Report, 12.
33. 2006 Annual Report. 11.
34. 2004 Annual Report, 8.
35. M. Quinn, December 12 and 14, 2018.
36. 2005 Annual Report, 12.
37. Ibid.
38. Email from W. Harris to W. Lewis regarding the Center's Program, June 21, 2005.
39. 2006 Annual Report, 11.
40. Minutes, March 16, 2007
41. *Discovering Montpelier* 5, no. 1 (2008 (1): 8.
42. See, for example, Center Marketing Review, November 1, 2005 [hereafter Marketing Review]. Also see Memo from M. Quinn to R. Smith, October 3, 2007.
43. 2004 R. Smith Letter. Also see TMF Proposal to Claude Moore Charitable Foundation dated August 29, 2006.
44. Memo from W. Lewis to Board dated October 11, 2005.
45. Ibid.

46. See Marketing Review.
47. 2006 Annual Report, 11.
48. 2007 Annual Report, 3. In 2016, the newly constructed Claude Moore Hall became the Center's academic building. The CEO and other senior administrative staff have offices in the adjacent Lewis Hall.
49. Description of Brick Stable (undated), prepared in 2007.
50. Ibid. Also see M. Quinn, December 12, 2018.
51. 2006 Annual Report, 13.
52. 2007 Annual Report, 3.
53. "Constitution Day 2007 Celebration" brochure, September 17, 2007.
54. See, for example, *Discovering Montpelier* 6, no. 2 (2009): 5.
55. 2007 Annual Report, 8. Also see Center for the Constitution Program Participation 2003–2014, April 23, 2014.
56. See, for example, James Madison's Montpelier Report on 2007. Among the major landscape changes required in the building of Lewis Hall was deconstruction of a large collapsing greenhouse. The removal was required to clear an area for Lewis Hall parking.
57. Minutes, February 16, 2007.
58. *Discovering Montpelier* 5, no. 1 (2008): 2.
59. Minutes, September 10, 2007. Also see memo from M. Quinn to R. Smith, October 3, 2007.
60. Memo from M. Quinn to Constitution Work Group, October 5, 2007.
61. Memo from M. Quinn to J. Grills, et al., November 14, 2008 [hereafter November 14 Memo].
62. Draft letter from M. Quinn to J. Vaughan, NTHP, undated.
63. November 14 Memo.

9. Visitor Center and William duPont Gallery Construction—2002–2007

1. The enslaved community pillar would also be a multiyear project (see chapter 13).
2. Agenda for Interviews, November 6, 2002.
3. Minutes, December 12, 2003.
4. Email from E. Waters to M. Quinn and W. Lewis dated May 20, 2002.
5. Email from L. Potter to W. Lewis et al. dated May 22, 2002.
6. Minutes, June 27, 2003.
7. See, for example, Minutes, September 12, 2003.

8. Minutes, June 27, 2003.
9. Minutes, July 9, 2004, and September 12, 2005. Also see M. Reeves Email.
10. Request for Qualifications, RFQ #2002-MGP-VC, issued 2002.
11. Agenda for Interviews, November 6, 2002.
12. Minutes, May 9, 2003.
13. Building Committee Report, May 9, 2003.
14. Glave & Holmes Visitor Center and Educational Gallery Questionnaires, February 2003.
15. Minutes, May 9, 2003.
16. See, for example, Minutes, December 12, 2003.
17. Minutes, October 31, 2003.
18. 2007 Annual Report, 2.
19. Minutes, March 26, 2004.
20. 2007 Annual Report, 2.
21. Minutes, September 8, 2006.
22. Groundbreaking Ceremony Statement of M. Quinn [hereafter Quinn Groundbreaking Statement], May 20, 2005, 3.
23. Ibid. Also see M. Quinn, December 28, 2018.
24. Quinn Groundbreaking Statement
25. Building Committee Meeting summary, August 19, 2004.
26. See, for example, Minutes, February 4, 2005.
27. Minutes, June 24, 2005.
28. James Madison's American Legacy Campaign brochure, 13.
29. Minutes, March 26, 2004.
30. Ibid.
31. Minutes, May 7, 2004.
32. Ibid.
33. Overview of Financing Alternatives, Morgan Keegan and Company, September 20, 2004 [hereafter Financing Overview].
34. Minutes, May 7, 2004.
35. Financing Overview.
36. See, for example, Minutes, July 9, 2004.
37. Minutes, September 17, 2004.
38. Letter from R. Moe, NTHP, to M. Quinn dated October 12, 2004, with attached NTHP Board Resolution dated October 3, 2004.
39. Minutes, November 5, 2004.
40. Minutes, December 20, 2004.
41. Minutes, November 5, 2004.

42. Minutes, March 21, 2005.
43. Minutes, June 24, 2005.
44. Minutes, March 21, 2005.
45. Quinn Groundbreaking Statement.
46. Minutes and attached Projects Update, September 8, 2006.
47. Minutes, November 4, 2005.
48. Minutes, November 3, 2006.
49. Visitor Center/William duPont Grand Opening statement of M. Quinn, March 16, 2007.
50. Minutes, November 3, 2006.

10. Program Highlights—2002–2008

1. *Discovering Montpelier* 6, no. 1 (2009): 3.
2. M. Quinn, December 29, 2018.
3. Ibid.
4. Minutes, March 7, 2003.
5. 2004 Annual Report, 3.
6. 2004 Annual Report, 5.
7. 2004 Annual Report, 9.
8. Minutes, December 16, 2005.
9. *Archaeology Sites at James Madison's Montpelier*, Montpelier Archaeology Department, 2017 [hereafter *Archaeology Sites*], 2.
10. *Archaeology Sites*, 12–13. Also see M. Reeves Email.
11. *Archaeology Sites*, "Meet the Archaeologists," pages unnumbered.
12. 2005 Annual Report, 11.
13. See, for example, *Archaeology Sites*, "Meet the Archaeologists."
14. Minutes, May 5, 2008.
15. See, for example, 2005 Annual Report, 4.
16. Ibid. Also see M. Reeves Email.
17. 2005 Annual Report, 11.
18. 2005 Annual Report, 4.
19. 2007 Annual Report, 1 and 3.
20. 2007 Annual Report, 3.
21. Roger Wilkins, *Jefferson's Pillow: The Founding Fathers and the Dilemma of Black Patriotism* (Boston Press, 2001), 131.
22. *Discovering Montpelier* 6, no. 1 (2009): 8.
23. *Discovering Montpelier* 5, no. 2 (2008): 8.

24. Elizabeth Dowling Taylor, *A Slave in the White House* (New York: Palgrave MacMillan/St. Martin's Press, 2012).
25. See, for example, 2005 Annual Report, 5.
26. See, for example, 2004 Annual Report, 6.
27. 2006 Annual Report, 13.
28. *Discovering Montpelier* 5, no. 2 (2008): 3.
29. See, for example, 2005 Annual Report, 13.
30. 2005 Annual Report, 7.
31. Working Group Report, 3.
32. A relational database stores data in table form (using rows and columns), enabling a user to access specific information distributed across multiple data records. New categories of data can be added without affecting existing tables.
33. Email from M. Kennedy to W. Lewis, April 29, 2019.
34. Minutes, September 17, 2004, and February 14, 2005.
35. Minutes, April 28, 2005.
36. Minutes, February 4, 2005.
37. Minutes, April 28, 2005.
38. Minutes, February 4, 2005.
39. Minutes, April 28, 2005.
40. TMF Interiors Research and Refurnishing Plan, 1 and 2.
41. Memo from M. Quinn to B. Lewis, et al., dated September 30, 2008.
42. Biography summaries of Board members who served during 1998–2008 are based primarily on summaries contained in a Montpelier Foundation document dated 2014, with the exception of the summaries for Roger Wilkins and Elinor Farquhar. Observations about their contributions are based on my fourteen years on the Board.

11. Leadership, Fundraising and Planning

1. Transcription of Remarks at Full Board Meeting on November 3, 2006, when W. Lewis turned over chairing of TMF to J. Grills.
2. Minutes, April 28, 2005. Also see Long-Range Financial Planning Worksheets, updated March 15, 2007.
3. Working Group Report, 4.
4. The Dolley Madison Coin is discussed in more detail in chapters 2 and 3.
5. Minutes, November 4, 2005. Also see Minutes, June 23, 2006, and Minutes, September 10, 2007.

6. Minutes, February 13, 2006.
7. Minutes, March 28, 2008.
8. See, for example, Madison Cabinet Plan (draft, September 5, 2001.)
9. The Madison 250th birthday celebration is discussed in more detail in chapter 5.
10. Minutes, May 9, 2003.
11. The Mellon Estate gift is discussed in more detail in chapter 5.
12. Minutes, October 31, 2003.
13. Montpelier news release, November 6, 2004.
14. See generally James Madison's American Legacy Campaign Brochure [hereafter Campaign Prospectus].
15. Undated draft letter from M. Quinn to F. Terry and B. Carter.
16. Letter from M. Quinn to Mr. and Mrs. O. Bruce Gupton, December 5, 2007.
17. M. Quinn, December 31, 2018.
18. See, for example, email from S. Hicks to W. Lewis, December 11, 2019.
19. Campaign Prospectus.
20. Minutes, November 4, 2005.
21. See, for example, Minutes, November 5, 2004.
22. Minutes, November 4, 2005.
23. Ibid.
24. M. Quinn, January 31, 2018.
25. Minutes, November 4, 2005.
26. Undated Master Planning paper for Montpelier and Center for the Constitution. Also see M. Quinn, December 31, 2018.
27. Minutes, October 31, 2008.
28. Minutes, November 4, 2005.
29. See generally Montpelier Master Planning Process, May 26, 2005.
30. Montpelier Master Planning Process, May 26, 2005, 2.
31. Memo from M. Quinn to R. Smith, October 3, 2007. Also see Memo from M. Quinn to J. Grills, et al., July 2, 2007.
32. Minutes, October 31, 2008.
33. Ibid.
34. Preservation Community Follow-up Meeting: Montpelier Farm Complex, Summary of Outcomes, prepared by B. Waters, November 4, 2009. Also see related undated Executive Summary.
35. Draft letter agreement between Montpelier and Bartzen & Ball, dated May 22, 2008.

36. Memo from M. Quinn to B. Remington, et al., October 19, 2008. Also see undated paper titled "Center for the Constitution, Infrastructure Phase and Minutes," October 31, 2008.
37. Patricia Sullivan, "Developer Robert H. Smith Dies," Metro Section/ *Post Mortem* blog with Matt Schudel, *Washington Post*, December 30, 2009.
38. See, for example, Letter from C. Miller, PEC, to M. Quinn, April 12, 2002.
39. Ibid.
40. Ibid.
41. See, for example, Memo from J. Moore, PEC, to M. Quinn, March 12, 2007.
42. Memo and attachment from M. Quinn to Montpelier Board of Directors, October 16, 2006.
43. Letter from C. Miller to M. Quinn, August 29, 2008. Also see Letter from P. Filer to M. Quinn, August 11, 2008.
44. Montpelier Interpretive Plan Committee, draft James Madison's Montpelier Interpretive Plan, June 2005, 2.
45. Draft James Madison's Montpelier Interpretive Plan, 3–8.
46. See, for example, Agenda, Meeting of the Education, Interpretation and Collections Committee, October 8, 2007.

12. Year of Celebration of Madison Monument—2008

1. *Discovering Montpelier* 5, no. 1 (2008): 1.
2. Ibid., 3.
3. Ibid., 1.
4. Ibid., 6.
5. *Discovering Montpelier* 5, no. 2 (2008): 1.
6. Ibid.
7. Ibid.
8. Ibid., 4.
9. Ibid., 1.
10. Ibid., 2.
11. Ibid., 5.
12. *Discovering Montpelier* 6, no. 1 (2009): 1.
13. *Discovering Montpelier* 5, no. 2 (2008): 2.
14. *Discovering Montpelier* 6, no. 1 (2009): 6.
15. *Discovering Montpelier* 5, no. 2 (2008): 3.

16. Ibid.
17. *Discovering Montpelier* 5, no. 1 (2008): 4.
18. Ibid.
19. M. Reeves Email.
20. *Discovering Montpelier* 5, no. 1 (2008): 5.
21. Ibid.
22. Only the enslaved community pillar still required significant additional initiatives to be fully recognized as a part of the monument, which would be undertaken in the second decade (see chapter 13).
23. *Discovering Montpelier* 5, no. 2 (2008):7.

13. Second Decade Highlights—2009–2016

1. *Discovering Montpelier* 6, no. 1 (2009): 1.
2. Ibid., 8.
3. *Discovering Montpelier* 6, no. 2 (2009): 1.
4. *Discovering Montpelier* 7, no. 1 (2010): 1.
5. Ibid., 1, 9.
6. Ibid., 1.
7. *Discovering Montpelier* 7, no. 2 (2010): 1.
8. Ibid., 1, 2.
9. *Discovering Montpelier* 8, no. 1 (2011): 3.
10. Ibid., 1, 2.
11. Ibid., 1–3.
12. M. Quinn, March 13, 2019.
13. *Discovering Montpelier* 8, no. 1 (2011): 1, 5. Also see M. Reeves Email.
14. *Discovering Montpelier* 9, no. 2 (2012): 3.
15. Ibid., 8.
16. Letter from S. O'Brien to B. Carter and F. Terry, July 30, 2012.
17. Report to the Estate of Paul Mellon on TMF Interiors Research and Refurnishing Project, July 2012, 2 [hereafter TMF Mellon Report with page number].
18. TMF Mellon Report, 1, 2.
19. Ibid., 4.
20. *Discovering Montpelier* 8, no. 1 (2011): 2.
21. Drew Jackson, "Montpelier Names New President," *Orange County Review*, November 9, 2012.
22. *We the People*, Fall 2013, 12.

23. Minutes and attached Resolution, October 31, 2014.
24. Ibid. Also see Montpelier Interpretation of Enslaved Community History Approach & Talking Points, December 5, 2014.
25. Memo from M. van Balgooy to TMF Board, June 1, 2015 [hereafter van Balgooy Memo].
26. Minutes and attached Resolution, October 31, 2014.
27. *We the People*, Spring 2014, 5–8.
28. Ibid., 12–13.
29. Ibid., 16.
30. Van Balgooy Memo.
31. Ibid.
32. *Inside the Gates* (February 2015): 3. This publication is an internal Montpelier newsletter.
33. Memos from D. Smith to TMF Board, June 1 and October 16, 2015.
34. Ibid.
35. Montpelier Media Advisory, March 2015.
36. Memo from E. Chew to TMF Board, October 24, 2016.
37. Memo from K. Imhoff to TMF Board Executive Committee, December 5, 2016. Also see Draft White Paper for Center for the Constitution, November 26, 2018.
38. Memo from E. Chew to TMF Board, October 24, 2016. Also see *We the People*, Spring 2017, 4.

14. Celebration of Montpelier's Becoming a Monument to Enslaved Community

1. *We the People*, Spring 2017, 2, 6–11.
2. *We the People*, Fall 2017, 6.
3. *We the People*, Spring 2018, 7.
4. *The Public Historian* 40, no. 4 (2018): 163.
5. *We the People*, Spring 2018, 5.
6. Ibid., 6.
7. Email from K. Imhoff to TMF Board and Emeriti, May 3, 2018.
8. *We the People*, Spring 2019, 5.
9. Ibid., 10.

Appendix A. New Foundation Directors 2003–2008

1. Biography summaries of Board members who served during 1998–2008 are based primarily on summaries contained in a Montpelier Foundation document dated 2014, with the exception of the summaries for Roger Wilkins and Elinor Farquhar. Observations about their contributions are based on my 14 years on the Board.
2. Adam Bernstein, "Roger Wilkins, Rights Champion in Government and Journalism, Dies at 85," *Washington Post*, March 27, 2017.
3. Ibid.

Appendix B. Board Establishment of Goals

1. The draft goals set forth in this section are excerpted from the "Concepts for Goal Setting Session of the Board," June 22, 2007.

INDEX

A

B

C

D

E

F

G

M

N

O

P

Q

T

V

W

Y

ABOUT THE AUTHOR

William H. "Bill" Lewis was a co-founder of The Montpelier Foundation and chair of the Board of Directors for its first eight years, serving for 19 years on its Governance Committee. Nationally recognized as an expert on clean air regulation and litigation, he is a retired partner and later senior counsel of an international law firm. Previously, he served as director of the National Commission on Air Quality, as well as executive officer of the California Air Resources Board. He was listed in *Best Lawyers in America* and *Washington, DC Super Lawyers*. He is a graduate of the University of North Carolina with an AB degree and a JD with honors from its Law School. He and his wife, Peyton, reside in Charlottesville, Virginia.